MARGARET BENNETT is a folklorist, singer and prize-winning writer. Brought up on the Isles of Skye, Lewis and Shetland, she studied in Glasgow then Newfoundland, and from 1984–96 lectured in Scottish Studies at the University of Edinburgh. Since 1996 she has been a part-time lecturer at the Royal Conservatoire of Scotland, and is also Honorary Research Fellow at the University of St Andrews. Described as 'wearing her scholarship lightly' Margaret is 'devoted to handing on tradition to new generations' and has recorded people from all walks of life to conserve Scotland's wealth of traditional knowledge. She has published 14 books and contributed to many more, and is the recipient of several awards on both sides of the Atlantic.

LES MCCONNELL is from Ayr. He studied at Edinburgh College of Art where he was awarded a graduate scholarship to study in Holland. Les trained as a teacher and settled in Fife. He has exhibited widely, including the RSA. He has continued to paint and illustrate books that have been reviewed with critical acclaim. Books illustrated by Les include *The Sair Road* (2018), *Saul Vaigers* (2021) and *Earth-Bound Companions* (2021) by William Hershaw, and *Dundee Street Songs, Rhymes and Games: The William Montgomerie Collection, 1952* (winner of the American Folklore Society Opie Prize for Children's Folklore, 2022) by Margaret Bennett.

Up the Glen
and
Doon the Village

STRATHEARN ORAL HISTORY & FOLKLORE

Margaret Bennett

Illustrated by Les McConnell

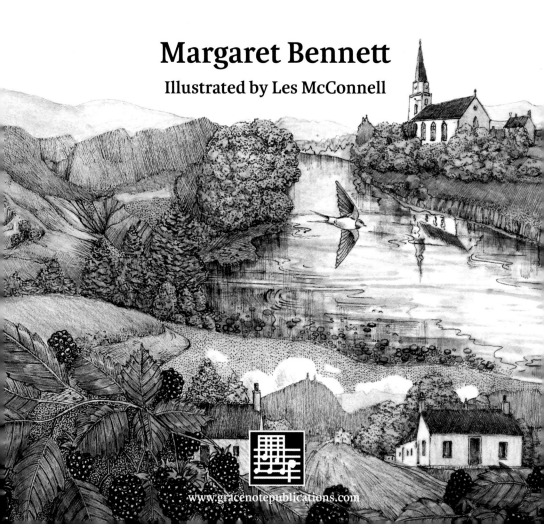

www.gracenotepublications.com

Up the Glen & Doon the Village
STRATHEARN ORAL HISTORY & FOLKLORE

With the announcement of 'Lockdown' in March 2020, all notions of 'normal life' were shattered, affecting everyone nationwide. Among rural folk in Highland Perthshire, where fireside visits were a way of life, suddenly it all changed: no visiting, not even a wee ceilidh by the fire.

This book records a 'pandemic project' that was devised so that folk in the glens and villages of Strathearn could still enjoy sharing stories, information, news and laughter without breaking 'lockdown' rules. Through these ordinary conversations we meet some extraordinary people; discover part of Scotland's history; learn about traditions that sustained a way of life, and listen to stories that might otherwise be forgotten.

'In the heart of Scotland, in the grip of a pandemic, Margaret Bennett created a virtual hearthside to counter isolation and depression. This wonderful book is the result. It is a unique record of rural life, a distillation of shared humanity, and a vivid demonstration of how stories and memories can leap across the generations to connect past and present. If you put Margaret Bennett in solitary confinement, somehow she would still start up a ceilidh!'

Donald Smith, Director
Scottish International Storytelling Festival

Up the Glen & Doon the Village

ISBN: 978-1-913162-21-4

Paperback/ 274 pages, photos & maps

Available at: https://www.gracenotepublications.com/

MORE INFORMATION: info@gracenotescotland.org

£15.99

Up the Glen
and
Doon the Village

Best wishes,

Margaret Bennett

Up the Glen
and
Doon the Village
STRATHEARN ORAL HISTORY & FOLKLORE

Margaret Bennett

Illustrated by
Les McConnell

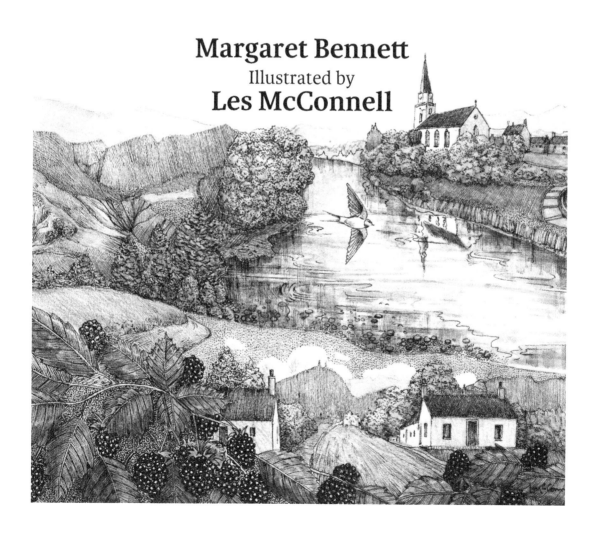

Up the Glen & Doon the Village: Strathearn Oral History & Folklore
First published in 2024 by Grace Note Publications

Grange of Locherlour, Ochtertyre, PH7 4JS, Scotland
www.gracenotepublications.co.uk
info@gracenotescotland.org

ISBN: 978-1-913162-21-4

A catalogue record for this book is available from the British Library

Grace Notes Scotland gratefully acknowledge the support from
The Weir Charitable Trust, Selkirk, Scotland

Dedicated with gratitude to
all who shared their memories and traditions

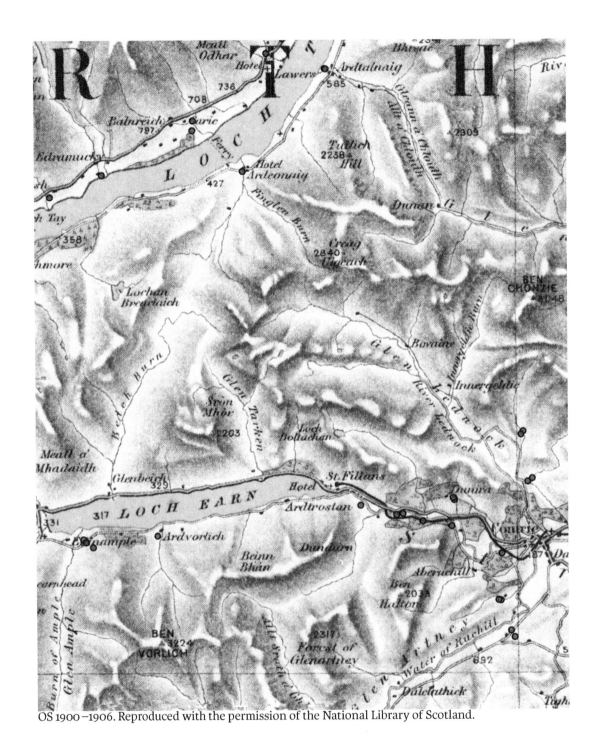

OS 1900–1906. Reproduced with the permission of the National Library of Scotland.

Contents

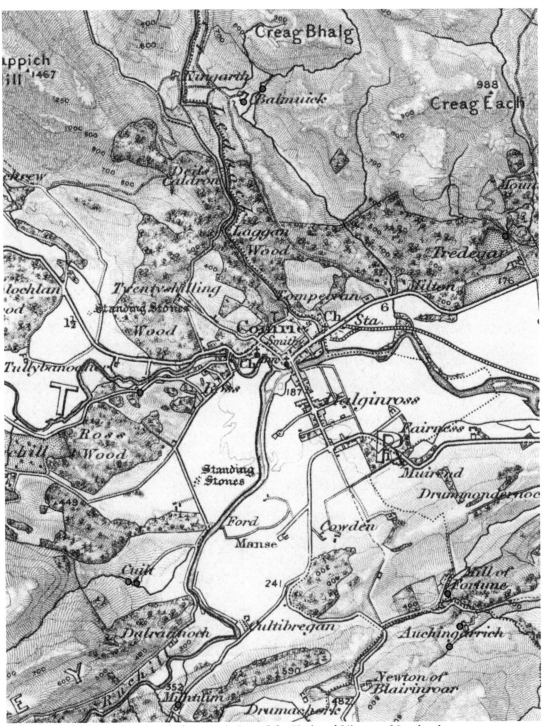

OS 1900–1906. Reproduced with the permission of the National Library of Scotland.

Introduction

March 2020 will long be remembered as the month when, suddenly, everything changed. On the 11th, the World Health Organisation declared the Covid-19 pandemic; on the 13th BBC news announced the first coronavirus death in Scotland; on the 15th we were all advised to stay at home; on the 17th schools, nurseries, colleges and universities were closed; and on the 24th we all heard the word Lockdown. It was a huge adjustment for everyone, and, as if at a loss for words, conversations often began with "the whole world has changed". The notion that it would be all over by Christmas had an eerie ring of the past: that's what our grandparents and great-grandparents said in 1914.

This project began as a response to some of the challenges faced during lockdowns and restrictions, particularly loneliness and isolation among the elderly and anxiety among young folk who had lost part-time jobs supporting them through college or training courses. And so this 'lockdown project' was devised along the lines of two past oral history projects completed in 2010 and 2015, when elderly folk shared their memories with young people.[1] The plan was to set up 'virtual visits' with residents of care homes or sheltered housing, or elderly people living at home, then, via a screen or telephone, enjoy time sharing reminiscences and laughter. With their permission, conversations would be audio-recorded, then transcribed by young people who would not only learn from the elderly but would also be paid for their work. Thanks to the generosity of the Weir Charitable Trust there is now a digital archive of several hundred pages of transcription, with copies deposited in Perth & Kinross Archive at the A.K. Bell Library, Perth.[2]

This book is compiled from transcriptions of conversations that keep alive stories and 'fireside memories' relating to life in the Perthshire villages of Comrie, Crieff, St Fillans, Killin and the surrounding glens. Most of the contributors were born before the Second World War, and all of them knew a way of life when the fireside, rather than the television (or a 'device'), was the focus of family and neighbourhood gatherings. Their social life included village hall dances and concerts, kirk soirees, school socials, pipe-bands, and associations such as the Scottish Country Dancing, the Young Farmers' Club, and the WRI. While their strong sense of community is firmly rooted in the villages and the glens, their conversations about life experiences, memories, and knowledge take us around the world – far beyond hearth and home.

The collective reminiscences date back centuries as several contributors recount what they heard from their parents and grandparents born in the 1800s. A few could contribute memories from previous generations, and, as with any fireside conversation, topics covered reflect the common interests of participants: family information and local characters remembered for their wit and wisdom; the weather, the war, the cost of living, 'The News', and so on. Through these ordinary conversations we meet some extraordinary people and learn about a way of life that might otherwise be forgotten. Those who took part deserve to be remembered for all they contribute to the history of the villages and glens of Strathearn and beyond.

Notes on recording and editing

Although contributors were recorded individually, mostly during 'virtual' visits, the book is set out as a conversation among neighbours and friends in Strathearn, Perthshire. Apart from a few 'visitors' with connections to the area, most of the participants live within a ten-mile radius of Comrie; some lived in the area their entire lives; several settled there during, or just after, the Second World War; and others chose to move to the area in retirement. As in any small community, several were already well acquainted, while others had never met, and, given their advanced years and restrictions during the pandemic, were unlikely to meet outside of this 'virtual fireside conversation'. My connection with many of them stretches back to the mid-1980s but, although I knew individuals who might enjoy a phone-call during the lockdowns, I began with an outreach to folk whom I had not previously met.

The 'virtual visits' resulted in a compilation of an archive of audio- and video- recordings transcribed by student helpers to create hundreds of pages, which I planned to edit. I anticipated creating a series of biographic sketches of participants, which would be meaningful to the families of those recorded as well as to the community. As I edited each one and gave (or sent) a copy to the relevant speaker, 'This is Your Life' with their name, it occurred to me that the entire corpus of recordings consisted of conversations that could have taken place by any of the firesides up the glen or down the village. The book is therefore constructed as a series of conversations among real people around an 'imaginary fireside' – they bring up the subjects, tell their stories, interject with memories, comments and occasional contradictions. They discuss topics that have almost been forgotten, talk about work and leisure, the weather and the state of the world. Some ask searching questions that begin with "see if you can find out...". Others make suggestions on who we should ask, or speak of a friend who could have told us, wistfully adding that it's "an awful pity they've gone now". Occasionally it has been possible to bring back some of these voices via recordings made over the years, and so they are included in our fireside conversations as if they had never left. In the text, their names are the only ones that are followed by the dates of birth and death. All the other 'speakers' experienced the world of lockdowns and isolation, though sadly several passed away before the book went to print.

In editing the transcriptions I have tried to be as faithful as possible to the speakers: retaining individual style, while balancing the variations in grammar and syntax between English and Scots, and ever aware that the printed page gives a paler image of the speaker. Occasionally I have made slight adjustments to the transcriptions, mainly for clarification, or because the speaker gave further information outside of the recording session.

Acknowledgements

Warmest appreciation goes to all who took part in this project and who made it possible. This book is a tribute to all of them: the 'speakers' (named on each page) who so willingly shared their memories, experiences, knowledge, and wisdom, and gave permission to be recorded; the care home staff and carers for their enthusiastic support; the team of transcribers – most of whom were 'locked down' at home, or in student flats or residences.[3]

In producing the book, special thanks must go to Comrie's local historian, the remarkable Billy Gardiner, who not only shared his memories and hand-written journals but also photographs from his collection. On the telephone and 'in person' Billy 'kept me right', explained dialect words, surprised me with parish records, gave me 'homework to do', and made me laugh with his droll and witty comments.

Huge appreciation goes to artist Les McConnell whose imaginative drawings illustrate the conversations; to Ros and Russell Salton who proofread several drafts, and to Gonzalo Mazzei who typeset the book. They all encouraged me with friendship, patience, and humour. Finally, on behalf of Grace Notes Scotland, we give special thanks to The Weir Charitable Trust for supporting the project, which brought a lot of joy to all who took part.

We hope the participants and their families will continue to enjoy the 'lockdown' conversations and take pride in the wealth of local knowledge recorded for future generations.

Endnotes

1   "Perthshire Memories" (2009–10), recording residents of rural Strathearn and "The End of the Shift" (2013–15) recording former industrial workers in Perthshire and Fife-shire. Publications by Margaret Bennett include *'In Our day...' Reminiscences and Songs from Rural Perthshire* (with CD) illustrated by Doris Rougvie (Ochtertyre: Grace Note Publications, 2010); *Nell Hannah: Aye Singin an Spinnin Yarns* (Ochtertyre: Grace Note Publications, 2013); *We are the Engineers! A History of Scottish Working People,* (Ochtertyre: Grace Note Publications, 2015). Recordings, transcriptions and photographs of these collections have been deposited in Perth & Kinross Archive, Acc11/52.

2   The material can be freely accessed at the Perth & Kinross Archive, Acc23/30 (M. Bennett collection) and can be used for independent research, educational purposes and general interest.

3   The project transcribers were Aidan Moodie, Anna Reid, Ben Muir, Brodie Crawford, Cameron Nixon, Cameron Sharp, Catherine McGoldrick, Deirdre McMahon, Emery (Kirsten) Law, Eoghainn Beaton, Hazel Cameron, James MacIntyre, Jennifer Meiklejohn, John F. O'Donnell, Laura Martin, Macaulay Ross, Mia Galanti, Michelle Melville and Tina Rees.

Dramatis Personae

Meet the Folk by the Fireside

Margaret Bennett is originally from Skye. She has a life-long interest in local histories and folklore and has enjoyed living in Strathearn for over thirty years.

Sarah Black is a resident of Dalginross Care Home, Comrie. Her family farmed at Dalrannoch, two and a half miles from Comrie. Sarah looks back at life on a hill farm, the work, the neighbourliness and the enjoyment of a close-knit rural community.

Jenny MacGregor [1911–2011] was a shop-keeper, church organist and music teacher in Comrie.

Ann Ross (née Dow) is a retired teacher. Her family farmed in Carroglen, though moved when she was very young. Ann and her husband Lamont settled in Crieff, which has been home to their family for many years.

Donald Ross, son of Ann and Lamont, now lives in Glasgow where he is assistant stage manager with Scottish Opera. He joined our 'fireside ceilidh' on a family visit to Crieff.

Billy Gardiner was born and brought up in Comrie. A retired joiner and undertaker with a lifelong interest in local history, Billy kept notebooks recording his memories of the village as well as his National Service, the only time he didn't live in the house in which he was born.

Sandy Gardiner, Billy's son, Comrie.

Bobby Thomson, from Forfar, has lifelong connections to the village as well as the glens. He holidayed with family and regularly visited the Doigs, especially 'Auntie Nan'.

Nan Doig, 'Auntie Nan' [1912–2014] was born in Angus on a farm near Kirriemuir. The extended family moved to Glen Lednock in 1929 leasing Balmuick and Braefordie. At the end of the lease Nan and two brothers farmed in Fife for 10 years, then returned to Strathearn, leasing a hill-farm, 'The Straid' at Blairnroar in Glenartney. Nan retired to Comrie, where she celebrated her hundredth birthday. (She died in Crieff two years later.)

Helen Doig, Nan's niece, was born in Glen Lednock, where her father (Nan's brother David) worked on the farm. At the end of the lease, they moved to Monzievaird then to Ardtrostan, overlooking Loch Earn. When that lease ended Helen and her brothers moved to a hill-farm in Lanark.

Elma Cunningham is Nan Doig's niece and Helen Doig's cousin. She was born in Glen Lednock and then moved to a farm near Muthill. Her father was a skilled cattleman and in 1946 was offered a job near Carlisle, then as cattle-breeder in Surrey where Elma trained as a teacher. Though she has lived in Surrey for over 60 years she returns to Strathearn every year.

Pat MacNab [1912–2010] was born on the Isle of Eigg. His father was a shepherd and in 1917 the family moved to Glenartney. After a lifetime of shepherding in Glenartney and elsewhere, Pat retired and in 1988 moved to Comrie.

Duncan McNab, son of Pat MacNab, grew up on hill farms where his father and grandfather shepherded. Though his early career was in the Royal Navy, then in 'civvy street' he retired to Almondbank, closer to the hills and glens that nurtured him.

Helen Gardiner (née Grewar) spent her formative years on a farm in Glenartney where she was known as 'Nelly Grewar'. Married to a farmer in Angus, Helen wrote weekly columns for the Dundee Courier entitled "Country Matters by the Farmer's Wife".

Jimmy Stewart [1921–2012] spent his life as a shepherd in the hills of Perthshire. In retirement he lived at Ochtertyre where, latterly, he was the cattleman at Locherlour Farm.

Tam Kettle grew up on Perthshire farms where his father was a horseman. Tam became a woodsman and estate worker and moved into Comrie where he was a resident of Dalginross care home.

Muriel Malloy [née McGregor] was born and brought up in Comrie. Her family has lived in Strathearn for many generations.

Alistair Work grew up on farms near Comrie before settling in Glenartney to work on the Drummond Estate where he was the Head Stalker.

Mollie MacCallum had a career as a schoolteacher at Morrison's Academy in Crieff. In retirement she takes an active role in community life and enjoys walking in the hills and glens.

Jane MacIntyre grew up in Comrie and for many years has been a member of the care staff at Dalginross Care Home, Comrie.

Jean Parker (Jane MacIntyre's aunt) was born in Glasgow in 1928; she was a wartime evacuee in Comrie.

Peter McNaughton was born in Comrie. He emigrated to Canada, and settled in Montreal though still regards Comrie as 'home' and visits most years. In retirement he follows his life-long interest in Strathearn, gathering photos and information for his website on Highland Strathearn.

Mildred Logan was born in Ayrshire in 1933. During the war her father, a minister, was an army Padre, stationed at Cultybraggan. She moved to Comrie in retirement.

Cathie McPhail grew up on a farm near Inverness. She retired to Comrie in the late 1990s, and in her mid-nineties moved into local 'sheltered housing'. She shared her wartime memories, recalling her services as an ambulance driver for the RAF.

Mairi Philp is a retired nurse from Comrie, which has been home to several generations of her family. Mairi organises and hosts regular 'sing-arounds' in Comrie Parish Church and thanks to a team of volunteers, folk get together for songs, chat, laughter, a cup of tea and excellent home-baking. Everyone is welcome – that's what the old folk called a 'real ceilidh'.

Nora (MacPherson) Hamilton [1920–2015] belonged to one of Comrie's oldest families,the MacPhersons. They had long-standing cultural, heritage and business interestsin the village, including her grandfather's shop, built in 1904 to a plan by Charles Rennie Mackintosh. (The Landmark Trust now owns the upstairs flat.) Nora's greatgrandfather was one of the early investigators of the seismic activity in the area, with an interest in the world's first seismometer, invented in Comrie in 1840. The presentday Earthquake House situated in the Ross, Comrie was built in 1872.

Ann Thomson was born and brought up in the Borders. She retired to Crieff, and in 2019 she was honoured for her wartime services at Bletchley Park. As Ann was hard of hearing she wrote down her memories and gave the pages to her neighbour, Austin O'Toole, who offered them to the project at Ann's request.

Austin O'Toole was born and brought up in Glasgow. Former horseman and contract shepherd and shearer, Austin lived at Monzievaird for many years. He retired to Crieff, where his neighbours included Ann Thomson.

Margaret Motherwell from Crieff was a member of staff of BLESMA Care Home before its closure in 2013. She continued to visit elderly residents as 'a friend to the end.'

Nan McPhail [1918–2016] was born and brought up in Gartmore. She trained as a nurse in Glasgow and worked in Scotland and overseas. She retired in Crieff and latterly was a resident at BLESMA.

Irene Addison [1934–2016] was born and brought up in Clydebank. She became a teacher and in retirement moved to Crieff. She was a resident at BLESMA.

Mervyn Knox-Browne was born and brought up in Donegal. In the early 1950s, he moved to Perthshire and began shepherding in Balquhidder and then Glen Lyon. In 1954 he bought a sheep-farm by Loch Tayside, keeping Blackface sheep and some cattle. A Gaelic-speaker (both Irish and Scottish), and a life-long conservationist, for 60 years Mervyn kept a journal of local wild-life, birds and plant-life and also recorded the rainfall and daily temperature for the MET Office.

Jean Innes 'Jean the Braes' [née McNaughton, 1900–97] was born and brought up on a hill farm in Balquhidder. Jean married a farmer, and spent her life in rural Perthshire, home to her family for generations. In 1975, when the county boundaries were changed and new 'regions' were created under the Scottish Regionalisation scheme, Jean was outraged to find that Balquhidder was no longer in Perthshire.

Arthur Allen was the resident engineer on the Lednock Dam. He graduated in civil engineering from Loughborough and London Universities and in 1947 his job took him to Comrie to survey the area prior to the start of the Breadalbane Hydro Scheme. In 1958, on completion of the Lednock dam, Arthur and his family settled in Comrie.

John F. O'Donnell ('Big John') was born and brought up in Perth. His father was one of the Donegal men who worked on the hydro scheme then remained in Scotland. 'Big John' runs the pub in Muthill's historic inn, The Commercial, which has a permanent exhibition of the Hydro workers, many of whom were Irish and settled in Muthill.

George Carson [1930–2014] was born and brought up in Glasgow. Comrie became his home after his marriage to local nurse, Mamie MacPherson, who ran the on-site medical base for the hydro workers in the Fifties. George was a keen hillwalker, loved Scottish Country Dancing and was well known in the village and surrounding glens.

Ed Miller was born and brought up in Edinburgh, though has lived in Texas since the late 1960s. He's a folklorist and singer and for over twenty years has organised 'Folksong Tours of Scotland' for American visitors. He has a life-long love of the hills and mountaineering, and got to know Strathearn as a schoolboy, camping at Cultybraggan.

Nigel Gatherer is an artist and musician who lives in Crieff. He's the founder and leader of the Crieff Community Band and the Ukulele Group and runs other music classes in Glasgow, Edinburgh and beyond. Nigel is also a prolific composer and a great supporter of community arts projects.

And we have a few visitors:

Eilidh Firth, former music student at the RSAMD, now a music teacher in Glasgow.

Ben Muir is a piper and graduate of the Royal Conservatoire of Scotland in Glasgow. At the start of the pandemic, confined to a student flat, Ben joined our 'virtual fireside' to share a visit with Duncan McNab.

Dolina (Doli) Maclennan from the Isle of Lewis is a Gaelic actress who has featured in film, television and the theatre. She lives in Edinburgh, having spent many years in Perthshire, where she had a guest house in Blair Atholl.

David Campbell from Edinburgh first came to Strathearn with a group of university students who worked at Cultybraggan Camp during the summer holidays. He became a teacher then joined BBC Schools as a programme-maker and broadcaster. For over 30 years David has been a storyteller.

Adam McNaughtan is 'Glasgow born and bred', a former teacher, singer-songwriter and stalwart of the 'folk-scene'. Though 'long since retired', Adam is well-known for his wit and humour; his songs include 'The Jeely Piece Song', 'The Yellow on the Broom', 'Oor Hamlet' and 'Cholesterol'.

Annie and Ian Young grew up in Glasgow. Annie's grandfather Samuel Comrie was from Comrie, a veteran of the Somme, who moved to Glasgow to work as a glazier. His daughter Margaret (Annie's mother) kept her Comrie connections and continued to visit. Annie and Ian settled in Edinburgh and the 'folk music scene' connects us in friendship.

Zoom *Ceilidh, 2021*

Left to Right

1. Jane MacIntyre, Dalginross Care Home, Comrie

2. Sarah Black, Dalginross

3. Tam Kettle, Dalginross

4. Mollie MacCallum, Crieff

5. Ben Muir, Glasgow

6. Duncan McNab, Almondbank

7. Alistair Work, Glenartney

8. David Campbell, Edinburgh

9. John F. O'Donnell, ('Big John'), Muthill

10. Cathie McPhail, Comrie

11. Margaret Bennett, Ochtertyre

12. Les McConnell, Fife

Céilidh (Scottish Gaelic), *céili* (Irish Gaelic) literally means 'a visit', traditionally denoting any visit or hospitable gathering of family and friends, pre-arranged or impromptu.

Zoom' is an internet platform that allows users to connect via video, phone and 'chat'. At the start of the pandemic, 2020, 'Zoom' was widely used to allow people to keep in touch, or have any kind of 'ceilidh'.

Billy Gardiner

Billy: "I aye kept a notebook ... When you write it doon you'll remember it better..."

Billy at 'Mill of Fortune', Glenartney.
"This is one o the mill stones"

Pages from Billy's notebook:
Reminiscences and examples of Comrie Scots

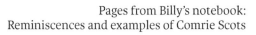

All houses had gardens and many KEPT hens
We started keeping hens at the start of the war
Dad had a hive of bees. You got a special ration
of sugar if you had bees. The sugar was usually used
in the house and the bees got old honey to feed on.
JOHN HAGGART had a big hen farm at Bofrauch.
They hatched the chicken in a down stairs room.
Paraffin incubators. Before the War beekeeper put
their bees to the heather. A lorry load would go up
to Blairichroad. Parson Kay had about 15 hives and
Won anton the same. People with a big garden
were at an advantage during the war, with room
to keep hens and grow veg of all kinds.
Coal was a problem, sometimes when we had bad
Winters. We had very bad snow and ice several
winters during the war. Early forties. 1947 was very bad
railways blocked with snow and severe frost
1962 was the worst Winter I remember for frost.
Water supply pipes were frozen and a blacksmith from
Fowlis Wester thawed out using an electric welding
When our house was built we had gas light in
the living room (Kitchen) and a gas ring in the scullery.
Only for a few Years. We went to lamps, and used
the range for cooking ALLADIN LAMPS. AND A TILLEY
                                        FOR SOME
                                        TIME

BOOT	BUT
SPOON SCHOOL	SPEEN SCHOOL
MEAT	MATE
SEAT	SATE
NEAT	NATE
PEAT	PATE
BREAD	BRADE
HEAD	HADE
DEAD	DADE
LEAD	LADE

Laying the foundation stone of
the Free Church, Comrie, 1879.
(Billy Gardiner collection)

Wool mill at the bottom of
Drummond Street, L (east end),
by the River Lednock, Comrie,
mid-1800s. (Billy Gardiner
collection)

After it ceased operation the
water wheel was transferred to
Dunira to power the sawmill.

Comrie Newsagent
(Billy Gardiner collection)

Ramsay Wilson, Rabbit Trapper, Comrie (Billy Gardiner collection)

Cousin John (John Findlay McIntyre), trapper, with a badger, Lechkin, Comrie (Alistair Work collection)

Ingin Johnnie: They came every year and sold onions round the village and up the glen. (Billy Gardiner collection)

Keith MacPherson beside his garage in Comrie, 1930s. (Billy Gardiner collection)

Stacking the harvest at Lawers Agricultural College (Billy Gardiner collection)

Students shearing Black-face sheep on the farm at Lawers Agricultural College, 1958. (Billy Gardiner collection)

Comrie WRI Granny parade, 1950s (Billy Gardiner collection)

Pat MacNab shepherding in Glenartney: "You need a good dog, a good pair o boots and a good stick" (Family collection)

Jimmy Stewart: "I met my wife Mary when I was shepherding in Glenbuckie, then after we were married we were in Glen Isla. After that we were in Glen Turret. There were a lot o shepherds up the Sma' Glen..." (Family collection)

Mervyn Browne, Lochtayside: "You got to know all the shepherds and all the glens ..." (Family collection)

Dalclathic House, Glenartney. 'The Lodge' rented by Rudyard Kipling (unknown Collection).

OS c. 1925, Glen Artney, The Ruchill Water flows through the glen. Dalclathic Lodge and cottage are to the north of the river, and to the south is Mailermore, home to the Grewars (Helen Gardiner) in the 1940s and 50s, and Pat MacNab & family in the 70s & 80s.

In 2022 only a few foundation stones remain of Dalclathic Lodge while the kennels and outbuilding have been refurbished for seasonal sports-people, and Pat and Isobel MacNab's first home, Dalclathic Cottage, lies empty. (Photo by Duncan McNab)

Nan Doig (centre) at a 'kirk soiree' in Comrie (2011) with her niece, Helen Doig (R). and Margaret Bennett (L)

Cousins Helen Doig and Elma Cunningham enjoying a ceilidh at Blairnroar. "This used to be Auntie Nan's old house when they farmed at the Straid (Blairnroar)"

Helen Doig, Bobby Thompson and Muriel (Doig) MacDonald at Auntie Nan's 100th birthday

Muriel (McGregor) Malloy, Comrie

Helen Gardiner (Nellie Grewar): "I grew up in Glenartney, at Mailermore ... most folk had a Tilley lamp in those days"

Drawings & plans for Lednock dam and tunnels and artist's impression of the Lednock dam.(Perth & Kinross Archive, MS140: Mott MacDonald, civil engineers, 1951–1972)

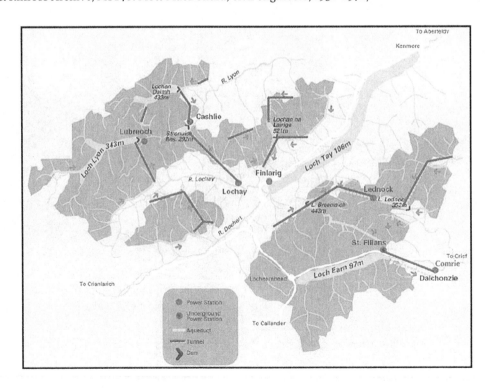

Chapter 1

Everyone Used to Visit

It only took one phone-call to set up a 'virtual visit' to Dalginross Care Home in Comrie. "What a good idea," said Jane, "We've got a few residents who'd love a visit.… Give me a few minutes … I'll set up the 'tablet' and call you back…" The purpose of my visit needed little explanation as Jane MacIntyre was on duty in Dalginross when I first recorded residents in her care in 2009.[1]

So begins our first 'virtual visit' on October 31, 2020. I'm at home in the kitchen, and Sarah Black is in her room in Dalginross Care Home in Comrie. We've never met before, so Jane introduces us.

"It's lovely to see you, Sarah, but I wish I could make you a cup of tea."

"It's all right, Jane has just brought me a cup; she's been showing me how to use this thing. Isn't it amazing we can see each other!"

I agree and tell her we can maybe have a real visit soon. Neither of us gives any thought to when that might be – we're hoping it might be over by Christmas. Meanwhile there's plenty to talk about.

Margaret Bennett: Have you always lived in Comrie, Sarah?

Sarah Black: No, we moved to Perthshire in 1945 when I was eleven – my folk were farming folk and my father took the lease of an arable small-holding, up at Dalrannoch Farm, a hill-farm up past the Linn – he rented it. It was mainly a family farm, so there weren't any hired hands. My brothers could do certain things, and help with the ploughing – we had two horses for a time, big horses, Clydesdales, and there was one that would run and get entangled in the fence. Oh, that was a job getting him out! And then my father got a tractor and he kept one horse. We grew potatoes and we had a flock of Blackface, they're perfect for the hill – when I was young I loved walking up the hill ground when my father was looking at the sheep, checking to see that they were all right.

MB: Tell us a bit about your family and why they decided to move here.

Sarah: My father's name was John Black, and my mother was Isabella but it was Bella usually she got called. I had two older brothers: Adam, who was born in 1924, and John, who was born in 1931, and I was the youngest – the 'ewe lamb', born in 1934, on the 18th of June. There was another brother between Adam and John, but he died when he was only three, so I never knew him. We were on a dairy farm, near North Berwick in East Lothian – my father had about 20 or 22 Ayrshires, and they were hand-milked. It was hard work – you'd be ready for your bed about nine o'clock and then get up about three o'clock to start the milking. They had a dairy, you see, and they had to put the milk through a cooler; it was water-cooled but I forget what it's called. And the milk was poured into big milk churns, and the milk lorry would come about six o'clock to collect the milk. There was a cream separator, on a table if I mind right, and you'd to wind the handle, so some of the milk would go through the separator so you'd have cream and could make butter.

We could see the Bass Rock from our house. I like the sea, but the sea air from the North Sea was pretty damp and cold at times, and the doctor thought the hill air would be better for myself and my father – better for our health. Father had been in the army in the First World War – he joined at Stirling and he was a sergeant in the Scots Guards. But was gassed and that affected him ever after. One year he had rheumatic fever and was very ill and took a long time to recover. When we lived in North Berwick, he and I both suffered from chest infections, and in those days they didnae have antibiotics, so the doctor thought the hill air of Perthshire would be better. Later on, I had to go for an operation tae get part of my lung off. They took me to Mearnskirk Hospital in old Renfrewshire – they took one of the lobes away, my left lung, so I just have one and a half now, but it's got me around a good lot – I'm still here and I'm 87!

MB: Can you remember the flitting, Sarah?

Sarah: A lorry came to take the house stuff, and another one for machinery and that – well, some of it anyway. And they took some of the cattle, the Ayrshires, for milk, but not them all, just a few so we would have enough milk for ourselves and for the cream to make the butter. Later it was Aberdeen Angus we had, mainly beef.

It was right after the war, 1945, and they were celebrating the end of the war. When we came up from East Lothian and arrived here, they still had all the flags and stuff up. And I remember when we were young, the army used to practice on the hill ground and you'd find empty cartridge cases on the hill, and my two brothers and I used to collect them because they were taking them in again, at Cultybraggan Camp – we'd get money for them. Not much, but it was always something.

MB: *What do you remember about the house?*

Sarah: The house up at the farm has been changed a bit over the years, but when we lived up the glen there was no electricity. We had a Tilley lamp, but the children didnae get to light that, because you'd to be awful careful with the mantle, you'd to watch you didnae touch it or it would just go to bits.[2] The Tilley would be in the kitchen, then when you went to bed you'd to go about with wee either candles or wee lamps, you know, in your hand.

We had fires, of course, and there was a stove in the kitchen, but it didn't work right, so for cooking there was gas containers – bitumen, I think.

I remember at the farm, up the glen, the cats used to come to milk as well! And they were sitting ready, and then they'd come in, they'd stand behind the cows a bit and whoever was milking used to squirt the milk! Oh, it was funny to see them! They got a lick o' the milk and I liked watching them – they'd be sitting waiting before they would get it.

MB: Did you go to school locally?

Sarah: I went to Comrie School – I was 11-year-old when I first went, so I was in the old school and then I was in what they called the new school. Of course, on the farm everyone has to be up early with jobs to be done before we went to school – the morning milking, but not so early as four o'clock because it wasn't a dairy farm, but it was before breakfast. When we got up there would be a cup of tea an a biscuit or a slice o bread an jam and after everyone had their certain jobs done, we got wur breakfast – porridge, with real oatmeal, but it's porridge oats now – with salt in it. And we liked to get the cream but there wouldn't be enough sometimes, so we'd have milk, though we usually got cream with our porridge. Then we would walk or cycle down to the village, to school, because we weren't quite far enough out to get the school taxi.

There were nice teachers, most of them, but there was some that were a wee bit nippy! You could learn if you wanted to. I think there was a belt... But I remember before I came here, when I went to school in North Berwick, the teacher kept the belt in a paper bag and if she wanted you to come up with it, she'd tell you to bring it up!

When we left home for Comrie School in the morning, we usually took a piece with us – some kind of bread or scone or something, or a roll. But then eventually we did get a midday meal at the school in Comrie. That was something they had, and oh, I liked the school dinners – I quite enjoyed them. And I was still at school when the school age went up from 14 to 15, and that's when I finished school. I was due to leave at fourteen, but I was actually fifteen when I left.

MB: What did you do when you left school, Sarah?

Sarah: My parents were a wee bit old fashioned [laughs] – there would be no word of having to get a job or leaving home, because it went without saying that I would stay at home and help them. So, I cannae say I did get a life o ma own because I was working at home all the time. I didn't really get going anywhere, which is a drawback, because you don't mix wi ither people the same. Oh, I had some friends and we used tae go tae The Young Farmers' Club. That was maybe about our late teens or whatever, and you made friends there and their parents came to visit us as well. That was nice, you know, an every year there was an excursion. I mind it was tae the Bass Rock one year! We got a boat fae North Berwick an sailed out; we didnae go ashore but oh, you could see aw the birds. I always mind o that. In fact, there's one girl I got to know at the Young Farmers' Club who was only about two years younger than me – she lives in Perth now, but she was on a dairy farm with her parents and she still keeps in touch – we're good friends, we're like sisters, you know, and it's lovely to stay in touch.

MB: *D'you remember Helen Grewar – she got called Nellie? She'd be seven or eight years younger than you – her father was Peter Grewar and he farmed up at Mailermore.*

Sarah: Oh yes, we used to visit them! [laughter] That's a long time ago!

MB: *Her married name is Gardiner, so I know her as Helen Gardiner. I was talking to her the other day.*

Sarah: Were you? Oh, my! I mind years ago when my mother and father would go visiting, I would go with them. We'd have some great nights out visiting – that's what folk did then, you'd visit one another, and we used to visit the Mitchells over at the Lechkin, and the Sinclairs at Craggish and other farms, and they'd come and visit your house. Oh some great nights, and there was always a cup of tea and a 'spread' – the home-baking. We did a lot o that. Mother used to make lovely currant scones, oven scones – they were a treat. She'd bake as often as she could get time, sometimes every day – griddle scones or oven scones, she could do both, and she'd have to make them on the gas stove cooker that we had. There was always baking to be done, and when we had the buttermilk, that was used in our baking because there's usually a wee drop butter through it, not much, but it made lovely scones.

When the milk was plentiful and we had cream, we used to make butter – we had a glass churn, and we used wooden ones as well, for a larger amount of butter. The wooden churn was on a stand and you'd put it on the table and wind the handle, but you could make a small amount of butter in a glass churn, maybe a quart of cream even, you could make a wee bit of butter. My mother also made a soft cheese, which was very good – she had the rennet an I think there was salt in it. When you used the rennet, the warm milk separated into curds and whey, and the curds made a lovely soft cheese – it didnae go hard or firm. Sometimes we used the whey for baking, and the pigs got some. But lo and behold, if we had visitors and they took too much of the soft cheese, if they weren't used to it, they had to truck to the toilet!

At Dalrannoch we always had to stock up for the winter so you wouldn't run out of things – bags of flour and sugar and oatmeal and anything that would keep. It's over two miles to the village so you couldn't always get the shops for things. I learned to drive when I was quite young because I didn't want my father or my brothers to drive me everywhere. I was wantin tae be independent, and I used to go to the country dancin – oh, I enjoyed that especially as the doctor said to me once, "I could stop you from going to that, but no, I won't do it because I know you enjoy it so much". So that was very nice to think he would say that. The country dancin was usually in the Rural Hall, but sometimes it was in the school. It wasn't records we danced to, it was usually a pianist or maybe a fiddle. Jenny MacGregor was a good pianist – she could sit and play for all the different dances! And I can remember it was in November when I'd started at Comrie, and then in December they'd a big Christmas tree in school with candles on it. And they'd to light the candles, you know – it could have went 'Whoof!' and gone up in flames! Oh, they wouldn't allow it now! It was in a huge classroom with a dividing wall that got folded up, and the janitor looked after the tree.

MB: *A lot of folk in the village still talk about Jenny – she was born in 1911 and she was over a hundred when she died. In November 2010 I visited her in Dalginross House along with a music student, Eilidh Firth, and we recorded Jenny.[3] Eilidh's a music teacher now, and she was interested in how Jenny became so involved with music.*

Eilidh Firth: When did you learn to play the piano?

Jenny MacGregor [1911–2011]: When I was a little girl, I had aunts who had a little American organ in their house. I went to visit them every Sunday afternoon and I played this organ for hours. I started piano lessons at the age of eight when a lady who came from Crieff taught me – she came to the house. After I'd finished primary school in Comrie I went to Morrison's [Academy in Crieff], and the music teacher there was Mr Mark Dobson, who had been the music master in Carlisle Cathedral before he moved to Crieff to the Music Department. But I didn't go to him at school – I had hoped to be a music teacher, but it didn't turn out that way. We never were all that well off, and Father was elderly when he retired; he had no pension because he was self-employed and so I took a job in David Richard's grocer's shop, which I eventually ran – I took it over in 1948. Anyway, it was only after I had started to work and could afford lessons I went privately on a Wednesday night after work. My teacher was Mr Dobson, whom I knew at Morrison's and he was very strict. When I was moving into Dalginross Home I had to clear out my house, but I had the great thrill of finding the receipt for my piano, bought in 1934 for forty-one pounds! I always played classical music – I sight-read a lot and became quite a good sight-reader, but I never got to play anything else but the classical music so I can remember you know ... Mendelssohn's music and so on. And he had a little American organ in his music room, and I said to him I want to learn the organ sometime – I had a pedal organ at home. So he put me to that when I was young, not needing very many lessons, just one or two, and in 1939 I became the organist of one of the churches in Comrie. And then in 1941, I started seriously to take an interest in the American organ – I had two American organs when my father died.

MB: What's the difference between an American organ and other ones?

Jenny: American is the one that you pump with your feet and a big pipe organ is the one you put in a bass part with your feet. They're a bit more intricate to play. I never felt that I was all that good at them you know, but I managed to play it once they got one in the church.

MB: You also played for concerts and dances.

Jenny: I had a great love of Scottish country dance music.

Eilidh: So do I – I play the fiddle and the piano, and I've also done Scottish country dance. Scottish country dancers are very particular about the music they like, aren't they? They like the music to be played a certain way.

Jenny: Oh, strict timing of course, you've got to play it like that. You're given so many bars to play for a dance and that has to be repeated. Thirty-two is general, sometimes forty and sometimes forty-eight... I quite like a little speed in it because it can become heavy for the dancers. My father was a great help with that because he and Mother would be in the living room when I was practicing – we had a sitting room, what I called my parlour, with my piano, and we had a living room, and Mother and Father would be in the living room and he'd shout to me, 'You've no' got the right lilt for that!' and he'd tell me what was wrong.

MB: Did your father play?

Jenny: Well, he did scrape away on the violin but he couldnae play it right [laughter] – he played the chanter, and he started up the pipe band in Comrie in 1923.

Muriel (McGregor) Malloy: My father was in the pipe-band – he was a drummer and so was one o his brothers, and three of my uncles were pipers, so there were five McGregors all in the one band. You could call it The McGregor Pipe Band! At one time we had three Comrie pipe bands. There was the Dalginross Pipe Band, the Drummond Street Pipe Band and another one, I cannae mind the name o't.

Pat MacNab [1912–2011]: When I was young there were sixteen boys in Glenartney learning to play the pipes. Every Friday night a piping teacher came by train from Edinburgh and when he arrived at Comrie Station someone from Glenartney went for him with a horse and gig. They drove him up the glen and he taught the boys in a bothy at the end of the glen, then he stayed overnight and returned to Edinburgh on Saturday. Back then, in the 1920s, there was over a hundred folk in Glenartney, but today there's scarcely a dozen. I had my Seanair's [grandfather's] silver-mounted pipes at home and we also had a clarsach – they came from Eigg. My father took them with us when we moved to Glenartney, but then his sister took them to Glasgow, so that was that. [4]

Jenny: My father loved the dances, and he had a great sense of timing. And now everybody says I've a wonderful beat for dance music, so I think I inherited that from my father – he had it in his feet. When I was in my early twenties, I used to go to the Scottish Girls Friendly Society – an organization for girls from working class families [giving moral support and friendship to girls who had left school, and were starting work.] They'd have meetings in the local hall, and then after that they would say, 'Ach, give us a tune Jenny,' and I'd play something, and they'd dance to it. And I used to play at the seniors Scottish country dance classes and I played for children's classes in the school. Everybody danced, and it was taught in all the schools.

MB: *I remember it well. In the mid-sixties I was a student at Jordanhill Teacher Training College, and teaching dance was a compulsory course for all primary school teachers – there was an exam on the RSCDS books. Did you play by notes, from the manuscripts, or did you also play by ear?*

Jenny: I played from sheet music. I wasn't good at ear, and everything had to be by the music because it had to be just right. I played for the classes in Ardvreck School – they had a teacher, the gym teacher, but they needed a pianist and the Headmistress asked me. I said, "Oh yes I'll come". I had my business at the time, but I said to her, "I've a very good assistant at the shop; I can leave for an hour or two in an afternoon". So I went once a week for three periods and played at a great school. Unfortunately, I was only there two or three terms when my mother fell and broke her leg and had to go into hospital, so I didn't carry on with the job. But I still played for dancing some evenings. There used to be competitions and I remember one night playing at a regional competition for Scottish country dancing – it was only for two different branches. I played for the dancers, and Miss Milligan was adjudicating. [She laughs].

MB: The famous Miss Jean Milligan [1886–1978] – founder of the Royal Scottish Country Dance Society, the RSCDS?[5]

Jenny: Yes, my old Headmistress at Morrison's knew her at that time, so she had asked Miss Milligan. I only met her that night – she was very much in the background, watching the dancing, watching every step, and adjudicating it. But I did play for one or two teachers at Ardvreck who all had Miss Milligan at the training college in Glasgow – she was a lecturer at Jordanhill, and from what they said, she was very, very strict.

MB: Jenny, did you have any favourite tunes you liked to play for the dancing?

Jenny: I don't know that I had a favourite, but I learned some nice ones latterly. See, what happened with the Scottish country dance music was that the Society published books of dances and tunes, and when new books came out I had to be able to play them all. I think there's about fifty books now, and a lot of leaflets as well. I played for years, because in 1975, not long after my mother died at the age of 104, I got a phone call from the Headmaster's wife and she said, 'Miss MacGregor, could you come and help us? I hear you might be free, so would you like your job back?' I was there for nineteen years, till I gave it up at the age of 84! [She laughs]. It was only four periods on a Monday, but it was lovely. I enjoyed it thoroughly and outside of Ardvreck I played for the local children's classes and the senior classes – Saturdays and some evenings.

Though Jenny died in 2011, folk in Comrie and Crieff still talk of her. Ann Ross , whose family once farmed in Glen Lednock, had known Jenny since childhood. When Ann left school, she trained as a PE teacher, then after she was married, she and her husband settled in Crieff. Their two sons attended school and Ann taught in the P.E. Department.

Ann Ross: Jenny and I were colleagues for quite a long-time, so I knew her pretty well. Being from the village myself, I had known her before that, because her parents had a shop in Comrie, so everyone in the village knew Jenny. When I worked at Ardvreck I used to give her a lift home sometimes – she lived in in 'Seaton Cottage' in Dalginross and her old mother lived to 104.

MB: *What was your connection to Ardvreck?*

Ann: I was a teacher. I trained as a P.E. teacher in Aberdeen, in Dunfermline College of Physical Education, at what they used to call 'DUNF'; so we were known as the "Dunfers" then, and they moved into Edinburgh, so I was there as well. The college became part of Moray House College of Education, which is now part of Edinburgh University.

MB: *Did you come across Miss Milligan?*

Ann: Oh, I did, yes! All the students had to learn the dances in the RSCDS books – you had to know the lot! Fortunately, by the time Miss Milligan caught up with me I was actually out teaching in Edinburgh, in a rather run-down school at the top end of Leith Walk. And of course, we taught Scottish country dancing – it wasn't exactly top of the pops with all the pupils, but we managed! But relating that to what Miss Milligan would've liked us to do was really quite fun … there was a lot of arm swinging, etc.

Though I wasn't actually one of Miss Milligan's girls, she used to visit schools and she adjudicated dancing. I remember she was extremely uncomplimentary – she was something else!

MB: *Did your own children go to Ardvreck?*

Ann: Yes, it's a long time ago, but my son Donald still remembers the dancing classes, even though he was just a wee boy.

Donald Ross: I remember Jenny MacGregor used to play the piano for my Mum when she used to teach country dancing at Ardvreck School on a Monday. And I remember her telling me and my father that she had this breadboard in her house – she was in her eighties at this point – and she had had the breadboard since she was a little girl. And the story of the breadboard was that when she was a little girl there was a flood in Comrie and she just referred to it as The Great Flood – I'm not sure what year that would be, probably around the time of the Great War, maybe. Anyway, during the Great Flood, this breadboard had floated past their cottage, and her father had picked it out of the water, and he had never been able to return it to its owner. Jenny had kept it all those years and she still had it as an old lady. And that was the story of the breadboard – to think that the flood was so high, just imagine, something like a breadboard would float past your house!

There could be few people more familiar with the village than Billy Gardiner [b. 1927], a retired joiner with a remarkable memory and lifelong interest in local history, dialect, and traditions of Strathearn. Over the years I've enjoyed many conversations with Billy – I wonder if he ever heard Jenny talk about this flood? I'll phone and ask him …

Billy Gardiner: I mind Jenny showing me the breadboard, an she told me this was the breadboard that cam intae the hoose – I don't know how it come in, but she still had it after aw those years. I remember her faither goin on aboot that flood, because it wasnae long afore it that he'd bought a carpet, an when the hoose was flooded the insurance wouldnae cover the carpet for some unknown reason. There was a bad flood in 1910, when Dalginross was aw flooded, an there's a postcard showing the local doctor comin in his car an he's stuck in the flood an it had to be a horse to pull him out. It was Mrs Kissack, Alasdair's mother, that took that photo – she was very keen on photography, an they were staying in 'Earnhope' at the time. The lower part of Dalginross got flooded quite often, an there's one of the hooses doon there, the gateposts were made o sandstone, an you'll see that when they were made there was two slots left in the sandstone each side o the gate for putting boards in to prevent the water comin through the gate. An some o the hooses had a pin on each side o the door – you know how they put a tail-board on a cart? They stick a pin on each side. Well, it was the same idea – they had these boards made an whenever the floodin was comin they would just put a pin on each side an stick the boards on.

Another year Mrs Kissack took a photo down at Dalginross Bridge an it's just pure water aw the way doon – completely water, the whole thing. Comrie is a dangerous place for flooding. Years ago I mind that some professor boy came, an he was advising the Council about the flooding an he said if they blocked the water fae comin down Dalginross it would spread out over the fields. But how can the water spread up the fields? It's just gaun tae go doon into Comrie, that's where it's going to go! And then there was the theory that when they made the dam, an controlled the Lednock waters, that that stopped the flooding. But there was bad floods there in 1990, an other years too.

MB: Yes, and we got cut off at Dunira when the A85 got flooded, and quite a few houses in Comrie were flooded; some folk had to be re-housed.

Bobby Thomson: (Forfar, visting relatives in Comrie): The worst one I remember was when Margaret and Irvine Walker were flooded out, on Glebe Road in Comrie, just along the road from Auntie Nan. She was lucky because the water didnae reach as far as her house, and there were a few steps up to her front door, so that might've helped. But Margaret and Irvine's house was in an awful state – they had to move out. They went to St Fillans, to Bobby and Cathie McLarty's – they were still in the big house, and there was a sort of annex place, and Margaret and Irvine stayed wi them for months until their own house was refurbished and they got back in again. It doesn't seem that long ago, the early nineties; there was a photo in the *Stratehearn Herald* of a boat being pushed along Glebe Road.

I mind Auntie Nan used to speak aboot the terrible winter they had in 1947. She said it was just awful, and it went on for months; the snow on the roads was up to the height of the telegraph wires. It was really a terrible storm. I don't remember the storm myself, because I would only be about three or four at that time, but she used to speak about it.

MB: Yes, I remember her telling me – she and Pat [MacNab] used to speak about that awful winter; so did some of the other older folk.

Nan Doig [1912–2014]: We were a few years in Fife, and in 1947 we moved back to Perthshire, though we didn't get the lease of a farm right away. We were employed by Mr Wood who had Dalchirla, one of the farms down the back road between Muthill and the Straid. (Relatives of his still have it, the Hunters.) It's on the Ancaster Estate[6] – miles of road, then a long farm track down to it, and very isolated, and so we moved into the cottage. That was 1947, well you know what that was like, nothing but snow storms one after another! And the road was blocked for weeks at a time. And the water froze underground, before it got the length of the cottage – it was terrible. I remember that keeping warm was very difficult because after the war fuel was rationed, coal was rationed, and there werena many sticks and no wood to be got. My sister Jean was teaching in Bridge of Earn and she was in lodgings there, but she came home to Dalchirla at the weekends. She came on the bus, but it was about four miles from where the bus stopped, and she had to walk up and back down again. It was a very difficult time.[7]

Pat: That same year we were ten weeks up Glenartney, blocked in by the snow. You couldn't get out for *ten weeks*! That was the time they got the Nazi prisoners from the Cultybraggan camp to dig out the roads. And they were good at it! There were 112 prisoners, and they took a week to clear the eight mile o road, all the way up the glen. When they started on it, they were hanging their jackets on the top of the telegraph poles, and the snow was that high they were doing a layer at a time, digging off the top layer and then going back to dig off the next layer. [8]

Helen (Grewar) Gardiner: Oh, I remember that! I was in primary school at Blairnroar and the school was closed for weeks on end. No school, so I went sledging every day. It was great!

Sarah: When we got snowed in at Dalrannoch and the road was closed, I had to walk down to the main road with my sledge and wait for the baker's van, then take whatever we needed up the hill. Some winters the river would be frozen solid, and our water supply that came from across the river would be cut off. But we managed to get water somehow – we didnae like getting it from the woods up behind our burn there because it was dirty, but ye had to do what you could. Oh, it was work, work, work!

Jimmy Stewart, Ochtertyre, [1921–2012]: After the war, late forties, we were up Glen Isla, above Alyth. There wis three shepherds in the place, a nice hirsel, nice sheep and everything, A married man in a house like that was only getting £3.15s.0d. a week, so you can imagine we couldnae save very much! But 1947 finished it – that was a terrible winter, and we were completely cut off, miles away from anything, planes dropping food to us. So, after that I came to Corriemucadh – that's from *muc*, the Gaelic for pig, the corrie o the pigs. It's just about a mile from Amulree, on the Crieff side and we were there for five years.[9]

Billy: That bad winter, 1947, the coal trains couldnae get through. But I was down in Aldershot, doing my National Service, as I'd been called up by then.

Tam Kettle: I can remember 1947, the really bad storm. I'd have been twelve, and we were at Millhill Farm, out near Auchterarder. An ma faither used to take the horse an cart up to Crieff to go for the shopping – the messages, as we called them. And that winter the road was blocked, and he used to go through the fields, wi the milk – they sold milk in Crieff, so he had to get there wi the milk.

MB: And he took the cart? I'm amazed that the cart coped with the snow.

Tam: Ah, well, they were broad wheels, rubber tyred, you know? They weren't thae modern ones.

MB: And did you ever use a sleigh behind the horse?

Tam: A slype, aye.[10] Well, around the farm, just for moving anythin heavy. And they used them in the woods, I used to be a woodcutter, and we used the slype when we were cutting wood. And they started off wi the horses an then used to roll the trees up the slype.

MB: And you were out in all weathers.

Billy: Have you heard the forecast? There's supposed to be a big storm on the way.

MB: Another one? It's only weeks since storm Barra [Dec. 7–8, 2021]. Did they say what they're going to call this one?

Billy: They didnae used to have names. I mind when I was still at school in Comrie, and there was great big snowflakes comin doon in April. And this Glasgow teacher, she said to me, because I was local, she says "What is this – snow in April?" So when I cam home, I asked ma faither an he said that was the gowk storm.[11] The gowk is another name for cuckoo, you ken. The cuckoo comes in April, in May it sings its song, in June it lays its eggs.[12] An there was the 'teuchit' storm, that was when the lapwings were nesting, round about March, an there could be wild, stormy weather: that was the 'teuchit' storm'.[13]

We used to have a saying about forecasting the weather on the second o February:

> If Candlemas be bright an fair
> Half the winter's to come and mair
> If Candlemas be wet and foul
> Half the winter's gone at Yule.[14]

MB: *Candlemas [February 2nd] was a lovely day, and our first daffodils are already in bloom, so I hope we're not in for bad weather.*

Diary entries:

February 23, 2022. We have a lot of snow today and the daffodils are buried.

Winter's not over and it looks like Billy's saying is right.

March 1, 2022: Beautiful sunny day, but –

> If March comes in like a lion it will go out like a lamb
> If March comes in like a lamb it will go out like a lion.

March 24, 2022: Sunny; clear blue skies; 18 degrees.

March 31, 2022: The garden is white with snow; temperature is −4°C.

Endnotes

1   Recordings, transcriptions and photographs of the collection have been deposited in Perth & Kinross Archive, Acc11/52.

2   The Tilley is a pressure lamp, named after John Tilley, who invented it in the mid-1800s.

3   Perth & Kinross Archive, Acc11/52: M. Bennett and E. Firth, interview with Jenny MacGregor (2010). Open access.

4   Perth & Kinross Archive, Acc11/52: M. Bennett, interview with Pat MacNab (2007).

5   Jean Milligan [1886–1978] was from Glasgow. She became Principal instructor in Physical Education at Jordanhill Teacher Training College in Glasgow, where she advocated the teaching of dance as an essential element in maintaining fitness and strength. Her keen interest in traditional dances led to her collaboration with Mrs Ysobel Stewart [1882–1968] and in 1923 they founded the Royal Scottish Country Dance Society. Miss Milligan succeeded in implementing Dance as part of the curriculum in all Scottish schools, thus it was also part of the curriculum of trainee teachers. Though Miss Milligan had long-since retired when I was a student (mid-1960s), she was still had a 'presence' at Jordanhill College of Education (Glasgow) as students were required to study her books of dances for the final exams. The RSCDS soon became (and still is) one of Scotland's largest societies with branches all over the world. See, <https://rscds.org/>

6   According to a survey of Perthshire's acreocracy (land-owners of three thousand acres and upward), conducted by the 'Perth and Kinross Fabian Society' in 1960, the Ancaster Estate, comprising Drummond Castle & gardens and Glenartney, covered 81,250 acres, the third largest estate in Perthshire. See, *the Fabian Society pamphlet, 'The Acreocracy of Perthshire', p. 8.*

7   Perth & Kinross Archive, Acc11/52: M. Bennett interview with Nan Doig, (2009).

8   Perth & Kinross Archive, Acc11/52: M. Bennett interview with Pat MacNab (2009).

9   Perth & Kinross Archive, Acc11/52: M. Bennett interview with Jimmy Stewart (2009).

10   I.F. Grant discusses the use of slypes in the removal of boulders from fields; *Highland Folk Ways,* p. 281, with sketch p. 283.

11   Charles Swainson discusses the 'Gowk storm' in *The Folk Lore and Provincial Names of British Birds,* p. 112.

12   Comparative sayings about the cuckoo, see Christina Hole, and M.A. Radford, *Encyclopaedia of Superstitions*, pp. 120–123.

13   Charles Swainson refers to the 'teuchit storm' in March in his discussion on the folklore of the lapwing (the peewit or teuchit) in Forfar and Kincardine, *Op. cit.,* pp. 183–187.

14   Robert Chambers includes the rhyme in his discussion of Candlemas-Day, see *Popular Rhymes of Scotland* (1826), pp. 365–367. Mary MacLeod Banks discusses Candlemas weatherlore in Volume II of *British Calendar Customs: Scotland*, pp. 156–57 and F. Marian McNeill cites 2 Candlemas weather-forecast rhymes in The Silver Bough, Vol. II, p. 31. David Kerr Cameron quotes a Candlemas rhyme from the North-East of Scotland in *Willie Gavin, Crofter Man,* p. 191, In 1985 I recorded Gladys and Charles Simpson from Banffshire talking about local weather sayings. Their Candlemas rhyme is very similar to Billy's rhyme and in referring to the 'teuchit's Storm' they added that some folk called it the 'gab o May'. School of Scottish Studies Archive, Edinburgh University, SA 1985/141. See also, 'Weather Sayings from Banffshire' in *Tocher* 47, 1994, pp. 310–313. In Roy Palmer's discussion on British weatherlore, he quotes several sayings about Candlemas, indicating its importance to farmers whose spring planting and harvest depended on favourable weather. R. Palmer, *Britain's Living Folklore,* p. 157.

Chapter 2

Doon the Village an Up the Glen

Billy Gardiner: I was born ben the hoose there, in that room doon there an I hope I die in that room, but maybe no –

Margaret Bennett: In this very house in Comrie? Not many folk live their whole lives in the same house, so tell us about the house?

Billy: Aye, ben the hoose – it was built 1925–26 an I was born in 1927, on June the 9th. My faither was a joiner an it was him that built this hoose. And when this house wiz built first, the kitchenette was where the bathroom is noo, an we'd a gas light there, an a gas ring – nearly everybody had a wee gas ring cos they were awfae handy.

MB: What kind of gas supply did you have?

Billy: There was a gas-works in Comrie in thae days – it's no there noo, but it was right doon the last lane: you get to Commercial Lane, then you get the Ancaster Lane an then you get Manse Lane … doon at the bottom o Manse Lane. I've got a picture of it, wi the big tall chimney. It was built in 1854, coal-fired, an people in the village were shareholders. It closed 1952.

But the family were here a long time afore my faither built this hoose. The one that bought this ground away back, my great-great-grandfaither, he was William Gardiner. He'd been a crofter over Muirend along there, an his brother was a weavers' agent. I've got it in my notebook: The feu was bought by William Gardiner in 1809, from Muirend on the Drummond Estate. 'Hedgefield' was the title to the feu on the South Crieff Road, so that's the name o the hoose.

Nowadays Muirend is regarded as part of Comrie but the parish boundaries can be confusing because back then, the burn was the boundary o the parish – it's changed over the years. In 1809 Muirend wasnae in Comrie Parish, so if you were born or died on this side of the Lednock Bridge, that had to be registered in Monzievaird Parish.[1]

An my folk went to the church in Comrie, which was in Comrie Parish, so you can see how the old Parish Records can be very confusing – I don't know exactly where my great-grandfaither was born [William Gardiner's son], because you won't find that in the Comrie Parish Records. He married Catherine Sharp an she was the first to be buried in Comrie new cemetery, 1874.

In their day, hooses were mainly 'but an ben', just two rooms doonstairs, the kitchen an the 'room' an a wee middle room. The 'room' was only used on special occasions like when the minister called; we didna say 'sitting room'; it was always the 'room'. The kitchen was the main room, an there was always a bed in the kitchen. The auld hooses had only a front door an no back door – that kept the heat in, an they had two windows tae the front, an one at the back, the middle room. Some o the auld hooses had two rooms upstairs, wi skylights.

There was no running water or WCs an folk had dry toilets oot the back. A lot o hooses had their own well, an some o them had a pipe coming from their well intae a pump in the scullery. There were village wells wi water from Glen Lednock – there was a public one at the wee Square [Mid Square, Dalginross] an one at the top Square [Melville Square]; they were cast iron, aboot 3 feet high. But people who lived on the outskirts o the village sometimes had to go a fair distance to get water, an there could be a problem in hot summers.

MB: Do you remember your grandparents?

Billy: My grandfaither was also William Gardiner, but I never knew him because he was dade afore I was born. By the way, we dinnae say 'deid' in Comrie [for 'dead'], it's 'dade' here an 'deid' in Glasgow [and other places].[2]

Anyway, he was a skilled gardener an he laid out gairdens an tennis courts at some o the big hooses in Comrie an St Fillans. He'd served his time at Lawers, the big hoose gairden, an after that he traded as Seedsman an Fruiterer. They kept a cow, an he rented a small field from Strowan Estate – part of it on Gowanlea Road was for the cow, an part of it was to grow carrots. He had a market gardening business an he bought the feu in Barrack Road – Uncle Andrew, my father's brother, worked with him, an they also rented two pieces o ground from the Steel family of Inverearn. So my grandfaither, William, was known as the Laird because of the bits o ground he owned or rented. After he died, the feu at South Crieff Road, 'Hedgefield' was left to my faither, Alec, an Uncle Andrew got the feu in Barrack Road. Half the field at the back of this house was kept in grass an Uncle Andrew made hay for his cow. He seemed to have the same cow for ages, Flecky, a Shorthorn cross, I think – it had horns. It had a calf every year – I remember it was always black, an it was always called Bobby. About October he would walk it into the market in Crieff, on Ford Road. In Grandfaither Gardiner's day, the story goes that one year he had a really good calf, an when he took it to the market several o the bidders were after it, so the price went up an up, an he finally shouted, "Stop! Stop!" Of course the calf had to go to the highest bidder – cattle dealers would want to bring it on for showing.

MB: *Though your grandfather had died before you were born, did the family talk much about him?*

Billy: My faither had a lot of stories an I wrote a few in my notebook: I'm told he had a rough beard an he spoke Scots. He married Elizabeth Drummond whose faither was a weaver in Drummond Street, but the Drummonds were not too happy about this, because William was a member of the Old Kirk an a Tory, an the Drummonds were U. P. [United Presbyterian] Church an Liberal. That's the way it was in their day, people who went to the Free church an the U.P. Church voted Liberal an the ones who attended the Old Kirk voted Tory.

Old Drummond was an elder in the U.P. for 40 years, an his daughter, my grandmother, Elizabeth, had been a lady's maid-companion to a lady in Edinburgh. When my grandfaither married Elizabeth Drummond he left the Auld Kirk an went to the U.P. – this caused a lot of talk because the custom was that the wife always took her husband's church.

One Sunday the minister announced that the fast day was to cease. William jumped to his feet an shouted, "Another game of golf for you!" My faither had these stories, but when he heard them he was too wee to ask more about them, like what happened. Apparently the Minister had been up to see his faither on the Monday an they had a long talk. Then another Sunday they walked past the U.P. Church an along to the Free Church, up to the back seat.

The Drummond family were still not very happy, even though my grandfaither was an educated man. My faither said he read the *Scotsman*, an could talk about anything. When a cousin o mine had his name in the paper for a project at school one of them said the Drummonds had put the brains in the Gardiners. What about another relative of ours, Mary Morrison, who got a New Testament at Comrie School for best in English? It was presented by the Gaelic Society of London an I still have it.

MB: Comrie had a lot of churches in the 1800s.[3]

Billy: The Church has changed – the Old Parish Church beside the river [built in 1805] is the one they call the White Church. [It became the community centre in 1965[4]]. Then there was the Free Church [built in 1847 following the Disruption of 1843[5]]. In the Free Church you sit for Psalms an stan for prayers, an there was no organ. A presenter struck his tuning fork on the bench an sang the first line. And in the Parish Church you sit for prayers, stand for hymns. Then they built a second Free Church – I have a photo taken in 1879 [see phot section] of when they laid the foundation stone of the new Free Church. That was a much bigger church – there's a wee rhyme:

> The wee kirk
> The free kirk
> The kirk without a steeple
> The auld kirk
> The cauld kirk
> The kirk wi aw the people.

The first Free Church got turned intae a hall because it wasn't needed when the two congregations combined [1925]. Our family were United Free, St. Kessogs, an I went to Sunday School an Bible Class but in thae days we never heard many of the terms used now, like Pentecost an Advent. And that's the Parish Church now, St Kessogs[6]

MB: Where did you go to school, Billy?

Billy: I went to Comrie School. It was built in 1910, an you could do all your schooling there, primary an secondary. That changed a while back, an my son went to the secondary school in Crieff – that one's demolished now an they've built another new one. D'you no think it would be better to build better quality in the first place? And in my day, there were schools in Blairnroar, Glenartney, Glenlednock, Monzievaird an St Fillans.

Helen (Grewar) Gardiner: I was at the wee school at Blairnroar and I remember when I went there we had a great teacher. Oh, she was brilliant, but she retired not long after we moved to Mailermore, then the one that replaced her, she was a teacher who came from Islay after a broken romance, or so the story goes. And then, d'you know what she did? She left and went back to Islay and married the man! [laughter] Figure that one out if you can, [laughter] but I hope it worked out. Anyway, that's where I went to primary school, a one-teacher school with about a dozen pupils, and for secondary school I went to Morrison's in Crieff.

MB: *And how did you get from Mailermore to Blairnroar every day?*

Helen G: I walked. There was a school car put on for pupils who lived a certain distance, but I didn't get that because I didn't live far enough away – a mere four miles! I used to be really late in getting home because I used to stop at all the burns and have a look and see what the fish were doing, and things like this! [laughter] That was in the late 'Forties, not long after the war.

Duncan McNab: My Dad went to the one in Glenartney but he was glad to leave it: he had some awful memories. When they moved there in 1916, he didn't have any English because my grandfather, who was the shepherd, came from Eigg. He was Peter MacNab, and when they came to Glenartney a lot o the shepherds spoke Gaelic. But the following year, when Dad started school the teacher leathered his bare backside for speaking Gaelic – he went home black and blue, so from then on it had to be all English.[7]

Elma (Henderson) Cunningham, niece of Nan Doig: There was no school in Glen Lednock, so when we were living at Balmuick the children had to go to Comrie School. Before I started school I'd only ever been used to mixing with relatives, my cousins, like Helen [Doig] and Muriel, who all lived up at Balmuick. So when I went to school, I was a very, very shy child, and when we had the assembly, I can still remember sitting in that assembly room with the tears rolling down my face. And one of the teachers took me to a side room and showed me how to make an envelope! [laughter] I just wasn't used to having lots and lots of children around me. I don't think I ever made an envelope after that, but I can still remember her showing me how to do it.

Helen Doig: When the lease at Balmuick ended, we had to move to Locherlour, so I went to the wee Monzievaird School. It's just a few hundred yards along the road and I liked the school.

Billy: These wee schools just taught as far as the qualifying class [primary 7] and then they'd go to Comrie for the secondary, though some went on to Morrison's Academy.

MB: *The Comrie School that you attended is a lovely old building.*

Billy: It's changed a bit since I was there. There was railings around the school, and you weren't supposed to go out those gates. The school had a playground for boys an one for girls, an there were metal fences an a gairden between them. At one time gardening was part of the school teaching. Then during the war the railings next to the road were

taken away, but the ones round the gairden were left. First thing in the mornin the janny came into the infant classroom to ring the bell – there was a rope came down through the ceiling, an when we heard the bell we lined up ootside the doors, girls East End, boys West End. Then we marched in lines to the corridor. There were a few R.C. pupils an they waited outside while the Headmaster, or sometimes a minister, gave a short prayer, then we sang a hymn, with a teacher on the piano, but the only one the boys liked was "Stand up, stand up for Jesus".

The school toilets were away in the corner of the playground an there was hand basins wi great big lumps o red carbolic soap. It was "Please miss I want to leave the room," an there could be six inches o snow, or lashing wi rain, an we'd have to go away outside!

Muriel (McGregor) Malloy: And mind the toilet paper? Wee squares o newspaper hanging on a string.

Billy: Aye, an the lighting was gas mantles. An when we were at school there was no school meals in Comrie, so you'd take your piece with you or if you lived near enough you could run home for dinner. Country bairns all took pieces, an for mothers who were making them every day it was difficult at times, providing pieces.

During the war we all got masks – they were to be carried at all times – an in school we all got air-raid drill. The air-raid siren was above the fire station – that was newly built, plus an ambulance garage alongside. An when the siren went, you'd to go to places of safety – under the railway tunnel, under stairs at Mitchell & Thompson office, the old jail, under the Old School.

MB: How many teachers were there?

Billy: The head teacher was Mr Murray – he lived in the schoolhouse. Most of the teachers were spinsters, an if they married they had to leave. All the teachers had what we called straps, what they called the tawse. The infant teachers, they were on their own, like a separate department, an the Infant Mistress was the most important teacher in the school, after the Headmaster. But to put it kind o bluntly, she was a bad bitch the teacher we had then. One o the classrooms had steps built up, an I was at the back an James Kemp, the butcher's laddie, was at the front. And he had chestnuts – dinnae ask me why he had chestnuts in August, that's a puzzle, he must have kept them fae the year before. An when the Infant Mistress was sitting at her desk we were throwing chestnuts up an doon, an one o them stottered on the step an rolled out in front o the teacher. She used to see o'er the top o her glasses, an James Kemp an I both got six o the belt for playing *chessies*. An that was in the infants' class, just six year auld. We didnae speak about conkers in Comrie – it was always 'chessies' we said. An there was one particular laddie, he was of the Traveller fraternity, an she made that poor laddie stand in the waste paper basket in the corner of the room. An when she was out of the room one day we tried it; just try it! Terrible!

Then when my brother went two years later she had a dunce's hat she used to put on folk; she was a bad teacher that. I was speaking to an old lady in Dalginross one day, an she was telling me she was left-handed, an when she was at school they tied her hand behind her back when the class was writing. An if they were doing anything else an children tried to use their left hand, the teacher thumped them across the fingers with

a ruler. My faither was left-handed an he never spoke about it. But I mind him tellin us about the man with a dancing bear that came to Comrie – that was before the Great War. I wonder how you'd transport a bear from Romania to Comrie afore the First World War?

Anyway, when I went to school in Comrie, there was Miss Dale, an she had a high an a low class; usually there would be 48 in a class, so she had a tough job. For the qualifying class, there was just the one teacher, then there was the secondary school, which was part of old Comrie School. We had a visiting teacher of PT, a Mr Bannerman, an we got different subjects. The literary ones, they got French an I dinna ken what else they got. I wanted to be a joiner, like my faither, an there was what they called the Technical Department so we got woodwork, technical drawing an all other things. There was a metalwork teacher, this sticks in my mind, his nickname was 'Purvey' an he was going to be teaching something to do with etching on metal, so at the start o the class he says to this laddie, "Go down to the chemist an get some petroleum jelly for me." So he's away doon the street, an when he came back he says, "They haven't got any." So the teacher said, "Away back down an ask him for Vaseline. That's what you put on top of the metal." We'd a woodwork teacher an he taught us how to do dovetails – that was a favourite with him, dovetails, so we made wee boxes all dovetailed. We learned how to do piano hinges an all that before we left school. Fourteen was the school leaving age, an most of the class was away at fourteen, but ma mother insisted that I stayed on for my Lower Leaving Certificate, so I stayed on till fifteen. Very few pupils stayed on an when I was in the third year, it was still during the war, I was the only local one in the class apart from one from Dunira – all the rest were evacuees. So I finished school during the war.

MB: And had you decided before you left school that you were going to be a joiner?

Billy: Oh well, I wanted to be an apprentice joiner, but of course everything was rationed an my faither an his partner got very little wood. You wouldnae see the amount they were gettin lyin in the bottom o a lorry. So, they couldnae take on an apprentice because there wasnae wood, except for special circumstances, an you got a licence. Then for some time after the war, you still werenae allowed to use wood on the bottom floor o a house, so that's why there's a lot of concrete floors; you werenae allowed to use hardwood, ken, birch an stuff like that.

MB: Could you go and cut timber?

Billy: Well, there were sawmills, an later on we got quite a lot of stuff fae the sawmill up at Dunira.

Sandy Gardiner (Billy's son): So that's why you worked as a baker?

Billy: Aye, there wasnae any work, so in the *Stratharn Herald* – that famous paper you ken, *The Stratharn Herald* – there was this advert for a boy doon the bake-hoose, so my Mother said, "Would you like to go?"

So I went doon there, an they took me on as an apprentice. It was six days a week, no holidays the first year, an the pay was fourteen shillings a week – that's less than 75 pence now. An I was doon the bake-hoose until I went in the army.

MB: Was that here in Comrie?

Billy: Aye. In thae days there wis two bake-hooses in Drummond Street an one in Dalginross. Three bakers in Comrie, an they all had Scotch ovens, like igloos, ken, brick. I was in the one – the bake-hoose, no the oven – at the bottom o Dalginross.

MB: *Can you remember roughly the dimensions of the Scotch oven?*

Billy: Oh they were a fair size. See that wee roomy there? They were about the size o that.

MB: *Say, about six feet by eight?*

Billy: Bigger than that, an there was two of them down there.

MB: *Brick, with a fire-box at the side?*

Billy: Aye, an you had to get the right heat up – highly skilled job, you ken. The other bake-hooses, Scotch ovens, are still in Comrie. You ken where Johnny Carmichael's yard is, well right across from there there's a bake-hoose there, on a triangle bit of ground.

MB: *And what fuelled them?*

Billy: Coke. Well you had to get it going, an that was a skilled part of the thing to get the coke going so there wasn't any smoke coming off it. The coke was in the corner of the oven, an first you had to coke it up so all the smoke was away an then get it right going – it had to be hot. Then you had to clean aa the floor wi like a mop wi a long handle, then you'd dust aa the floor wi rice flour, so you got that nice crust on the bottom of the bread.

You've heard about folks talking about a half loaf? An some folk wonder what you're blethering aboot – they think it's a loaf cut in half, but it's not that at all. [To the baker], a loaf was like two loaves baked side by side, baked together, that's how they made them all, so a loaf was half of one of those baked together – a half-loaf. An my job as a laddie, I was the boy that put them in the oven, on the peel. That's the thing like a shovel, wi a big long handle an a flat thing at the end for the loaves, that was called a peel. That's what they called 'running the batch', an you had to watch the clock an no burn it. There was a wee boley-hole for looking in – d'you ken what a boley hole is? Mind, a boley hole can mean two meanings: it can be a room in below a stair where everything's chucked in, that's a boley hole as well.[8] But in the oven it's just a wee lid that you opened up, an you just looked in to see how the oven was going, but you aye had to watch the clock.

MB: *You'd have an early start every day.*

Billy: Aye, the bakers started at 6 o'clock an you got half day Saturday, just working mornings, but you had to start God knows what time on a Saturday to make up for this! All the shops were closed Sundays an Wednesday afternoon – that was the half-day in Comrie. An we got a Monday holiday once a month – I used tae go doon to Muirend Farm because I liked the horses, an I got to work wi them. An in the bakehouse, if there was anything wrong with the oven, mebbe a brick or something, there was this oven boys came an they were stripped tae the waist, you ken. They left the oven off till Monday, as long as possible, an then they went in there, crawled through this door in there – what a job!

MB: *It never did cool down then, did it?*

Billy: No, it would aye be warm, Scotch ovens aye stay warm. Mind you, it was gey cold in the bakery, because there wasnae an awfu lot o heat come into the actual bake-hoose.

MB: *Was all the mixing done by hand or did they have mechanical paddles of any kind?*

Billy: No, we had a machine for that, a dough mixer, an then it went in this what you call the big troughs[9] that's another name, trock or troch, great big wooden thing, then it went in there, an was covered with flour bags until it rose.

MB: *Any idea where they got the machinery?*

Billy: Hobarts was one of the firms that made machinery for mixin the bread dough, Hobart. It had an oil engine when I went doon there first, an this oil engine would start about four o'clock, five o'clock in the morning. There was a man come in once, he was lodging across the road, for a holiday, he come in one morning an he says, "I'm interested in that engine," he says, "I hear it going off every morning", cause the boss would start it up first thing in the mornin. An he says, "What kind of engine is it?" He come in, enquirin, you see. But [not long after that] the baker I worked for wasnae long there an he kind o renovated the place. He got this old oil engine chucked oot an got a braw electric thing instead.

MB: *And what about pies and pastries?*

Billy: There was a machine, like an auld-fashioned mangle for manglin yer washin, an you put the pastry dough in there to roll it, an they called it the 'brake'. I suppose it would be called that because, you ken when you're makin puff pastry, you put it through the rollers, then put the brake on, an then you double it up, an put it through the rollers again, an that's how when the pastry rose it comes like layers on crust of a pie. But ken Scotch pies, wi pie crusts? The Scotch pies were all done by hand. You just got a lump o dough an then you just worked it like that, wi your knuckles [kneading it repeatedly]. A lot o work, but then there was another improvement the new baker made: he got a pie crust machine, so you stuck your bit o dough in this metal thing an pulled the handle down, an the machine steamed it, an you got a pie crust like that.

MB: *A lot of learning for the apprentices! So how long did you work in the local baker's?*

Billy: Till I was called up for the army.

MB: *When you got your call up papers was baking not deemed to be essential work?*

Billy: I didnae bother applying so I didnae ken – I wasnae wantin to stay onyway; I was wantin tae get intae the Army.

Endnotes

1   The name Monzievaird is from Gaelic, 'monadh a' bhaird' meaning 'moor of the bard'. The current spelling with a 'z' found on Ordnance Survey maps suggests that the map-makers had no knowledge of Gaelic as there is no 'z' in the Gaelic alphabet. The older spelling was in use in nineteenth century as can be seen from *The Statistical Account of Scotland, Monivaird and Strowan, Perth*, Vol. 8, Edinburgh, 1793. The Rev. Colin Baxter, Minister of Monivaird [sic] and Strowan notes that these "originally distinct parishes, have been united for at least a century and a half." (p. 567) This information is repeated in 1845 by the Rev. John Ferguson, see *The New Statistical Account of Scotland, Monivaird and Strowan, Perth*, Vol. 10, 1845, p. 732. For an early description of the adjoining parish of Comrie, see *The Statistical Account of Scotland, Comrie, Perth*, Vol. 11, Edinburgh, 1794. Mr Hugh McDiarmed, Minister of Comrie, described the parish, which extended from Comrie to Lochearnhead and into 4 glens: Glenairtney [sic], Glenlednaig [sic] and Finniglen and Glentearkin [sic]. See p. 178 ff.

2   Billy kept a notebook listing Strathearn Scots words as he wanted to record regional variations of the language. Before resuming the conversation, and to make sure I had noted the differences in dialects, he demonstrated with further examples (English, Comrie and Glasgow): bread, brade, breid; lead, lade, leid; head, hade, heid. James Wilson from Dunning (20 miles west of Comrie) discusses the distinctive pronunciation in Perthshire's district of Strathearn. He also compiled a list of local vocabulary and examples of Strathearn sayings in his book, *Lowland Scotch as Spoken in the Lower Strathearn District of Perthshire.*

3   For a site map of church buildings in Comrie see "Places of Worship in Scotland": <https://powis.scot/sites-map/#searchdbInstr>.

4   See <http://www.comriewhitechurch.co.uk/>.

5   In the debates that led to the establishment of the Free Church in 1843, the most contentious religious issue was the Protestant church's stance on 'patronage' – i.e., the right of a church 'heritor' (the landlord or 'laird') to select ministers for church vacancies, regardless of the people's views. Experience had shown them that, in exchange for favourable living conditions, ministers supported the landlord in parish matters, even over issues of poverty, starvation and ruthless conditions. After the break-away, the newly formed Free Church had no funds to build elaborate churches, far less churches with steeples, but their congregations out-numbered those that remained in the established church.

6   For a history of St Kessogs, which is the present Church of Scotland, see <https://comrieparishchurch.org/history/>.

7   Pat MacNab's school memories, see M. Bennett, *In Our Day...*, p. 48.

8   Scot. Dictionary: In Dumfries-shire, boley hole is a space for stowing junk; Also, boal (Ayrshire) is a hatch; a pay window (in factory); a ticket window (eg at railway station).

9   Pronounced 'trows'.

Chapter 3

Paraffin Lamps, Tilleys, Gas Lights and a Warm Fireside

Margaret Bennett: Muriel, the McGregors have been in Comrie for a long, long time. Were you born in the village?

Muriel (McGregor) Malloy: I was born in Drummond Street, on the same side as the library – the Morrison's Buildings it was called then. Six of us were born there: Bunty was the eldest (Catherine Anne's her name – she was born in 1935); then Agnes (she died when she was 60); then me. I was born in 1939 an I was called after my Mum. Then there's John, two years younger than me, then Lawrence, an then Jennifer. During the war my Dad was called up – the early 'forties. He didnae want to go, because he thought it was terrible getting taken away fae his bairns. He was nearly becomin a conscientious objector, but anyway, he went. He drove a tank transporter an I don't know where he was but he got shot through the stomach. So, he was in an army hospital – after the war he used to show us where the bullet went in! When I was about eight, we moved to a house over on the glebe, an there were three more: Fiona, then Allan an then Audrey. So, there were nine of us altogether an we all went to Comrie school.

MB: Can you remember your first day in school?

Muriel: Yes. I went hand in hand wi Johnny Carmichael an we both left at fifteen, the same day. He was a great friend o mine, Johnny. I loved the school an I got on great with all the teachers. Looking back, I think they must have thought our family were poor, because they used to bring in clothes – costumes an blouses an that. But children all wore hand-me-downs then; it's different now, everybody's trying to be better than the next. They'd wonder now how on earth my mother did all the washing an drying for all of us, wi no washing machine.

My Mum grew up on a farm – Logiealmond, near Harrietfield. She was Muriel Webster afore she married, an ma Dad was Jimmy McGregor. They were married in Monzievaird Church, which is no longer there, an the reception was in the wee Monzievaird Hall. So, whenever there's a Burns supper or anything in the hall, I always like to go; I think, oh, this is where my Mother had her party for her wedding.

My Dad was a stonemason, an so was his father, so he grew up with it. He built grates in a lot o the houses around here, an he made the fireplaces out of stones from the river. It had to be stone from the Ruchill or he wouldnae build it! My Dad's brother, Uncle Willie had the blacksmith's – you know down Drummond Street, opposite the library? That was the Blacksmiths shop, an Uncle Willie did the horses. There was a lot o horses in those days, an it was all horses at Logiealmond.

During the war there was an awfu lot o changes on the farms – most o them were leased from the big estates, an I'm not really sure what happened, but Grandad lost the lease of Logiealmond an they all had to move. He got a job near Comrie at Locherlour Farm, so he an my Granny an the family stayed in the cottage across the road from the steading. Grandad an three o the boys worked there. There were five boys, but Allan moved away an Ronnie joined the army, so the three who worked at Locherlour were Uncle Davie (he was the eldest), Uncle Bob and Uncle Jock. They'd all been used tae workin wi horses at Logiealmond, and the farms round about all had horse-mills. So they were all workin at Locherlour mill doing the corn [oats] or whatever it was – but that was a water-mill, an the old water-wheel is still there. I don't remember a lot about my Grandad but when we were children we used to go doon there to play. Then after Grandad died, the family left Locherlour and moved into Comrie. They got a house on Dundas Street, 'West View' – it's just on the corner there. They lived there for years an years, an Granny was in her nineties when she died. Uncle Davie got a job cutting bracken – he had the contract all over this area, and Uncle Bob and Uncle Jock bought Tomperron Farm so they lived there.

I had another Uncle Jock on my father's side, Jock McGregor, an after the war started he worked at the Cultybraggan Camp. He cut the grass an did all the things round the camp, like a groundsman.

MB: *Was that while the prisoners were there?*

Muriel: Oh, aye. They couldnae have the prisoners workin wi a scythe. It was a high security camp – all the bad ones were up there.

MB: *Can you remember anything about them?*

Muriel: The railway station wasnae far fae the school, an when we were children we used to sit on the pavement so we'd see the German prisoners comin off the train. They used to line them up an then head for the Lednock Bridge. They'd be marching up the road wi their long coats on, an their big steps, aw singin at the top o their voices. We didna ken what they were singin but I remember that alright.

Where we lived in Drummond Street, there was two Nissen huts just at the bottom o the garden, an they were the cook houses for the camp. It was all Polish soldiers there, an they used to throw oranges out to us!

MB: Oranges! I thought nobody had oranges or bananas during the war.

Muriel: Aye, I know, but they did! And they made lots o nice toys too. I remember the Polish soldiers, an a lot o the local lassies went with the officers.

MB: So the cook houses were quite a distance from the camp?

Muriel: Aye, but there was another camp in Comrie – you know, when you go to the top of Dalginross an go round that corner where the new houses are built? There was a camp there. It was all fenced off, an they werenae allowed to come near to the fence or anything – they were all under guard.

Billy Gardiner: When the war started there were troops under canvas at Strowan before coming into Comrie an that camp continued through the war. Then a lot o soldiers came to the village, an they were billeted in halls an empty houses, an then they erected Nissen huts an timber huts at various points. They built a camp at the top o Dalginross, where the Eaglesfield hooses are noo, an 1939–40 they built the big camp at Cultybraggan, for Italian and then German prisoners. There was an awfu lot o soldiers here: the Glasgow Highlanders, the Cameronians, The Buffs, and there were Poles, French-Canadians, Sherwood Foresters, all stationed around Comrie.

Alistair Work: I remember that camp where the housing is now. Everybody talks about Cultybraggan Camp [Camp 21], but nobody talks about the other prisoner of war camp. We stayed at Cowden Farm – my Mum an my Granny milked the cows there. Mr. Kenyon was the farmer – he was originally from Kirkcudbrightshire, an the Kenyons had two farms: Cowden an the one beside Cultybraggan. An when I was of an age to go to the school, I used to leave the house an cut across a field, an I could see all the prisoners. Half o them were in Cultybraggan an the other half were in this second camp nobody mentions, Cowden Camp [Camp 242]. But anyway, we stayed at the farm, an on my way

to school I had to go down past this camp, an the German prisoners were as near as could be, hardly a couple of yards away. I was just a wee, wee boy an I'd see them behind the barbed wire fence, wearin big, long coats down to their ankles, standing there, smoking their wee cigarettes, roll-ups, an just glowering at me.

MB: *That's some memory for a wee boy starting school!*

Alistair: Aye, but that was just the first problem on the way to school. The next one was down the lane before the top of Dalginross. Every morning, Narth Grant used to walk dogs for Miss Cairns who bred these Cairn Terriers, an he would be comin down that lane wi fifteen, maybe eighteen o these yelpin dogs, no leads or anything! I don't know what was the most frightenin, the German prisoners standin glowerin at ye or these Cairn Terriers comin flyin out that lane! At least I didnae meet the dogs on the way home.

MB: *You'd be used to working dogs, Collies, being on a farm.*

Alistair: Yes, all the farmers had workin dogs. I'd have been about two when we went to Cowden. It was a dairy farm, Ayrshires, an my Mum an my Granny were both hired by Mr Kenyon who sold milk in the village. So, they hand-milked about 40 or 50 cows twice a day. They'd start around four in the morning to bring in all these cows, wash the udders an milk them all. And there always seemed to be kickers among them, young ones, heifers that had had their first calf. They weren't used to being milked and they'd be kicking out at the pail – oh, not easy! They'd get used to it, but it's no fun at the start.

After that, they'd strain the milk, put it through the cooler, an then my mother would yoke the horse to deliver the milk around Comrie. The horse was called Paddy, and the milk was in big flagons on the cart. She used tae fill it frae there into a big jug, and customers would leave a jug at the back door, so she'd walk in each entrance, wherever their jug was, then pour the milk into their jug. There was always a saucer on top of it so the bluetits couldn't get at the milk, like they did once they started bottling it wi silver top an the birds would peck-peck-peck-peck. And Paddy always got an old roll or a piece of bread at the baker's, so when he got near, they'd stop just by the Newsagents in Comrie. My mother would maybe be on the right-hand side of the road delivering milk, and when she was out of sight, Paddy used tae nip round and she'd find him trying tae get in tae the Baker's, with his hames, because he got a piece there! He didnae like a thunderstorm, so if there was a rattle of thunder Paddy'd be off along the road. By the time she'd finished delivering the milk she'd scarcely be home when it was time to start milking again.

MB: *They worked so hard, both of them.*

Alistair: Especially in the winter, getting up in the dark – there was no electricity in Cowden, just paraffin lamps or a Tilley, an of course no hot water supply. They'd heat up water on the stove an carry out a bucketful to wash the udders, an after the milking, the milk-pails all had to be washed.

MB: *Did you learn how to milk?*

Alistair: I learned to milk, but I was only very young. When I was growing up, I was never away from farm work; there was always something needin done. Alistair Gillies used to work for Kenyon, driving the tractor, and I'd go with him and I'd sit on the toolbox

when he was ploughing. No cabs then! I'd be sittin on the toolbox and sometimes I'd get sleepy wi the drone o the tractor and he'd tell me "You gonna have to get off a tractor or you'll fall in below the wheels if you fall asleep!" On a lot o the farms it was horses, Clydesdales, but it was mostly tractors that Kenyon had.

Tam Kettle: It was a pair o Belgians ma faither worked when he was at Mill Hill – oh, big, burly beasts they were. He was wi the Stewarts o Mill Hill – they're the ones wi the famous herd o cattle, Shorthorns. It was mixed arable, cattle and sheep, Blackface if I remember aright, an the herd o Shorthorns. Actually they had their own cattlemen, an my faither was the horseman – it was just the one pair on the fairm, the Belgians.

MB: *Is that where you grew up, Tam?*

Tam: I was born in Bankfoot, 28th of March 1935. I was the second eldest an I was called after my dad, Thomas – Tam. Ma mither was a Gardiner, Wilhelmina Gardiner, but everybody called her 'Meenie'. I lost a brother, an one of my sisters an after I was born we moved tae a farm called Towford near Bankfoot – ma faither always worked wi horses, right from when he started workin. We lived in a farm cottage an I remember it was made o steel – it wasnae one o thae corrugated hooses; it was a steel hoose. An I remember when it come hard frost it shrank, an it cracked in the really cauld winter. Aye, I remember that.

MB: *Was it insulated?*

Tam: Mebbe a wee bit, but no a great deal. There were big open fires then, in all the rooms, an an auld cast-iron stove in the kitchen. Hard work keepin them going but an being on the estate we could cut our own firewood, mostly windfall, and that was it. You could aye cairry in a few sticks gaun intae the hoose. But I'd no long started the school in Bankfoot when we moved to near Crieff, Mill Hills Estate.

MB: *Was there a big difference in that house, Tam?*

Tam: Oh aye, it was more modern. It was just a single cottage, and we didn't have a stove in that one, just the open fire. All the cooking at Mill Hill was done on the open fire; there was a kind of a hob that swung out, and then back in again, over the open fire. And there was a chain up the lum for hingin the kettle on. I mind when the embers went down, we used tae make toast wi a fork. Mind the lang toastin forks? You couldna make better toast than that!

MB: *I remember we used to toast the day-old scones – you toast them, and they were brand new!*

Tam: Oh aye – you wouldnae waste bread or scones.

Then we moved to Auchterarder – Dunpatrick Ford, that was the name of the farm an that hoose had a range in the kitchen. There was a bothy at the side of the fairm cottage, so we used that as part of the hoose because there was eight o a family of us. I was the second eldest so my older brother an I slept in the bothy.[1]

Billy: I mind there wis quite a few fairms wi bothies. There was a man in a bothy along at Fariness, no far fae here [South Crieff Road], an there was a bothy doon at Dalginross

Farm. Maist o them were across fae the back door o the fairm hoose – the steading was like a square, an so the ones in the bothy just had tae go across the steadin for their food.[2] There was one at Dundurn, no quite the same kinda bothy, but they had a wooden hut, an there was a lad in that. He was in the bothy an he went intae the kitchen for his dinner an that, an then he went back at night an slept in the bothy. He had his stuff in the bothy. An there was aye fairmers needin a joiner so ye got to know everyone. I used tae cycle aw thae back roads, up Glenartney an everywhere. You'd get to know aw the fairmers, the fairm workers, an the bothy men.

That's a good while back – noo many o these bothies were turned intae a wee hoosie, like the one doon the road there. I remember it was converted intae a wee hoose – just a wee room [ground-level] an the loft was made intae a bedroom up the stair. That had been a bothy, ye ken. I mind goin up to Blairnroar, to the Miss Doigs, the two sisters an their brother – they had the fairm at the Straid. There was a saut backie in their kitchen – a salt box, on the right side of the fireplace. The Carmichaels had the same, just like a hole in the wall about 15 inches square, wi a wooden front. The warmth kept the saut dry, you put your hand in when you needed it. And the Doig sisters had an old flat iron they used, the kind you heated on the fire, wi an iron bolt.

Helen (Grewar) Gardiner: Oh I remember the Miss Doigs! They used to go to the Blairnroar WRI with my mother – the hall was quite near their farm.

Sarah Black: The Straid was one o the farms my parents used to visit – oh, yes, I know the Miss Doigs. An I remember when there was a dance on in the hall we used to go an I'd always get at least one dance fae the brother – I think he was called Duncan.

Billy: An just alang fae them, there was a smiddy at the Cullach, an I used to go up every year because Miss [Nan] Doig had the smiddy hoose under her control. She let it out to summer tourists, so every year afore she'd let it, she used to phone me up, y' ken, aboot a pane of glass, or various things needin done. So I used to go along to the Cullach in the spring, to help her get the place ready. An you'd always hae a *stroupach* – d'ye ken what that is?

MB: Is that what we'd call a strupag in Skye – a cup of tea and maybe a scone or something?

Billy: Aye – in Comrie it's stroupach. Miss Doig would be a fair age noo.

MB: Yes, she was born in 1912 – I had many a strupag with Nan, but that was long after she'd moved into Comrie. On her hundredth birthday all her nieces and nephews came – some o them had moved to Lanarkshire but they always came to see Auntie Nan. She told me that when she was young, two of her elder brothers, Davie and Dunc, lived in the bothy, because there was quite an extended family in the house – elderly aunts as well as themselves. She had a great memory – will I send you one of the recordings?[3]

Billy: Aye, that'd be good. Ye miss that kinda thing thae days.

MB: I asked Nan about the bothy and said she remembered they used to keep the 'spartie' [esparto grass] in the loft.

Billy: Oh aye, that was a great thing on a wet day, when you couldnae work outside, the bothy lads would make ropes for the stackyards.[4] They were aw on this, the fairmers. On wet days some were awright, other anes would be, oh! I remember, there was one lad, a man in the bothy up at St Fillans there, he told me he'd been wi a fairmer outside o Crieff there, an he said they wid keep them workin in pourin rain, ye ken? Some o their stories were famous, like one this man told me, he says it was pourin rain, an he was oot in the field an he went in an knocked on the fairmhoose door an said tae the fairmer "Ah cannae wirk in that," he says, "I cannae sort oot neeps in the pourin rain; the dreels is full o water." So the boy [farmer] says, "Ach, pit a bag ower yer hade an sweep the close there." Noo, mind, we dinna say 'heid' in Comrie – that's Glasgow; it's 'hade' in Comrie.[5] Folk speak aboot the 'big cheese', aboot folk who think they're important, but here it's the 'hade polydacus'.[6] Anyway, when the bothy lad was walkin away tae get a bag to put ower his hade, an a brush, he heard the fairmer shoutin, "Ah'm puttin the dug in the barn, its nae so cauld there." Oh, they used to tell thae stories!

I remember one time I was up at the Straid an we had a great night up there. That was when her brother was alive – Duncan, an Miss Doig was on aboot gettin a poem for the WRI competition; she was needin a song or a bothy ballad, or a poem aboot fairmin. She knew I was interested in that kinda thing an she said she'd found one fae a Border poet but that wasnae suitable. So I cam hame – it wis a Saturday, an on the Sunday I wrote this thing … I'll gie ye a copy so you'll get it right.

The Bothy Lads o' Blairnroar

Haud yer weesht ye gentry folk
An listen tae oor tale,
We're ploomen cheils fae Blairnroar
Wha live on brose an kale.

Up till noo we've deen no bad.
Braw male fae Mill o' Fortune
But noo they're gaun tae close it doon
We'll hae tae start the poachin.

Oor horse whin they were needin shod
We took them tae the Cullach
An noo the smiddy door's bin shut
We miss oor smoke an *stroupach*

Whin we foregaither at the Toll
There's aye the nixt ane missin
Anither gane tae Comrie toon
Tae wark for wright or mason

For mony a day the grund wis plooed
Roond Glasnafate an Cornoch
Ruined noo an hapes o' stanes
Their tenants sailed fae Greenock.

Noo Black-faced sheep are aw the go
There's hunters up Glen Ertney
A hazel stick an a collie dug
Are aa they need tae work wey

So noo guid folk, see whut we mean
Oor days are nearly o'er,
The whaup an peeweep tak oor place
Fae Trian tae Arrevore

Billy: You ken what a whaup is? A curlew, an a peeweep's a lapwing.

MB: *We used to call them peewits but you don't see so many these days.*

Billy: No, lot o thae birds seem to be disappearin. There's an awfu lot o changes, even the names o the places. 'Arrevore' is one of thae [farms] up the Langside, away up to the right. On a sunny day you'll see a cottage away up there.

MB: The name , 'Arrevore', would that have been from Gaelic? It's pronounced exactly the same: Airidh mhòr, the big sheiling.

Billy: Oh aye, it would be. An the Culloch, that was a Smiddy – it was aye called that, an that's where Miss Doig had that wee hoosie. They tell me it's aw been sorted up noo an there's someb'dy in it. Anyway, I think she won a prize at the WRI for her poem.

MB: She could still recite poems when she was a hundred! I remember her reciting "John and Tibby's Dispute" – and that was another one she'd done at the WRI.

John and Tibbie's Dispute[7]

John Davison and Tibbie, his wife,
Sat toastin' their taes ae nicht,
When something startit in the flair,
And blinkit by their sicht.

"Guidwife," quoth John, "did ye see that moose?
Whar sorra was the cat?"[8]
"A moose ?" – "Aye, a moose." –
"Na, na, guidman, – It wasna a moose, 'twas a rat!

"Now, now, guidwife, to think ye've been
Sae lang aboot the hoose,
An' no to ken a moose fae a rat:
Yon wisna a rat – 'twas a moose."

"I've seen mair mice than you, guidman –
An' what think ye o' that?
Sae haud your tongue an' say nae mair –
I tell ye, it was a rat.

"Me haud my toung for you, guidwife?
I'll be master o this hoose!
I saw't as plain as een could see't,
An' I tell ye, it was a moose!"

46

"If you're the maister o' the hoose,
It's I'm the mistress o't;
An' I ken best what's in the hoose –
Sae I tell ye, it was a rat."

"Weel, weel, guidwife, gae mak' the brose,
An' ca' it what ye please."
So up she rose, and made the brose,
While John sat toastin his taes.

They suppit, and suppit, and suppit the brose,
And aye their lips play'd smack;
They suppit, and suppit, and suppit the brose.
Till their lugs began to crack.

"Sic fules we were to fa' oot, guidwife,
Aboot a moose" – "A what?
It's a lee ye tell, an' I say again,
It was a moose!" – "'Twas a rat!"

"Wad ye ca' me a leear to my verra face?
My faith, but ye craw croose!
I tell, ye, Tib, I never will beer't –
'Twas a moose !" "'Twas a rat?" "'Twas a moose!"

Wi' her spoon she struck him owre the pow –
Ye dur auld doit, tak that!
Gae to your bed ye cankered sumph –
'Twas a rat !" – "'Twas a moose!" – "'Twas a rat!"

She sent the brose cup at his heels,
As he hirpled ben the hoose ;
Yet he shoved oot his head as he steekit the door,
And cried , "'Twas a moose! 'Twas a moose!"

But, when the carl was fast asleep,
She paid him back for that,
And roar'd into his sleepin' lug,
"'Twas a rat! 'Twas a rat! 'Twas a rat!"

The de'il be wi' me if I think
It was a beast ava –
Neist mornin as she sweepit the fluir,
She found wee Johnnie's ba'!

Bobby Thomson: Oh, Auntie Nan was a great one for the Rural! It used to be held in the Blairnroar Hall – the old corrugated iron hall just next to the school, the wee crinkly tin hall – that's where the Blairnroar WRI was held, and they used to do plays and everything. There used to be regular dances in all the village halls round about here, and Country Dancing classes too. Auntie Nan loved that, and she was very keen on the drama – they used to put on plays an they'd rehearse these and put on a concert. Sometimes they'd have a night with the Comrie or Muthill WRI. Oh it was a great thing at one time.

Sarah: Oh yes, I remember the two sisters, Nan and Jean, from the Blairnroar Rural. I went to the Rural in Comrie and there was a WRI in Muthill and in Auchterarder and other places. When they'd put on a concert, or a dance we'd go to that – and I always got a dance wi Nan's brother, Duncan. I was a bit shy to do the drama but there used to be some great nights when they'd put on a play – there was always a great laugh.

Helen G: Oh yes, all the women went to the Rural. That's where some of them got their recipes for jam! And don't forget the scone competitions or the peg dollies! They used to have great nights – same thing in Perth, and in Angus and Fife too.

MB: *Yes, Nell Hannah [in Perth] gave me some photos of the drama nights they had – she was laughing even talking about them! And an old man in Fife gave me a copy of one of the plays from the WRI – it was apparently written by a miner whose wife was in the WRI. He'd been badly injured in an accident in the pit, and when he couldn't work anymore, he used to busk around the villages. Robert MacLeod was his name – he used to write poems and songs for local folk.[9] This one was almost thrown out, but the local barber, Arthur Neavey kept a copy. Maybe we can do this one on Zoom?*

A SCOTS DRAMA IN ONE ACT
LOVE ON THE FARM

A Play by Robert MacLeod

A Scots Drama in One Act.

LOVE   ON   THE   FARM

by Highlander.

(Characters)

Effie McLean   ....   A Widow
Willie Buchan(A Bachelor) ..... A Shephard
Mary McLean (A Milkmaid) ..... Effie's Daughter
Donald Stewart(The Farmer's Son) A Young Ploughman

Scene: The kitchen of a cottar's house.   Dresser, Table, Two Chairs and Fireplace.   Time: An early summer morning.

Effie: (Sitting just finishing her morning cup of tea) Aye, Aye, folk say farm life is a gey healthy yin; weel, it is; but a' the same ye hiv tae work gey hard.   At least it his aye been that wey wi'me ever since I wis ony thing worth.   But they say that wark's guid for ye, although ower muckle sune tires ye oot, but I believe in the auld proverb, "Tae bed wi' the lamb an' up wi' the lark".   And ever since I lost my man John McLean, Ive aye tried tae mak' the best o' it; me an' Mary, this bit lassie o' mine, she's the only ane we ever had an' a' the comfort I hae left noo, and she's aye dune her best tae keep the bit hoosie abune oor heids.   But let me see, whit time is it?(Looking at timepiece) Five o'clock!   By my certy, it's time Mary wis up.   She wis at a maiden-dance last nicht and she'll be gey tired this mornin'.   I'll hae tae wauken her.   Haw Mary!   (Mary does not hear the first time) Mary! Come awa' lassie or the kye will be cryin' on ye this mornin'.

Mary: Aye mither, I'll be there the noo.

Effie: It's the mornin' that tells. (Effie working about the house

Mary: Whaur's my shawl mither?

Effie: On the back o' that chair at yer bed.

Mary: Oh aye, I see it noo mither.   (Mary comes into the kitchen yawning with shawl in hand) Ay aye mither, but I'm a tired lassie this mornin'.

Effie: Ye will gang tae the dancin' ye see; but I needna say that, for I wis jist as daft mysel' when I wis like ye.   Haud ye a guid nicht Mary?

Mary: Oh aye mither, it wis something graund, the best I've been at for a lang time; plenty dancin' and guid singin'.

Effie: Wis Willie Buchan the shepherd there?

Mary: Aye mither, and he sang durin' the nicht.

Effie: Aye, Willie wis a guid Scotch singer in his day. Whit sang did he sing Mary?

Mary: He sang "The Bonnie Lass o' Ballochmyle". Aye, and he came ower and sat beside me efter he wis finished and asked me hoo ye were keepin' mither.

Effie (Smiling) Did he Mary? That wis gey mindfu' o' him. Dae ye want a cup o' tea Mary?

Mary: Oh, no, mither, I'll no hae time; I'll hae tae rin or I'll be gettin' the kick this mornin'. Weel mither, guid mornin' wi' ye.

Effie: Guid mornin' Mary. (Mary goes away) Oh aye, she gangs awa' singin' like a wee lintie. Aweel, Aweel, when the hert is young, everything gangs bricht and cheery. (She comes in and shuts the door).

(Willie Buchan starts to sing outside)

Ca' the yowes tae the Knowes
Ca' them whaur the heather grows
Ca' them whaur the burnie rows
My bonnie dearie.

Effie: Ay! That's Willie Buchan the shepherd singin' tae his sheep and bits o' lambs. Willie and my man John McLean were aye dear cronies. Aye, it wis Willie wha sat his death-bed wi' me nicht and day and seen him breathe his last. Aye, it wis a bad harvest day that for him, the drenchin' he got brocht on the trouble and that wis the end o' it; but ye hae jist tae thole it a'. Aye, jist tae thole it a'. (Effie sits lamenting)

(Willie Buchan enters with stick in hand)

Willie: Weel Effie it's a fine mornin'. An' hoo is the warld usin' ye noo wumman? Are ye aye keepin' in guid health?

Effie: Weel, I canna complain Willie. Are ye no' sittin' doon a wee while?

Willie: Naw Effie. I'll hae tae gang and be watchin' they sheep. Dae ye ken I've lost ane some wey, and I'm feart tae tell the maister, so I'll be gang Effie and mak' a guid search for it.

Effie: -Mary wis tellin' me ye wis at the dance last nicht. Did ye enjoy yersel' Willie?

Willie: I darsay I did; an' I saw Mary there richt enough. Dae ye ken Effie, I think Donal' Stewart the fairmer's son has a bit notion o' Mary. He had her up at very near every dance.

Effie: Oh, Willie, dinna say that! Mary's faur ower young tae hae a laud, an' I dinna think she'll leave her mither for a lang time tae come yet.

Willie: It's hard tae say Effie, but time will tell. Noo I think I'll be gaun an' hae a look roon' for that sheep I lost, but I'LL gie ye a ca' in when I'm passin' this wey and let ye ken if I get it.

Effie: Jist that Willie, an' I'll aye mak' ye welcome for auld times sake.

Willie: Ta-ta the noo then Effie; an' tell Mary I wis askin' for her, will ye?

Effie: I'll dae that Willie. Ta-ta wi' ye. (Willie goes away) Aweel, I think I'll hae a scone or twa bakit tae keep me frae wearyin'. (Knocks heard at door) Wha can this be noo I winder. (Effie opens the door) (Mary enters with arm in sling and Donald Stewart supporting her) What in a' the warld's happened Mary?

Donald: Oh, jist a wee accident Effie. Dae ye ken it wis that new coo we bocht last week. Its a bad yin. Mary wis jist sittin' milkin' quite the thing, when she lit oot an' knocked Mary kickin', milk can an' a'. I dinna think its awfu' bad, altho' she's got a guid lick. Hiv ye ony-thing in the hoose tae rub it wi' Effie? I'm a bit o' a doctor, I yist tae be in the ambulance class ye ken.

Effie: I think I should hae a wee bottle o' embrocation some wey in the hoose. Oh, aye, here it is Donal'. (Effie hands the bottle to Donald from off the dresser)

Donald: Come on Mary, I'll be yer doctor lassie. Let me tak aff that sling. (Takes sling off Mary's arm)

Mary: Oh, Donal' be canny wi' it laddie.

Donald: Oh, I'll be canna Mary. Dae ye ken whit Rabbie Burns said.

Mary: I dinna min' the noo Donal'.

Donald: (Sings) Bonnie wee thing, canny wee thing,
                   Lovely wee thing, wert thou mine.
          (Keeps on dressing Mary's arm while singing)   Noo I think
          that will be an awfu' lump better in a while Mary, an' if
          ye feel onything weel in the efternune, ye'll jist gies a
          ca' up tae the field, ye ken the yin I mean Mary?

Mary: Aye, Donal' , if my mither agrees tae that.

Donald: (Goes over and claps Effie on the shoulder)   Will ye Effie?
          Let her up for a wee while.   The fresh air will dae her a
          lot o' guid.

Effie: Och aye Donal', seein' ye were kind in bringin' her hame
          and baundagin' up her arm sae weel.   An' that wis wan guid
          thing, we didna need tae send for the doctor.

Donald: Aweel Effie, I'll awa, an' jist gie Mary a het cup o' tea
          tae refresh her.   She'll be a'richt in a wee while.
          Ye'll try an' come up Mary?   (Mary nods, smiling)   Ta-ta
          then Mary.

Mary: Ta-ta Donal'.   (Donald goes away)

Effie: He's a fine féllow that Mary.   Is his faither keepin' ony
          better?

Mary: No mither.   Donal' wis tellin' me he wisna makin' muckle
          o' it.   The hert's a place they canna trifle wi' ye ken.

Effie: Willie Buchan wis sayin' tae me this mornin, that you an'
          Donal' wis gey lovin' like at the dance last nicht.   I
          doot he his a bit notion o' ye Mary, his he no?

Mary: Oh, mither, we could be freenly enough at the dance, an'
          still no nae love between us.   Aye, an' Willie Buchan
          wis in here this mornin'?   He's shairly been awfu' early
          afit efter last nicht's fun.

Effie: Och, weel, Mary, he jist ca'd in a wee while in passin'.
          He wis tellin' me he had lost a sheep an' he gaed awa in
          a hurry tae hae a look for it.

Mary: Aye, mither, but believe me Willie Buchan has some regards
          for you.   Dae ye ken, he wis aye speakin' aboot ye tae me
          at the dance, an' there's nae man wad speak aboot a wumman
          sae muckle if he didna care for her, I ken that muckle
          onywey.

Effie: He wis a dear crony o' yer faither's Mary, an' that's the
          wey we like tae keep up the freenship.

(Willie Buchan is heard singing outside)   Oh, wert thou in the cauld blast, on yonder lea, on yonder lea.

Mary: That's Willie Buchan the noo mither.   Will he be comin' in?

Effie: Oh, very likely Mary.   He said he wad ca' in an' let me ken if he got the sheep he lost.

          (Knocks heard at the door. Effie goes and opens it)

          Ay, jist come awa' in an' sit doon Willie; I've got an invalid since ye ca'd this mornin'. (Mary sitting at fireside)

Willie: (Taking a chair) Oh, its you Mary; an' whit's went wrang wi' ye lassie.

Mary: Oh, jist a kick Willie I got frae frae yon new coo that wis bocht last week.   She's a richt wicket yin.

Effie: Its naething serious Willie; it'll sune get better.   Did ye get the sheep ye lost?

Willie: Aye Effie, I got it wanderin' up at the auld castle yonder. Ye'll ken the place I mean, whaur John and you yist tae walk on the bonnie summer efternunes, an' I often thocht there wisna a brawer couple in the hale country side.

Effie: Ay, Willie, ye're bringin' up happy memories o' the past noo.

Willie: Aye Effie, that's quite true; but keep up yer hert wumman, there micht be happy days in store for ye yet. We never ken whit's in front o' us.

Mary: Weel mither, I think I'll tak a bit walk an' get the fresh air.

Willie: Its a fine day Mary, an' it'll no dae ye a bit o' hairm lassie.   Are ye gaun up tae the farm?

Mary: No Willie, I'm gaun up tae the field whaur Donal' is ploughin'.   I promised I wad gang up an' see him wi' my mither's consent of course.   Weel I'll awa, but I wis gaun tae say (Mary looks shy)

Effie: Whit wis ye gaun tae say Mary?

Mary: Twa's company three's nane. (Mary closes door slowly)

Willie: (Laughing) Dae ye ken Effie, them that's in love are no like ony ither body. Aye an' believe me, there's love between Mary an' Donal' Stewart as shair as I'm a shepherd.

Effie: Weel Willie, I'm beginnin' tae think that tae. Donal' cam' doon wi' her when she got the kick frae the coo this mornin', an' he wis gey cheery on it a' the time he wis sortin' her airm.

Willie: I'm tellin' ye, they're in love Effie. And mind ye, she'll be wrang if she disna wire in for him, for if onything should happen his faither, Donal' wad become heir o' the farm, him bein' the only son, and that wad be something for her. Jist fancy her becomin' Mrs. Stewart and mistress o' the farm as weel. By, mind ye its something tae look forrit tae Effie.

Effie: Aye Willie, but I'm lookin' at it in a different wey. What wad I dae if that should happen?

Willie: What wey Effie? Ye're quite young yet, an' ye can aye dae yer ain turn as regards farm wark; or ye micht tak a thocht o' mairyin' again for a' that I ken; that is, if ye got a rale weel dae'in man. Wad ye no?

Effie: Oh Willie, that wad set the country side a-talkin'.

Willie: But ye can please versel' in that respec' Effie. Never mind what folk say. Dae ye ken Effie, I've ha'en somethin' on my mind tae tell ye this lang time wumman, an' ye're no tae think ony harm o' me when I tell ye what it is.

Effie: Weel, Willie Buchan, dinna be blate an' tell me. It's a gey true sayin' "Open confessions are guid for the soul". So its you tae explain versel'.

Willie: (Rather Backward) Oh aye, if I only could tak the courage wumman; but I suppose I'll hae tae try. Weel Effie, I'm gettin' tired o' bothy life, an' I've been a lang time a bachelor, so I wad like a bit hame o' my ain an' a cheery, smilin' wife something like versel' for the rest o' my days; so I maun tell ye noo Effie, that I love ye wi' a' my hert. Will ye be mine?

Effie: (Shyly) I half jaloused that a' the time Willie, an' ye've been a lang time a faithfu' servant tae the maister, an' if ye look ower a bit hoosie o' yer ain as weel as ye've watched ower yer flock, I maun jist accept yer offer Willie.

Willie: Ay! Effie, an' ye'll be mine! An' we'll be happy the gither for the rest o' oor lives; will we Effie?

Effie: Aye Willie. But hoo can I break the news tae Mary?

Willie: Weel Effie, ye hae a chance tae break the news richt enough. Dae ye ken I didna like tae tell ye, but I heard for truth that Donal' Stewart wis comin' doon tae ask for yer consent tae mairry Mary.

Effie: I doot Willie, this has a' been made up between you and Donal' Stewart, but we'll find oot later on.

(Donald and Mary listening outside door, then come in laughing loudly.

Donald: Oh aye, we heard a' yer conversation. Aye, Wille, an ye've popped the question hae ye. Weel, look here Effie, since Willie has brokeen the ice for me, I'll no be sae backward as him in askin' ye. (Donald looks simple) I've come tae ask for yer consent tae mairry Mary. Say aye Effie, say aye wumman.

Effie: Weel Donal' what can I say but aye, when I hae consented mysel' tae become Willie Buchan's wife; an' I ken fine Donal', you an' Mary will mak a guid match.

Donald: Oh, thank ye Effie, an' I'll try an' mak Mary gey happy. (Donald goes over to Willie and shakes hands) Weel, Willie, ye've managed it gey weel, so we'll jist mak a double event o' it, an' hae the banns cried oot on Sunday first at the auld kirk, an' that'll be a big surprise for a' the folk aroon this country side.

Willie: Jist that then Donal', an' when we get mairret and sett-led doon side by side, we can baith look back on the happy days when we made Love on the Farm.

(Willie Embraces Effie and Donald Embraces Mary)

(CURTAIN)

Endnotes

1   David G. Adams interviewed retired farm labourers (bothy men) who described in detail their living quarters and general conditions in the bothies. *Bothy Days and Nichts,* p. 30–42 (with photos) and diagram of a typical floor-plan, p. vi.

2   In his discussion of the layout of the farm buildings David Kerr Cameron suggests that the 'shrewd placing of the byre among the farmtoun's *biggings* [buildings] – between the turnip shed at one end and the straw-shed at the other – gave notice of its importance.' *Cornkister Days,* p. 230. In his book *The Ballad and the Plough a Portrait of the Life of the Old Scottish Farmtouns* Cameron provides invaluable insight into the way of life of farmers and farm labourers.

3   Digital copies of the recordings and verbatim transcriptions can be accessed at Perth & Kinross Archive, Acc11/52: M. Bennett interviews with Nan Doig, 2009–12.

4   Discussion on heather and horse-hair ropes and the tools used for twisting ropes (included drawings), see I.F. Grant, *Highland Folk Ways,* pp. 205–05. The device used was generally known as a 'thrawcock' in the Highlands. See also, photograph of a thrawhook from the croft in Auchindrain, Argyll, and now in the museum: <https://www.auchindrain.org.uk/our-blog/the-art-of-making-rope/>.

5   Billy kept a notebook listing Strathearn Scots words as he wanted to record regional variations of the language. Before resuming the conversation, and to make sure I had noted the differences in dialects, he demonstrated with further examples (English, Comrie and Glasgow): bread, brade, breid; lead, lade, leid; head, hade, heid. Sheila Douglas discusses features of regional pronunciation and dialect in 'Perthshire Scots' in D. Omand, *The Perthshire Book*, pp. 219–226.

6   'Polydacus' is the person in command, or the 'big cheese'. The Scots word is also rendered as 'pilliedacus'; see, <https://www.dsl.ac.uk/entry/snd/pilliedacus>. Further examples of the Scots phrase, particularly in Tayside, <https://www.dsl.ac.uk/entry/snd00078648>.

7   Though Nan didn't have a printed copy of the poem, it was among poems and songs sold at the feeing markets, printed on a broadsheet. Copies were also sold at the Poet's Box, 182 Overgate, Dundee, (Price one penny). It is included in the collection of broadsides at the National Library of Scotland; digital copy can be accessed at <https://digital.nls.uk/broadsides/view/?id=15095>.

8   "Where the devil was the cat?"

9   Biography of Robert MacLeod and his poems, see, M. Bennett, *Robert MacLeod: Cowdenbeath Miner Poet. An Anthology by Arthur Nevay.* Ochtertyre: Grace Note Publications, 2015.

Blairnroar Recreation Hall: Constitution and Rules, drafted by Nan Doig, 1959

Draft   Blairnroar Recreation Hall.   1959
Constitution and Rules.

1. *Name.* - The Hall shall be known as The Blairnroar Recreation Hall.
2. *Purpose.* The purpose of The Hall shall be to provide a place to hold meetings, Concerts and Dances, and to provide recreational facilities for the residents in Blairnroar and District.
3. *Annual General Meeting* :- (a) There shall be held an Annual General meeting of The Trustees and Members of Committee within two months of the THIRTIETH day of November in each year after the closing date of the Accounts. (b) The following business shall be transacted, (1) Secretary's Report, (2) Treasurer's Report and Audited Statement of Accounts (3) Appointment of Officials, (4) Appointment of Committee of management, (5) Appointment of Auditor (6) Appointment of ordinary Officials (7) Any other Competent business.
4. *Officials.* - Officials of The Hall shall be (a) Four Trustees one of whom shall be The Factor ex officio of The Drummond Castle Estate: *note:*- The three existing Trustees shall remain in office until they retire and vacancies shall be filled at the next succeeding Annual General meeting. (b) 1. The President (2) Vice President (3) Secretary (4) Treasurer The offices of The Secretary and Treasurer may be Combined.

5. *Committee of management:* - The Four Trustees and Three other members of the public as may be appointed shall act as The Committee of management.
6. In the event of The Hall buildings falling into disuse and no longer being used as a Hall for the benefit of the community, the whole structure together with the site, will immediately revert to the Proprietor of Drummond Castle Estate.

Rules and Regulations

1. The Hall will be open on week-days only all functions held on Saturdays will terminate at 11.30 p.m.
2. No gambling or obscene language shall be permitted. The sale of or consumption of intoxicating liquor on the premises is prohibited.
3. Parties using The Hall will accept responsibility for all damages to the premises, furnishings and parked cars. They shall also be responsible for leaving the hall clean and tidy at the end of the function.
4. The following shall be the Scale of Charges for the use of The Hall.   1983.

Whist Drive	£
Whist Drive and Dance	£
Dance	£
Dance to 11.30 p.m	£
W.R.I meeting	£
Political	£
Religious	£
other meetings	£ Charges to be fixed by COMMITTEE OF MANAGEMENT

Nan Doig papers, family collection, used with permission.

Chapter 4

Working from Home and Earning Your Keep

"Sandy's workin fae hame," Billy began, "he's ben the hoose on his computer.... Awbody's workin fae hame." The national radio and television reminder to work from home sparked off local conversations that ran along the lines of "if ye didna work ye didna eat … children were told that many hands make light work … and even little hands can help. They might not be able to bring in logs, but wee hands can carry in a few sticks." At home or on the land, there was a sense of pride in being able to 'earn yer keep,' and paid or unpaid, children developed a sense of responsibility and learned skills that would last for life.

Muriel (McGregor) Malloy: We all helped at home – you didn't expect to do anything else! You'd help your Mum, and when you were maybe nine or ten you'd wee jobs, like going the messages for somebody. If you got a sixpence or thruppence it was great, because people didnae have a lot o money, especially big families. I was still at the school when I got my first job wi Jenny MacGregor – she had the grocer's shop in the village. There was always someb'dy needin a hand.

Margaret Bennett: Muriel, what did you do when you left school?

Muriel: I worked in the shop wi Jenny MacGregor and I worked there for eight years till I got married. I've got lots of photos of her – oh, she was great, Jenny was, and a lovely pianist. She played the organ in the church and she taught a lot o people to play, an she'd play at concerts an everything. Her father had the shop and Jenny took over. It was a right grocer's shop, serving at the counters. Everything was loose – oatmeal, flour, barley came in sacks and you'd weigh it out, but it used to get wee black things, thae wee beasties, weevils, and I spent hours picking them out! Tea was loose – it came in a big tea chest and you'd have to make up the bags, a quarter or a half pound. Things like tins and packages were on the shelves and you'd be running up and down ladders to reach them. The sago and the rice and stuff like that was kept in drawers, all loose, so you'd weigh that and put it a brown paper bag. And a man used to come round once or twice a year, an inspector, and he'd measure everything that you'd done to make sure none o the shops were short-changing the customers. But I got a right lecture one time for putting too much in the bags. Oh, he gave me a right lecture, that was as bad as having too little, so I didnae do it again!

MB: Did you sell broken biscuits?

Muriel: Oh, aye. We sold paraffin as well. And the cheese came in a great big round thing and you'd have to cut it with a cheese wire, like a piano wire, wi two wooden handles on it. It was a busy shop, an you knew everybody – then when I got married I had to give up workin wi Jenny. We moved to Crieff an I was there for years, till I came back to Comrie.

MB: Did you work in Crieff at all?

Muriel: Oh aye, I worked in the George Hotel – that's the old hotel in Crieff that's just been demolished, on the corner of King Street. That used to be a busy, busy place wi a restaurant, bed and breakfast, and they did bus tours. I was a waitress and I worked there for years and years. Scottish Brewers had the hotel then, but it's been sold several times over, and now there's nothing there. I imagine they'll be building something else. They're building an awfu lot o houses in Crieff – all that land used to be farms.

Billy Gardiner: I mind just after the war when you could count over forty farms around Comrie. I wrote down the names in one o my notebooks:

> *In 1948 there were 40 small farms not far from Comrie, all rented from e.g. Strowan Estate (Major G. Stirling not Strowan Crieff), Dunira Estate, Drummond Estate. Near the village: Dalginross, Muirend, Fairness, Drummond Earnoch, West Cowden, Mid Cowden, Cultybraggan, Ruchillside, Mill of Fortune, Bogton, Auchingarroch, Glentarf, Bishopfauld, Lechkin, Dalchonzie, Cuilt, Dalrannoch, East Meiger, West Meiger, Mailermore , Dalchurn, East Ballindalloch, West Ballindalloch, Lawers, Locherlour, Carse of Lennoch, Carse of Trowan. Brae of Fordie, Ballaig, Braincroft, Balmuick, Carroglen, Kingarth, East Tullybannocher, West Tullybannocher, East Dundurn, West Dundurn. Farms up, Loch Earn: Middleton, Tighablar, Ardtrostan.*

There was a lot o fairms.

Helen (Grewar) Gardiner: We lived at Mailermore Farm in Glenartney – it's on the Earl of Ancaster's estate. Dad had grown up on a sheep-farm in Glenshee, then he worked at Bridge of Earn before he got the lease of Mailermore Farm. I'm not sure of the year, but I was born in 1942, during the war, and that's where we lived when I started school. Dad's name was Peter Grewar, so I was Helen Grewar. He'd been married before, but his wife had died, and I was from his second marriage, an only child.

MB: *What a beautiful place to grow up, though quite a distance from the school.*

Helen G: Yes, and I had to walk two and a half miles to play with other children but eventually I got a bike from one of the relatives – it was too small for her, so I got a bike.

MB: *Was it Lord Ancaster who was in in Drummond Castle in those days?*

Helen G: Yes, I didn't know him, of course, but I remember their son got drowned – I think he was just in his early or mid-twenties; a right nice-looking lad he was. Very sad... I think they were away out at sea when it happened. It was so sad... His sister is the one they call Lady Jane; I think she was a wee bit older – she'll be well over eighty now. [1]

MB: *I imagine you helped on the farm, Helen.*

Helen G: Everybody helped in those days – and children all helped on the farms, but I was an only child and I think sometimes I was the extra sheepdog! I didn't bark but I think I did everything else! Whatever was to be done on the farm, I had a role – and I did plenty of running! I remember one time Dad had bought sheep in Perth and we usually got a float to take them to Comrie, because they were local firms that did all that. This was when the Cultybraggan Camp was in full operation and some of the German prisoners were employed on local farms. We didn't have any working at Mailermore, but they helped the labour situation when a lot of local folk were called up. But this day, when we came home from the Perth sale, there was some parade going on around the camp. And this sergeant, or whoever was in charge, had been told not to let anybody through the gate – they used to have a gate across the road up the glen. So we were there with all these sheep, ahead of them, and the soldier guy came out and said, "You have to get these sheep out of there! There's a whole parade on! We really can't have all these sheep in the way!"

And Dad said, "These sheep are all in lamb, and they're not running." He was a fairly quiet guy, but the sheep were not to be running and that was that. [laughter]

But I did plenty of running! When the lambing season started, and the orphan lambs had to be bottle-fed, I used to feed them through the garden gate – I'd just put the bottle and the teat through spars then they'd take it out of their mouth and put it into the next one. They have strong jaws! And when it was bitterly cold weather some of the new-born lambs got brought into the kitchen, in cardboard boxes for overnight, and in the morning, you woke up, you heard bah-bah-bah-ah! [laughter].

MB: *What crops did you grow?*

Helen G: We had potatoes and we had grain, or corn, as it was called – oats. I don't think we had barley, just oats.

MB: *And did you have hay, or did you have to buy it in?*

Helen G: Well, it just depended on the summer weather. The trouble with the hay was, the farm was on quite a slope, so if it came on heavy rain the hay could be flattened pretty quickly. Sometimes we'd have quite a good summer for the hay, but otherwise we had to buy it in.

MB: *Was it all stored in the barn or a stackyard?*

Helen G: The grain went into the stackyard into stacks and anything else more or less just went into a shed on the floor. But it had to be dry, of course, good and dry.

MB: *Did your dad have any hired help?*

Helen G: We had people in from time to time, like when the sheep-clipping was going on, we'd get help with that. Ploughing, not so much, because we had a tractor reasonably early on. But you know what the ground was like, very, very steep. The farm was mostly run by the family, and when we were planting the potatoes, we had one or two relatives that didn't live far away, so they'd usually come here to help. Now and again some of the lads would turn up and help, because they always got a good feed of dinners – they'd say, "We'll just go along to Peter's and we'll get our dinner," and they'd lend a hand. There was always cooking to be done, but we had a gas stove as well as the Rayburn in the kitchen – we used to burn a lot of logs as well as coal. There were quite a lot of trees on the farm got knocked down by the wind, so they were used for wood.

MB: *And who did the wood cutting?*

Helen G: Oh, usually somebody that was needing some wood themselves would come up and offer to help. It was a matter of, "Are ye needin any wood cut, Peter?" And Peter would say, "I wouldnae mind," and that usually meant somebody else to get fed, and they'd get a load of wood. When anyone came to help you always gave a 'wee mindin' – that was the phrase, a 'wee mindin' – and everyone got a pot of jam or something. I remember it well. And in the winter, Dad and his brother-in-law who lived in the farm down the road, drove the snow plough – it might have been the Council unless the Council didn't do things like that, because it was way off the beaten track, as Cultybraggan was.

We were at Mailermore Farm for about fifteen or sixteen years, but then Dad died very suddenly one October night. He'd been helping somebody clipping the sheep and then the fellow was in visiting us, just like they do. And Dad was sitting, joking and laughing, just enjoying the company and then the fellow went away home and we were getting ready for bed and Mum started shouting up the stairs. I said, "What's wrong, what's wrong?"

"It's your Dad! There's something far wrong with him. I can't get him to move, and I can't get him to speak." I was sent to the phone-box at the cross-roads to phone the Doctor – hardly anybody had a phone then, and my bike didn't have any lights. It was October, so of course was dark and there was no moon. There was nothing. And by the time I got back he was gone. It was very, very quick. And that was the end of that. I was going on for seventeen, '59 it would have been. It was so unexpected and there wasn't even anybody with him when it happened.

MB: Oh, what a shock for you all. And he wouldn't have been that old.

Helen G: I think he was 70. We stayed on at the farm for a while, but it wasn't easy. I was still at Morrison's in Crieff, Mum didn't drive and neither did Auntie and, in the end, we moved Perth. We could walk down the town and do the shopping, and I could walk to school. But we enjoyed living up the glen, the land and the people; folk were happy and friendly.

Tam Kettle: I'd been workin on fairms long afore we moved to Auchterarder. I always liked the outside work an ma faither aye worked on fairms. I'd sometimes go with him when he took the horse an cairt to Crieff wi the milk. But no the milkin – I never had naithin to do wi cattle. I left school about fourteen an a half – you were supposed to be fifteen, but I wouldnae hae learnt anyway! I got my first job working on a fairm just half a mile away, workin at Dornach Mill – that was the name of the fairm, an Kirkland wis the name o the fairmer.

MB: Did you move there?

Tam: No, I still bade in the same bothy wi ma brither. The rest o the faimily were in the hoose an we bade in the bothy. We preferred that, goin hame at night an it was late, they wouldnae hear us in the rest o the hoose! [laughs]. When I got ma first job, the fairm workers used to get their milk an meal an the tatties fae the fairm; "The Milk, Meal and Tatties", that's what they called it. That went with the job.[2]

MB: Did you have a meal kist?

Tam: I don't think it was as big as that. It may hae been a wee box, wooden, but it was the oatmeal that was aff the fairm.[3] Aye.

MB: So did they have a threshing mill on that farm?

Tam: No, they used to bring in a traivelling mill, an it was it powered by a tractor, wi a belt.

MB: That would be a big day when the threshing mill came.

Tam: Oh indeed, aye, it was all go, but there was a lot a fairm workers then.

MB: The farm workers and their families must have done a lot of flitting.

Tam: Aye, but it was aye Perthshire wi me, I never lived anywhere else except for my National Service. When we were young, my brither an I both started on the fairm, but he finished up fencin an I shifted tae the forestry.

Alistair Work: You went where the work was. We moved from Cowden when my Mum got a job in the village, workin as a waitress in the Royal Hotel. But we couldnae get a house in Comrie although the council were building a lot o houses after the war. They'd put your name on a list, but they made my mother wait for thirteen years for a house – thirteen years – and that was because we didn't have a man in the house to speak for us. It didn't make any difference that we were local, and I went to Comrie school – they made my mother wait all that time.

We got a place to stay on Dalginross Farm; the Bells had the farm then (where Tainsh is now), and there was a cottage at the back o the farm house, so we rented that, and she cycled the two miles to work every day and back, summer and winter. At that time, the Royal Hotel opened to the public at 7 o'clock in the morning and people could go in off the street for breakfast. And when the Masons had a 'do' in the Royal, it would finish quite late, and afterwards she'd have to clear up and have the tables ready for breakfast. So it was sometimes three o'clock in the morning when she'd be coming home, then she had to be back in the morning at seven o'clock to serve the breakfast.

I was still at school, but I'd always be over at the farm, working away – weekends, harvest time, or whenever, always wi the farming, wi auld farmers, picking tatties, driving the wee Fergie tractor, emptyin the baskets o tatties, takin them to the pit. Always. During the school holidays in October, the tattie holidays, the potato farmers would always hire a squad for the tattie liftin. I mind one year being up at Dalrannoch, Black's farm, liftin tatties for Sarah's ol' man. Sometimes whole families would go to the tatties – it was hard work, but you had a chance to earn a bit o money and your pals would be there too, so there was always fun.[4]

Sarah Black: We usually had two acres o tatties, because it's one o' the main crops that we had – Perthshire's famous for the potatoes, and we used to sell them to a tattie merchant. They'd come with the big lorry and they would take the whole lot (apart from what we'd keep for ourselves), and eventually they'd go into bags. I forget the name of the kind we grew – it was what we'd call a 'wet tattie' and they made very good chips.

Billy: When the war started, Dad got Willie McDougall in with a pair of horses an got the field piece ploughed up. We dropped tatties in every second furrow an when they were ready in October we all went up to the Bogton Braes and got ferns, bracken, and made a pit to store them for the winter.[5] Later in the war he fenced off part of the top and we started keeping hens, Rhode Island Reds, and then Anconas. Mam tried turkeys once, an put 4 eggs below a clucking hen, but they'd roost away up in the trees.

Alistair: Another thing we did when we were still at school, Jock Spence and I used to set snares for rabbits and hares, and we'd pull rabbits out of the dyke and take them down to the butchers, and he gave us a wee bit money for them.

Sarah: Oh yes, there was a lot o' rabbits about, and sometimes they were shot and sometimes they were in snares. It was mainly ma father who did the snaring when we had rabbit. They were very good.

Alistair: And there were thousands o rabbits – oh, there's nothing better than a good rabbit. D'you remember the thick gravy your mother made when she cooked the rabbit? Nothin better! And even when there was rationing nobody here needed to be hungry.[6]

MB: I imagine you'd have wanted to work on a farm when you left school?

Alistair: I never thought of doing any other work, but I couldnae get a job. When I was about to leave the school, fourteen year-old, goin on fifteen, I thought I would just go along with the first farmer and ask, "Are you needin anybody to start?" So I started in Comrie and I went right around the back road all the farms and I come back the other way.

"Are you taking anybody on?"

"No, sorry laddie, I'm no takin anybody on."

Not one farmer was hiring, though I was always on a farm, all the time, but when I left school I could not get a job on a farm.

MB: *So what did you do?*

Alistair: The Forestry Commission opened an office in Comrie, so I went there and asked, "Are you taking anybody on?"

"How old are you?"

"Oh, I'm no 15 yet."

"Well, you cannae start till you're 15."

So I had to wait for a week or two till I was 15, and I got a job. I was there for two or three years. just general planting trees, cutting trees down, fencing, general work wi the Forestry Commission. Then they told me that if I wanted, I could work three years practical and then go to the Forestry Training School at Faskaly or Pitlochry and become an Under Forester wi the Forestry Commission. But och, I just didn't want that – it wasn't really for me. A man's wage then was about seven pound odds a week, and I think mine's was about four or five pounds the age I was, seventeen.

And I had a mate who'd served in the Merchant Navy, and oh, he was a strong guy and he and I used to work together. You could do piecework wi the Forestry Commission an make a lot more than seven pound odds a week, so that's what we did, putting up fences an that. We worked really hard an some weeks we earned more than they thought we should an one time the head forester says, "Oh I cannae, give you that!" We'd made 25 pounds wi fencing an he said, "You've made too much, we're no payin you that."

We said, "We've done the job! We put the fence up!" They weren't used to that, because most of the older forestry workers wouldnae do piecework; they wanted an easier life, home every night at the same time an that.

MB: *Were you still living at home at the time?*

Alistair: Aye, still at home, but we'd moved to Earn Place by then, when we got a house in the village. And there was a rabbit trapper stayed in the house just round the corner from us, Campbell MacIntyre – he worked up the glen, trapping, workin wi the ponies and other jobs. This was when Fisher Ferguson was the farm manager up the glen – he'd been the head stalker on the Drummond Estate, then he got the job of farm manager.[7] And when Fisher left, a man called Willie Bennie took over as head stalker. He wasn't from around here, and he wasn't from a keepering family either. His people were from a big firm to do with shipping, tug boats: Bennie & Co. It's a pretty specialised operation, bringing these big ships wi tug-boats. He was from that family an he decided that he wasn't going to be working in an office. He was drawn to the land, so he opted for keepering. He told me his first job was at Rowardennen on Loch Lomondside, looking after pheasants, then he went on to fox-hunting, wi terriers, and looking after thousands of acres of farmland around. He moved from one farm to the next farm, and he was in Argyll before he came here. Anyway, he told Campbell MacIntyre he was lookin for a pony-man, an Campbell said, "Oh, there's a laddie in the village there, an by God, he's keen on that sort of thing."

So anyway, one night – it was a Thursday night – there's a knock at the door. I went to the door, and this wee mannie was standin there, an he said, "I'm looking for a pony-man an Campbell MacIntyre was telling us you're quite keen."

An so I says, "I'm your man. When do you want me to start?"

An he said, "Could you start on Monday?" And this was Thursday.

So I said, "How am I going to get up the glen?"

"You'll need to get a motorbike."

I hadn't even a licence! I had a driving licence because I'd bought an old car from Keith McPherson who had the garage at the bridge there. But you couldnae drive a car all the way up the glen. I'd need a motorbike, and there was an ad in *The Courier*, Duncan of Brechin – they had motorbikes by the square yard. So I phoned him up, and "Yes, I've got a trials bike," and he took this trials bike down to the house, and then I went down to the Post Office and got a provisional licence, and on the Monday morning I went up the glen. And the mist! You could hardly see a thing in front of you for the mist!

So anyway, I got there, an I went down to the farm an got a couple of horses, an they said the guest will be here for 9 o'clock. It was a Major Edwards – I always remember his name, and he went to have a practice shot, and I was noticing his rifle. "That's not like

the old rifles," I thought. It was a hexagon barrel, and I'd never seen one before – like a thruppenny bit.[8] Seemingly it was his father's rifle from the Boer war. So away we went, set off up the glen but you couldn't see the glen, it was nothing but mist, right down the glen, but on we went, the stags were roaring – it was October.

MB: Had you ever done any stalking before this?

Alistair: No, but I knew the glen since I was a laddie, snaring rabbits. Anyway, on we went in the mist, wi this Major Edwards, an eventually when we were about four miles up the glen the mist was startin to lift, and we came to the wood. I was told to wait there wi the pony, and he disappeared in the wood, and the next thing I heard a shot. An I went in – there were no wirelesses then, like they have now; it was a white hankie that was the signal to come over, or they would light the heather. You'd see the smoke about four miles away.

MB: *And would you gralloch the stag on the hill?*

Alistair: Yes, but by the time I got to where they were, they had it gralloched. I couldnae get the pony in to where it was, but we dragged it out to put it on the horse, then we carried on to get the second stag.

MB: *So that was your first stag?*

Alistair: Aye, my first stag.

MB: *How heavy a stag, would you say?*

Alistair: Well, that one was a very big stag, it was seventeen stone. But the heaviest I've seen up the glen was 21 stone.

Janet (Alistair's wife): Remember we brought back a huge stag – was that one not about 27 stone?

Alistair: Oh yes, that was the one we got at Dalmally.

MB: *And what kind of pony was it?*

Alistair: A garron.[9] It was always garrons on the Drummond Estate. They used to have their own stud up here at one time, but by the time I came there was only about twenty horses. But when they had the stud, they used to hire him out, so much a week, a pound a week – you would have made your fortune then, when they had their own stud. And there would maybe be a hundred horses up there, all Garrons and Dales – they're a lighter coloured, lighter boned, the Dales. The old folk used to talk about the war when they wanted horses, the First World War, and they took hundreds of horses from this area. They took them away through *Bealach an Drobhair*[10]– there's a track over to Doune. There's a wee bridge out Findhu Glen – you'll need to go out to see that wee bridge and photograph it. It's still there, and that's where the drovers used to bring the sheep and cattle down from the north, long ago. They would stay there maybe the night and then go away through *Bealach an Drobhair*, they called it, and down in to Doune then on to the market [at Stirling].

At one time they used to hire out horses to other places, and they'd take them down to the village to get shod. D'you remember the mirror in Comrie?[11] The blacksmith shop was in there, and he would shoe them. When I was a boy, we used to see all these horses, and sometimes line them up along beside the church, waiting to be taken into Crerar's, the blacksmith. There used to be horses waiting to be shod over at Keith McPherson's garage, and somebody had to hold them then they were told to bring another half dozen or whatever round to the smiddy. And there was a field beside the Caledonian Stables and sometimes they'd train the horses in there.

Sandy Gardiner: How many blacksmiths were there in Comrie, Pop?

Billy: When I was young there was aye the two: there was Crerar's an then there was one doon Drummond Street. I've got a photograph of Crerar's, with the horses, the ponies from the glen – they used to come doon every year all tied in a row. They'd lead the ponies doon tae the old station where they had the Caledonian Stables. The Caledonian Railway had the stables at the station, an Ancaster Estates used to rent them for their ponies, because they used to hire out these ponies to different estates, you see. They could send them away on the train to wherever they were needin ponies. And they'd wait in the Caledonian Stables to be shod.

MB: Pat MacNab used to speak about all the ponies – he was a great man for the horses; he mentioned taking them down the glen, all tied together.

Duncan McNab (Pat's son): I remember Dad talking about bringing the ponies in off the hill and taking them down to Comrie. He and his brother Duncan were involved in 'breaking' the ponies in a corral at the back of the train station in Comrie. They were then loaded onto rail wagons to be sent out to various shooting estates around Scotland – that would be another source of income for the estate. It had stopped long before my time, but they still kept ponies in Glenartney – they need them for the shooting and that. I remember one time after my brother Peter and his wife moved to Somerset, I accompanied Dad on a visit there (after he retired), and we visited a pub high up on the Mendip Hills near the village of Priddy. It was a beautiful summer's evening, and we were sat outside the pub, which was called The Hunter's Inn. Then some folk turned up on horseback, dismounted, and tied the horses up while they went inside to get a pint. When they came back out, Dad headed across to speak to them – you know what he was like! And my brother and I were just looking on, when he showed them something they had never seen before. He took the reins of one horse and with a lightning-quick move, he secured it to the tail of one of the other horses. I can't explain exactly how he did it, other than to say it was a very simple move that could be easily undone. I presume he told them how or why he knew this – it was a trick he had learned as a young man working with the ponies in Glenartney; that's how they used to lead a string of ponies down the glen, all connected, rein to tail, one behind the other. The people were fascinated and got him to repeat the move two or three times so that they could learn it for themselves.

Pat MacNab [1912–2010]: My father was a shepherd in Glenartney – and it was nothing but Gaelic at home, an he always spoke Gaelic to his dogs. It was Lord Ancaster who was in Drummond Castle – that's Lady Jane's father, but this was before she was born. And when we came to Glenartney, there was over a hundred people at the top of the glen, between shepherds, and gillies and pony-boys and so on. There were twenty pony-boys alone because there were no cars or vehicles so there was a pony-boy allotted to every horse for the toffs, taking them out on the hills and all that sort of thing.

I was just in my early teens and old Jimmy was our blacksmith – he wasn't a big man but he was a powerful man. I'd ride doon to Jimmy, maybe wi fifteen ponies ... doon tae the foot o *Beinn Mhùrlaig* (Ben Vorlich) Now the smiddy is a ruin... They had the big anvil, but I don't know what happened tae it, an Jimmy shod the horses himself – he cold shoe'd them. Many a time I shod them myself; aye, we cold-shoe'd them. [laughs] When I'd get there with all those ponies, Jimmy used to say to me, "Right laddie, what are you gonna do? Are you getting the jacket off [to work] or are you going o'er the road?" So I'd help him shoe the horses and that was for a half bottle of whisky! He was a powerful man, the blacksmith, and I was scarcely in my teens, and he'd give me the whisky then he'd say, "Man, laddie, you're going to come to an awffy end!" [laughs].[12]

MB: Was that your first job, Pat, working with ponies?

Pat: No, my first job was trapping rabbits. After I left school, to begin with there was plenty work. I didn't turn fourteen till December, but I left anyway, just thirteen because there was plenty to do in the glen – the lambing, and the hay and everything and then when the shooting came we'd work at that. But when the shooting was finished there was nothing for you except to go an kill rabbits. So that was my first job [away from home] and there was about eight of us killed rabbits. Every man had his own beat an he'd live there, in a bothy. I was four mile out at the head of the glen, Gleann Ghòinean, [between Glenartney and Loch Earn] and before I started I took the horses up and prepared myself for the season. I took up a load of traps and snares and about three of four hundredweight of coal for the stove, and an axe and a bushman saw. The bothy was beside the great big wood, there was about a hundred acre of wood and the water ran right by, so I used to go wash mysel in the burn.

MB: What sort of a bothy was it?

Pat: It was wooden and all lined and there was no lock on the door or anything, just a plain sneck.

Duncan: And to stop it being blown away in any winter storm it was held down with wires over the roof, anchored into big posts in the ground.

Pat: Aye, and there was a round stove in the corner, and of course plenty of dead wood, so I'd burn a mixture of coal and wood. There was an old lantern, a paraffin lamp, so before I started I took up enough paraffin to last, and I took up potatoes afore I started. I had a gun in there and a dog and everything else.

MB: What about oatmeal?

Pat: Oh aye, plenty of oatmeal and a sack of barley, and Indian meal [maize] for the dog. I had tea, and there was plenty of water in the burn, only yards away from the bothy. Plenty to eat – I cut and stewed rabbits; and there was bacon – I'd fry that. My Mother had an account with Sorley the Grocer in Comrie, and he came up the glen with the van – [the road went as far as the houses, but after that it's just a track]. And there was a man who went right round all the trappers with about half a dozen horses an he came in an lifted the rabbits –there was eight different trappers and we had our sections so he would start above Dalclathic and go right round by St Fillans to old Archie's and then mine and then back down the glen. So Mother could send stuff with the pony-man – she'd send the likes of condensed milk to me and she sent up venison an everything, and when the pony-man came to gather the rabbits, he left the messages for me at the bothy. I didn't see him because I'd be out all day. And every now and again I'd leave my stockings an trousers an my shirts, and he'd take them to my mother to wash and he'd bring them back. I had a change of working clothes – I used to have a khaki shirt on, and shorts and a Scout belt; they had to last a while [without washing] but of course you didn't wear [under] pants or anything else – just the shirt. And I lived on my own from the 20th of October until the middle of March.

The only person I would see now and again was old Archie McNaughton from St Fillans – he was a decent old fellow, an I used to go and speak to him occasionally. And if they were at the gathering, old Archie would come and have a blether with me, and my father, when they'd be up gathering the sheep. They would come an speak to you. But apart fae that, they would never know if I was living or dead – I never saw a soul nor nothing else, four mile out at the head of the glen, fourteen-year-old, living there in the bothy, killing the rabbits. I didn't know what day it was, and I don't remember a calendar being there and I had a guess at the time When I was up at that bothy, I was never near the kirk and I neither was down for Christmas or New Year; I just worked on, but [in those days] there was nothing up the glen for Christmas.

MB: Same thing in Skye, the old people didn't keep Christmas, but after the war they did. In the 'Fifties we hung up our stockings, and we had Christmas dinner, but I remember the postman came on Christmas Day, and my Dad was at work.

Pat: There was a lot of keepers lifted their tackle at the weekend, but no, I just carried on, and I was quite happy – ye imagined you were away in Hudson Bay, young an fit, aye, an I didn't give a rap for nobody! But these are the things that hardened you up, I'll tell you, because there was nobody to help you if you went wrong and you were always most careful among the rocks and things. And then snow an everything else – I was in snow for days up there, doing it all and then I used to come doon out the rocks and go in at the burn and I would go in there with the dog an everything else. I had a collie, and by gosh that dog could kill rabbits, catch rabbits! It was just myself and my dog and never saw a soul.

MB: Did you use ferrets for rabbiting?

Pat: And nets, aye. I had about three ferrets up there – I kept them in the ferret box and fed them rabbits. Then after I'd been working among earth and stuff, because I dug them out, I'd wash in the burn when I got back. But it's surprising, I was quite happy there. Did I read? No, I didn't get time to read! I had to come in and cook my dinner, and then you were always sorting up broken snares at night and awthing else like, an keeping your tackle right. I'd get finished up and go to bed, and when the stags were rutting and I was in the bothy, sometimes I'd wake up when they'd be rubbing their horns up and down the wire cables that were holding down the roof. But that never put me up nor down.

MB: How often would the pony-man come to collect the rabbits?

Pat: Twice a week they came in an lifted the rabbits, and they went right round all the trappers and at every bothy there was hangers for the rabbits. They were all gutted and you'd try no to have any blood or anything about them, and the pony-man lifted them. I didn't see him, so I wasn't speaking to them; I'd be away working at the top of the hill, and they would just lift the rabbits there themselves, aye.

Duncan: There were two posts with a wire stretched between them, and my dad would take the rabbits and couple them together by the hind legs and hang them over this wire. You count rabbits by the couple, as opposed to grouse and pheasants – you would have a brace of pheasants, a couple of rabbits. And he would leave them hanging on the wire and he'd be off doing his bit, and when he got back the rabbits would have been taken away. And maybe once a month he would get a set of clean clothes brought up by the pony-man, and he would leave his dirty clothes to be taken away.

Pat: The pony-man kept [a note of] the numbers he lifted, and you kept your numbers – you didn't get paid till the end of the season. You'd get a pound for every 30 couples, and I'd trap sixty rabbits a day, thirty *couples*. You had to carry the rabbits for miles there, to put then on the hangers, all gutted and cleaned, but you didn't skin them –they didn't want you to skin them. It was blooming hard work, but of course I knew the ground so well, right out to Glen Ghòinean and Craignaharry[13] – it was great, just great.

MB: And what happened to all those rabbits? Did they go to the butchers?

Pat: Oh they werena sold in the *local* butchers – they were put in a hamper and they were going away on the railway, to Glasgow and Leeds. The hamper had a bar across, and the rabbits were coupled and put across the bar. They'd put twenty-five couple into a hamper and the hampers went away on the train.

Duncan: But when he finished his six-month contract, the pony-man came to collect him and take the stuff back to Glenartney and my dad was taken down to Muthill to the estate office to collect his pay. It was piece work. and you got your money at the end of your six-month contract. And the factor was waiting there to see what he was due, to tally up. But when the factor looked at how many rabbits he had killed, and worked out what he was due in recompense, he said, "There's no way a boy of your age is getting that money – that's ridiculous, that's obscene, I'm no payin a boy o your age that amount. Children of your age don't deserve that kind of money!" He was just fourteen, and the factor wouldn't pay him. He had worked for six months, and the factor refused to pay him, so my grandfather went into the estate office and said, "Now look here, I paid for the supplies– it was my oats, my barley, my coal that set the lad up in Glen Ghoinean. That cost me, and the money will come to me, and he's earned it, so you 'better blooming

76

well pay him.' And there was a bit of an exchange but eventually the money was paid over, but I don't know how much of it my dad received.

Pat: Fisher's father [the factor] wasn't pleased, but he paid me, and as soon as I got my money, I went to pay my bill with Sorley the grocer; it was forty pound something to pay. But the second year I went up there he said to my father, tell that laddie of yours to come in and get his money [sooner] an it was Christmas Day, so, an I went in an I had twenty-five quid tae lift and he said , "That's scandalous, a young laddie like you getting that amount of money, but mercy me, look at all we were carrying, loads of traps an snares an every other thing!

I was two winters up at the head of Glenartney, and then [the next winter] I went to Glen Beich and I was going to do wonders up there, killing rabbits. But there was nothing there but the granary for me to live in. They had a bed in the granary, and you never saw rats like it! I had the frying pan [hanging] from the rafters on a rope and everything else and they were running down and into the frying pan! I just stuck it for a week and I said, "Well, I was never reared on this," so I lifted all of my tackle and went away to Morven. Fisher [Ferguson] took me [to the station] to put me on the train for Morven.

I bought a motor bike with money I earned rabbit-trapping. I went to Dundee with big Jimmy MacLean and bought an Ivory Calthorpe, and there wasn't a mark on it. [When we got there] it was there with a cover over it, an I said "What's in below the cover?"

"Oh," he says "that's the Manager's bike." An I said ,"Are you selling that?" "Oh, I've no idea, I never heard him selling it, I'll go and ask him." An then he said , "Aye, we'd sell it." And I think it was forty-five pound, And I was the first person in the area to have electric light on my bike, an old carbide motorcycle lamp, an I bought it in Dundee.

MB: *Is your old bothy in Glenartney still there?*

Pat: I went up with the keeper two or three years ago, Alistair Work, and all I found was my frying pan and there was thousands of ants in it.

Duncan: I made a song about Dad's time as a rabbit-trapper.

The Wilds of Glen Ghòinean

He was just a child, only thirteen years, when he set out on his way
To the wilds of Glen Ghoinean, on that warm October day
He was leaving behind his family, leaving behind his home
For the wilds of Glen Ghoinean, where herds of red deer roam

He arrived with a sack of barley, and oats for making brose
Two hundred and fifty rabbit snares and a change of working clothes
And a sack of coal to fuel the stove in a tiny wooden shack
And six months would come and go before he'd walk back down that track...

From the wilds of Glen Ghoinean, where herds of red deer roam
The rabbit-trapping laddie, he lived there all alone

He had a six months trapping contract in Glen Ghoinean's wild hills
Through the mellow months of autumn and through winter's bitter chills
And the trapper lad, in solitude, would check his lines of snares
No one to share his thoughts with, his worries or his cares...

He dined on freshly guddled trout, brose and rabbit stew
He slept upon a hard camp bed, and his comforts they were few
He gathered fuel from a nearby wood, drew his water from the burn
But all the while the boy he dreamt, of the day he would return...

December fifth it came and went, just like any other day
No one to help him celebrate on his fourteenth birthday
No gifts to open on Christmas morn, no bells on New Year's Eve
Just two more months of loneliness before the boy could leave...

The boy saw out his contract, and six months to the day
He bid farewell to Glen Ghoinean and he set out on his way
He was leaving behind the wild hills where herds of red deer roam
And the time had come for the trapper lad to return to his home...[14]

Duncan: So that would've been 1926, '27, when he was just fourteen.

Sarah: I remember seeing Pat wi the rabbits, in the Forties and Fifties, oh definitely, and there was also Cousin John who used to catch rabbits, and Jim Mitchell too. I've seen Pat comin doon the lane (past Dalrannoch) and Cousin John, he'd have them laden all over the bike, so many hanging on the bike they couldn't cycle, they just walked them down to the village.

Muriel: And you'll mind the "Onion Johnnies" with all the onions hanging on their bicycles – they'd go round the village selling onions. We aye said 'ingins' – *Ingin Johnnies* – I don't know if it was the same one would come every year but they wore the same kinda hat, a flat sort of a beret.[15]

Alistair: Oh, yes, you need onions for a good rabbit stew.

MB: Alistair, is anybody trapping rabbits these days, 2021?

Alistair: Well, the thing is, the law has changed now. You cannae snare a hare and I don't think you'd be able to snare a rabbit [without a licence]. There's some people still keep ferrets. When they used to bring rabbit trappers in, they would have a part of the hill and you would have another part, and a good rabbit trapper would see the run, so he'd know where to set the snare. Most people wouldnae see it, and if you got them out on the hill and showed them, "Now this is what you do," then take them out tomorrow and asked, "Do you remember where you set them?" Well! Find 200 snares and check for rabbits! Not a chance! The trappers used to say that a rough night was the best because the rabbits would come out of the burrows and run, whereas if it was a good night they were just hopping here and there, but when they'd come out the burrows on a rough night, they'd run like the devil, to get shelter, and that's when you would get the best kill. There were thousands and thousands of them, and the young rabbit trappers all had motorbikes. But that was stopped by the time I started work on the estate, so I don't know how many rabbits they put on a horse. It was hares in my time, and we used to put seventy hares on a horse – you would bring them back and hang them in hampers and then they had a lorry up the glen, and they would take them from there down to the station in Comrie. And if you had any deer as well, they'd be put in the train and they'd be in London in the morning.

Cousin John was one of the rabbit trappers, and he sometimes worked wi the ponies. Everybody called him 'Cousin John', I don't know why.

Mairi Philp: He was my Grandpa's first cousin. His name was John Findlay McIntyre.

Alistair: Oh I see! Well, we used to see him when we were going to school. He lived at the Lechkin, and he had this old car he used to leave on top of the bridge because it wouldnae start cos the battery'd be flat. So, when we were passing, we'd give him a push down the brae to start it, past Keith McPherson's garage right at the end of the road; we used to give him a push and he would get going. I can see that wee green car yet! He was a hardy old fellow – and oh the stories! You would've loved him! And strong! Cousin John (John Findlay McIntyre, Lechkin, Comrie) could carry about twenty-five, thirty hares – that would be like carrying a stag! I have a photo of him: that's old Cousin John holding a badger! Look at the wee thin legs, and he could carry all those hares!

I mind sometimes he would be looking at the sky, and he'd say, "Aye, that's the Banff bailies..." and he'd read the sky to tell the weather. The 'Banff bailies' as he called them, were the kind of clouds, like goat's hair, and he'd say that was an indication of wind, we'd be getting wild weather.[16] Oh, Cousin John was a great character.

Endnotes

1   When Helen's family lived in Glenartney the owner of the Ancaster Estate was the 3rd Earl of Ancaster (Gilbert James Heathcote-Drummond-Willoughby), Baron Willoughby de Eresby. His only son Timothy Gilbert (born 1936), went missing in the Mediterranean Sea in 1963 and was presumed drowned. His sister, Lady Jane Willoughby de Eresby was born in 1934. She was one of the Queen's Maids of Honour at the Coronation, June 2, 1953.

2   David G. Adams notes that the general allocation was 6 gills (one and a half pints) a day. *Op cit,* p. 23. He also cites a bothyman who said they got as much as they needed, but there wasn't always an allocation of tatties on the Angus farms where he worked, so at night they'd sometimes steal them from the field. p. 35.

3   Adams notes that the use of the meal kists in the bothies declined after the Second World War when some meals were served in farmhouse kitchens. Thereafter, a smaller allocation of meal was provided in a small barrel or wooden box. *Op cit,* pp. 34–39.

4   The annual October holiday in Scottish schools is referred to as 'the tattie holiday' as thousands of families worked as well as Irish migrant workers at potato harvesting. See, Ian MacDougall, *Hoggie's Angels: Tattie Howkers Remember* (1995) and Heather Holmes, *'As Good as a Holiday': Potato Harvesting in the Lothians from 1870 to the Present* (2000).

5   The potato pit was common practice in the Highlands and Islands. In 1988 I tape-recorded Murdo Stewart (my uncle) explaining how it was done in Glenconon, Skye: School of Scottish Studies Archive, SA1988.23; Listen: < https://www.tobarandualchais.co.uk/track/72242?l=en>.

6   In her classic collection of recipes, *The Scots Kitchen: Its Traditions and Lore,* (1929), F. Marian McNeill records details of traditional methods of cooking wild meat, game, and poultry, including *maragan* (puddings), haggis, tripes and offal discussed in Chapter 9 of this book.

7   Duncan Fisher Ferguson is included in the collection of character sketches by Ben Coutts, *Auld Acquaintance: Great Scots Characters I Have Known,* pp. 85-92.

8   The pre-decimal three-pence coin was 12-sided (dodecagon) and was Britain's first non-circular coin.

9   The word 'garron' is from Gaelic, *gearran,* a gelding, pony or small sturdy horse.

10   The pass of the drover.

11   The A85 goes through Comrie and there was a traffic mirror above the bend beside the church.

12   Perth & Kinross Archive, Acc11/52: M. Bennett interview with Pat MacNab 2008.

13   Anglicised from the Gaelic place-names, *Gleann* Ghòinean (Glen of the couch-grass) and *Creag na h-Àiridh* (Rock of the Sheiling, or summer pasture).

14   Listen to Duncan singing his composition at Edinburgh Folk Club on <https://youtu.be/vQFjo_bodFk>.

15   Ian MacDougall, *Onion Johnnies: Recollections of Seasonal French Onion Sellers in Scotland.*

16   In his *Notes on the Folk-Lore of the North-East of Scotland* (1881) the Rev. Walter Gregor notes (p. 153) that 'The large, white snowy-looking clouds that rise along the horizon... were called the 'Banff bailies' and at all seasons of the year were looked upon as the forerunners of foul weather.' According to Gladys Simpson from Keith however, "the Banff bailies were big black thundery clouds" so-called because "the bailies of Banff thought an awful lot of themselves." Recorded 1984, see, M. Bennett, *Tocher* 47, p. 310.

Chapter 5

Local Worthies, Characters and True Stories

Alistair Work: A lot o the old worthies are away now ... we dinna get the same craic at all, and you miss that. I remember when Jock Spence and I were young we used to go over and visit Billy. We were just at the school, ye ken, but Billy had time for everyone – I always like to have a craic wi Billy. He used to show pigeons and he allowed us into the loft where he was handling them and then explained all about pigeons. Bald-headed Tumblers, that was the breed he kept, and then he got into canaries and budgies; he still keeps them.

Margaret Bennett: Oh, yes, you can hear them singing as soon as you reach his gate. [After the strict lockdowns] when we were allowed to visit in the garden, Billy put a couple of cushions on the bench beside the canaries – I was trying to count them!

Billy Gardiner: Sandy's the hade man wi the canaries noo. I just sit an watch them – it's ma damned legs that's the problem, getting aboot, ye ken, but I still like tae watch them.

MB: What got you interested in birds, Billy?

Billy: Och, I was aye interested an so was ma brother but I think ma faither wis kind o disappointed cos he was a great football player an neither ma brother or I had any interest in football at all. But we would tame jackdaws an anythin like that. Ye just get them when they were young in the nest, an then carefully let them go aboot the gairden. They got tae know ye, they'll eat out o yer hand.[1]

MB: And when you tamed a Jackdaw, was it just a pet?

Billy: Aye, just a pet, aye; I caa'd him Joey. We were quite young at the time, an Joey was quite tame. He'd follow us aroun the gairden, an if ye were workin an there were stones there, ye'd aye turn the stone up for Joey tae see if there'd be a beetle or somethin in below the stone.

MB: I've heard it say that Jackdaws steal things – is that true?

Billy: Well, that one used tae steal things. I remember there wis a woman along the road there an she hud one o thae things ye put on yer eye, like if ye got a watery eye or somethin, an she came an said, "Joey's stolen my –" whatever-you-call-it. "It came in the bathroom window an pinched it, an it's the only one I've got." Oh, she went an awfae length, so I says, "Just a minute," an [I told her] Joey had a wee boley hole where he'd hide things, wi a kinda box inside. So I went tae huv a look, an it wis in there! Aye, right enough he'd taken it hame. But another time, this man who used tae stay in Dalginross, I met him on the road this day an he said tae me, "Have you got a tame Jackdaw?" An I says, "Yes."

An he says "It came to our bedroom window an took my wife's diamond ring away."

"Well," I says, "I know where it puts aw the stuff so I'll hae a look."

"Oh no," he says, "dinnae bother, because he came back half an oor later, an laid it back doon where it got it."

But what can ye believe? I don't think a jackdaw'd take it back an put it back where it was, in the exact same place – makes ye wonder if it stole the ring in the first place!"

They used tae huv aw thae stories aboot poachin salmon, an aw this cerry oan. They wid say, "Oh ye remember So-an-so, an So-an-so, an they'd talk aboot characters, the likes o auld Keith McPherson an aw that. Ye never hear anything aboot anyb'dy like that noo – they've aw this blinkin Facebooks; Sandy'll no have anything ti dae wi Facebook.

Sandy Gardiner: Pop, did you tell about when you used to show pigeons all over the country?

Billy: Oh aye, fancy pigeons – the ones aw different colours an shapes 'n' sizes an everything. I liked the black ones, wi white wings, a white tail an a white hade, the Bald-headed Tumblers, they were my favourites.

Sandy: Was it the pigeon show in London you got a big win?

Billy: Aye. We used to take pigeons by train, all over the country. In the old days, say, if you wanted a day out, or wanted tae go shoppin, you could take a train fae Lochearnhead, stop off in Comrie for a few hours, an still get tae Perth for the afternoon. An you could go fae Comrie to London, all the way by train.[2] Aye, trains were a good thing – but now we have none, thanks tae Dr Beeching.[3] There wis a lad here no long ago, askin me aboot racin pigeons – we used to race with the North-West Federation an there wis six o us in

Comrie in the racin pigeon club. I think there was more in Comrie than what there was in Crieff, and we'd train them for racin. Yer birds were aw rung, wi a rubber ring on the leg, an we aa had a special clock for timing them. An you took the ring off an put it in this wee metal thing, an put the metal thing in yer clock.

In the pigeon club there was a man who had a car – no many had cars in thae days – an on a nice day he used to take the pigeons so far out and release them to fly home. There wis a milestone above Cultybraggan Camp, an that's where he'd go to start them off – they'd fly hame an we'd be sittin in the gairden by the pigeon loft, an used tae watch an see if ye could see a pigeon landin.

Then there was another milestone up at Blairnroar – that would be the next training day, a bittie further away, an he went on like this, until we got away oot towards Stirling, oot tae where thon battle was, Sherrifmuir, an they'd fly hame. An when the pigeons got to Sherriffmuir an they could fly hame, that was them supposed tae be trained.

They always talk aboot their 'pigeon lofts' but it wisnae really a loft, it was just a shed or somethin like that, but for some unknown reason they always caa'd them 'lofts'. But it doesnae metter, they were aw fur keepin pigeons anyway, or 'doos'. We caw'd them 'doo' [doves].

MB: What was the difference between a dookit [dovecot] and a pigeon loft?

Billy: I think a doo's dookit wid maybe been the ones that wis on the top o a buildin, like some fairms had pigeonholes, dookits, into the attics, the lofts. Maybe that's where we got the term 'pigeon loft' – but here it'll only be a shed. An when ye joined the pigeon club first ye got an Ordnance Survey map an ye put a pin through where yer loft wis, then ye turned it upside down an where the pin was, ye wrote yer name an address. There wis one pigeon in the Strathearn Pigeon Racin Club, fae Crieff, used tae go tae France – that wis a long way tae expect a pigeon tae fly hame, fae France – Rennes, that's where they spoke aboot. An there wis one o mine went four hundered an thirty miles, tae Christchurch, doon in Dorset, in the south o England.

MB: Billy, did you ever hear pigeons being used in war for carrying messages or anything?

Billy: Oh aye! Folk in the Air Force used tae take two pigeons wi them an if anything happened to the plane, they wid release the pigeons an they'd fly back hame. This fella in Dundee went intae his loft, an there was this bird arrived wi this message on it. [A bomber returning from Norway to Leuchars had been shot down and the crew were in the North

Sea.[4]] So, he phoned up the authorities right away, and they managed to save the crew that were in the airplane! An that pigeon got, the owner got the Dickin Medal, the Victoria Cross ye get fur animals.[5] I think there wis a dog got the medal recently for war services in Afghanistan.

I mind there wis a bank manager in the village who was very keen on shootin an natural history, an he was friendly wi the gamekeeper at Invergeldie. And this bank manager used tae write notes tae a gun & rod magazine that was printed in Yorkshire. An this editor came up here for the Game Fair in Perthshire – he had a big bushy beard, an he'd meet up wi the bank manager an hear all about the local goings-on. An this time, the bank manager must've been tellin him aboot some o the implements we use here, an the editor decided he wanted a spade for cutting peat and a Scots sned – that's what we ca a scythe. Well, he managed to get a peat spade but they were wonderin where he could get the sned when the bank manager saw the gamekeeper coming towards them. He'd be sure to know, so they asked for his help findin a sned. The gamekeeper took one look at the editor, wi his big bushy beard, an he said "Will a razor no tak it?" and walked away.

I mind a story I heard aboot auld Jock – I'll no name him, but he lived in Comrie. And Jock was cairting stone fae Dalness, an his dug was running oot in front o him. It was the month of August an one of the shooters from Auchinner was drivin up in a bull-nosed Morris, an comin roun that bad corner he hit Jock's dug, knocked the dug over. An Jock came roun the corner to find the man standing ower the body o the dug.

"Is this your poor dog?"

"Aye."

"I'm frightfully, frightfully sorry – etcetera, etcetera. I will have to compensate you", he said. So he put his hand in his pocket for his wallet an Jock was just wondering whit tae ask for, when the dug jumped tae its feet an was aff doon the road. So that was the end o that. An when Jock arrived at the hoose, the dug was lyin in front o the fire wagging its tail. "Some dug you" says Jock. "If you'd jist lain another three meenits I mighta got three quid for ye".

The same Jock was "a martyr tae the bile" as they used to say, although he lived to well over eighty. An during the first war, 1914–18, when things got tough they started calling up men well over the usual age group. So Jock an five other local men were called tae Perth for a medical exam. The six were all in the same railway coach an they got talking – one had a sore back, one had a bad eye and so on, an Jock was a bit surprised to find that he seemed to be the only fit man of the lot. When they got tae Perth they went tae a well-known pub an had a beer an a pie, before going to the medical centre. A pie might no be the best thing tae eat if ye've got the bile, but away they went. An when Jock was under examination the M.O. asked him what he did for a living. "I'm a carter". "Carting what?" says the M.O. "Wood", says Jock – at this time he was cairtin wood fae the Black Planting to the railway station. The M.O. shook his head and said, "It must be very light wood, my man" and told Jock he would not be needed. Of the six in the coach Jock was the only one who failed!

There was a lawyer here one time, a bit o a character, who was known as J.P. an one time he had a fairmer in from West of Loch Earn askin him to act for him in a dispute aboot fences. J.P. told the fairmer he was sorry he couldnae represent him because he was acting for the other party in the dispute, but he knew a good lawyer in Perth, a friend o his, an he'd gie the fairmer a letter tae tak tae him. This was afore the Second World War, when the train service was very good – you could get the mornin train fae Lochearnhead Station, to Comrie, Crieff an so on, and he'd still have plenty time for Perth Markets. So, as they were headin doon past the Carse of Lennoch (between Comrie and Crieff), the man thought he would open the letter an see what J.P. had said:

> Twa fat sheep fae the Braes o' Balquhidder
> You fleece the tane and I'll fleece the tither.

You used tae hear a lot o auld sayings roun here, like,

> As we gade up past Clachnadu
> St Fillans Hill cam intae view.

An you'd hear "So-an-so's jumpin aboot like a puddock wey clugs on"

MB: Quite a sight, a frog in clogs! [laughter]

Billy: Aye, an there's one aboot a dispute atween two fairmers on a very wet day: one o them was kinda sharp-faced an he was wearin a large felt hat, an the other fairmer says tae him. "You're like a mouse lookin oot ablow a bowl!"

They had a lot o sayings, like it was bad luck tae go into a hoose by one door an oot another, so you wouldnae dae that. And you wouldnae you cut yer nails on a Sunday, or put your shoes on the table – that was bad luck, and so was breakin a mirror, or

bringin certain floo'rs intae the hoose. You wouldnae want to sleep in a bed facin the door; the foot o the bed mustn't face the door, or that was bad luck. Touching wood was common an they'd various stories aboot crossed forks an knives. An if you get a gift of a knife, or anything sharp, you'd give a coin in return.

They had a lot o good stories – I mind one aboot The Mill of Fortune. There used to be a very large oak tree stood near The Mill o Fortune – I'll show you where it was ... An for years people used say that the spirit of Thomas Brough, the onetime mill owner, resided in the tree. People believed it was haunted, so eventually orders were given to fell the tree, so, as usually happened, it was sawn through near the root an wedges were driven into the cut so it would fall in a certain direction. However, the tree refused to fall, so they brought in a horse an fixed a heavy chain so the horse would pull the tree, but to no avail. So another horse was yoked, but when the pair o horses pulled, the chain snapped. They decided tae leave it till mornin, an the next day the tree was felled with the aid o a block an tackle, so they loaded it on to a wood-bogie to take it to Morgan's Sawmill in Crieff. These wood-bogies were of a low-wheeled lorry-type construction – the basic construction was two pair o wheels an axles, with a long beam aboot 9-inches square doon the centre, an there were stilts, uprights, which could be removed when loading. For heavy loads like this, they'd have one horse in the shafts an another in traces. A good horseman could load a tree on his own – he drove the bogie alongside the tree trunk, took the horse from the shafts, chained it to the bogie at the side, pulled the bogie over the tree, tied the tree with chains, then the horse pulled the load intact. So away they went to Morgan's Sawmill in Crieff, but when the tree was being unloaded from the wood-bogie it rolled back an broke the carter's leg.

Have you been to the old Tullychettle Churchyard? It's over near Cultybraggan, by the Ruchill – it's long since closed. In my great-grandfaither's time bodies used to be stolen from graveyards an sold to the medical college in Edinburgh – people were scared o body-snatchers, the burkers, so, when anybody died, they made great efforts tae guard

90

the graves for a few days after burial.[6] As a young man, my great grandfaither took his turn at Tullychettle, an one night it was very wet an windy, an although the churchyard was surrounded by large trees back then, there wasnae a hut tae shelter. On a wet night, the usual practice was to lie under the McGrouther table stone, facing the gate, so that's what he did, just crawled in there for shelter.

He was half sleepin when he was aware o someone crossin the dry stane dyke behind him. Stones rattled, then he heard a chain clinkin an comin his way. Half turnin in the narrow space he saw a pair of eyes shinin an heard a pantin sound. As he tried to swing his stick. the hair on his neck stood on end an thought his time had come. But the explanation was simple: a friendly collie dug had broken his chain at nearby Cultybraggan Farm.

Duncan McNab: When we lived in Glenartney I was in my teens and the only way I could get to anything, like a dance, was to walk down to Comrie – a three mile walk down the village an then I had a three mile walk back after that. My dad was a busy man on the farm, an anything as frivolous as me wanting to go and see a friend it was, "Well, you want to go, it's just Shanks's pony – walk there, and you'll get there." And I remember one particular night, I was walking down the Glen road and there was no moon, it was pitch black. And there's one place, oh, I've forgotten the name of it now, but there's a tight bend on this single-track road, and I was walking down towards this Z-bend, when I suddenly heard something in front of me. I'd no idea what it was, and it was pitch black, so I stopped, thinking it would be an animal of some sort. There I was, staring into the darkness trying to work out what the hell it was – I could hear it, down on the left-hand verge of the road. Staring at it, I could just make out that it was about half a metre high, and it was long, and it was certainly no sheep or any animal that I knew. I'd no idea, but I thought, well, if I want to get down to the village, I need to walk on so that's what I did. And it turned out, as I discovered on my way home, it was soldiers from the army come out on night manoeuvres, and they'd split them up into two groups. They were trying to find one another and attack one another, and this was a column of about a dozen soldiers on their bellies crawling along to try and ambush the other group. But I only realised this when I was walking home again and I met the other group coming the other way and they were shouting "Who goes there?" On the way home, the mist had settled on the glen, and the manoeuvres were still going on, and they were sending up signals with pyrotechnic flares. There were parachute flares of different colours, and when they landed, and when they exploded in the mist, the parachutes would come down with the flares and the whole glowing with top and all the multicoloured mist and it was just – I remember I thought it was just a magical thing to see.

Ben Muir: It must've been really scary as well – were you not scared?

Duncan: Some people would probably have been scared, and there's lots of things that could have scared me, but when you're brought up in the country you're used to be out and about at night, hearing animals and birds, it was more puzzling than scary. More than anything else I was baffled, trying to figure out what was crawling along on the side of the road.

Muriel (McGregor) Malloy: Did ye notice the earthquake last night? [Aug. 20, 2021]

MB: I did! I was sitting on the bench in the garden, and all of a sudden this thunderous noise ripped through the sky – I thought it was one of those low-flying jet fighters but I couldn't see a thing; I felt the whole bench shaking!

Muriel: I ken – we felt it in the village. I think the tourists got a bit of a surprise!

MB: I bet they did! I remember the first time I realised why Comrie gets called the 'Shaky Toon' – at school we'd been told about the Highland Fault Line, but I don't think it sank in. It wasn't until I lived in Dunira and felt an actual quake, and heard the dishes rattling, I realised why Comrie is Scotland's earthquake capital.

Billy: Oh, there were some years a lot worse than others. Way back in the 1700s, the old ministers used tae keep a record o the earthquakes – you can read aboot it in the *Statistical Accounts*.[7] In Comrie we're aw used tae earth tremors. There's a story told aboot a Comrie woman who emigrated wi her faimily tae a volcanic region o New Zealand. An durin a heavy shock, which alarmed aw the New Zealanders, inducin them tae leave their hooses in terror, our sturdy native of Comrie carried on makin bread.

When spoken to on the matter she replied "An earthquake? Dear me! I thocht it was a horse rubbin his haunches against the hoose."

There used to be a number of coal merchants in the area because every hoose burned coal. The lorries would go everywhere, an in Comrie a lot o folk got their coal fae Gilfillans. When I was young we were friendly with the Gilfillan family, coalmen – they had a field at the glebe and we got a drill of potatoes off that – you supplied your own seed an planted them, and in October you lifted them an helped them wi the rest. This was common practice at that time, pre-war. I mind when the wagons full o coal would come into Comrie station an then the Gilfillans used to load up the lorries. But before the railway[8] came in it was aye horses that cairted the coal fae Crieff – the Gilfillans were known as Carters and Coal Merchants. They had a story about one o the family back then, Duncan Gilfillan who left school aged thirteen an worked wi his faither. An one time he was going along the South Crieff Road wi an empty cairt, an he was drivin a pair of horses in tandem. An as he was passing 'Woodside', he knocked a cherry aff a tree wi his whip, an it landed in the bottom o the cairt. Now this was the hoose where the widow of old Rev. Samuel Gilfillan lived[9] – no relation to the coal merchant. He'd died over thirty years before that, an his widow moved into 'Woodside' wi the three daughters. Anyway, later that day when Duncan Gilfillan returned fae Crieff wi a load of coals, this Mrs Gilfillan was waiting for him at 'Woodside' an she handed him a religious tract. The words "Thou shalt not steal" were underlined in red ink! That's way before our time, but they still used to tell the story.

I remember the coal merchant's daughter, Lily Gilfillan – she was older than me, an she used to keep the books for her faither. We knew Lily quite well, an for a long time she kept hoose for the Miss Hodges. They were fae that big publishing company in Glasgow, Hodges, an educational publishers or something, an they had one o thae big hooses in Comrie, 'Clairmont'.

Muriel: I remember the Miss Hodges, they lived in a big house on Barrack Road, and we used to be able to cut down through the garden on a path that took you to Bob's Yard – he used sell second-hand stuff, furniture an that. It's not there now, an it's aw hooses. I think the Miss Hodges were cousins to Miss MacLagan who stayed at The House of Ross.

Billy: They'd come for the holidays or just to get away from the city. That's where Lily worked, an during the war the Miss Hodges were there, but anyone who had a big hoose, or even a spare room, they'd have to make it available for soldiers. A lot o big hooses were completely taken over, an when the Buffs East Kent Regiment were stationed in Comrie some o the officers were billeted wi the Miss Hodges. At the end I the war, when they were leaving, a young lieutenant lad had to inspect the hoose, checking everything – like, if a soldier had damaged anything he'd be fined for what they called 'Barrack room damage'; they still have that in the army. So he approached Miss Gilfillan to be a witness for barrack room damages at Clairmont because Lily had worked in this hoose when it was taken over by the army, an she could tell if anything had been damaged. "Barrack room damages?" says Lily, "Don't speak tae me aboot barrack room damages! My brother was charged barrack room damages during the First World War when he was sleeping in a tent! Get oot o here wi' ye!" Exit officer. It was very sad, though, because Lily's brother Tam was killed in France with the Black Watch – his name's on the war memorial.[10]

Lily was still wi the Miss Hodges after the war, an this day, they'd maybe be havin their afternoon tea, Rudyard Kipling came into the conversation – they were aye talkin aboot books, an one o the ladies turned to Lily an said, "Of course, Lily, you wouldn't know anything about Kipling". As if folk didnae read, or hadnae heard o Kipling or *The Jungle Book*! "Aye fine I do" says Lily, "a wee shauchly buddy, he used tae get coal fae ma faither."

Apparently, Rudyard Kipling rented Dalclathic for his summer holidays. I cannae tell ye which hoose that could've been, an Lily's long since gone. There's a hoose in Dalginross caa'd 'Dalclathic', but there must've been another one o that name. It's before my time, but I wonder if there's some way we could find oot?

MB: *I hear the libraries are opening again*[11] *– if I'm not mistaken, Kipling was a great one for writing letters, so I could phone the Mitchell Library and ask if they have Kipling's letters.*

[Three weeks later, telephone call]

MB: *Good news, Billy! I was in Glasgow and made an appointment to go to the Mitchell. It was fantastic! They'd laid out the books for me, 5 volumes of Kipling's letters and they even reserved a wee study desk for me. And guess what? There were three letters written in Dalclathic in 1919. It seems that he and his wife and daughter went on holiday to Glenartney, probably to get some peace and quiet after the war – they lost their only son. I wonder if Lily's father told Kipling about his son, Lily's brother? The librarian made photocopies of two of the Dalclathic letters so I'll put them through your letter-box.*[12]

Billy: We're allowed tae visit noo, so we could sit in the gairden. I've got a wee bench there; I was sittin there the day, watchin the canaries, an it's supposed to be a fine day themorrow – jist come on roun.

The context of Kipling's Dalclathic visit is summarised from several letters, notes by the editor Thomas Pinney, and various online dictionaries of biography: Rudyard Kipling drove to Scotland with his wife Caroline (Carrie) and daughter Elsie. They left their home in Sussex[13] on September 3, 1919 and their route took them "to Ascot to see Lady Roberts, to Oxford, Astley and the Baldwins, to Aunt Louisa's at Wilden, and on to Dalclathic Lodge, Perthshire, on the 76,000-estate of the Earl of Ancaster." Arriving at the Lodge September 11, they holidayed until the 25th with Daisy Low, who was related to Kipling's American wife. Juliette "Daisy" Gordon Low was the widow of a wealthy Savannah cotton merchant with an estate in Scotland, a friend of Robert Baden-Powell, and founder of the Girl Scouts of America.

On September 16, 1919 Kipling wrote his first letter to a fellow-writer and friend, Frank N. Doubleday, who had sent him a manuscript to read. Addressing him as 'Dear Old Man', Kipling deals with the 'business' then continues in a personal vein:

> We came up here by car a few days ago from Bateman's and are living in "lone Glenartney's hazel shade" (v. Lady of the Lake, W Scott)[14] on terms of almost indecent familiarity with the stags.
>
> [The] Day before yesterday, crossing a path, we slid down on a couple of 'em and had to stop and let them cross the road – which they did in one bound of what looked like 50 feet. It's breathless, burning blue weather – which has dried all the rivers so we get no salmon – but it's almost good enough merely to be alive. I wish to goodness I had you sitting up on those dried lumps of Heather looking over what seems like the end of the world – [sketch of barren hills with an arrow]
>
> Carrie has begun to get a little rest at last: Elsie is enjoying herself and eating enormously, and I have done literally not one stroke of work for 10 days. [......*page of the original was missing*]

Rudyard Kipling, September 23, 1919, letter to cousin Stan (Stanley Baldwin) in Ireland:

Dalclathic Lodge/ Comrie/ Perthshire/ Sep. 23, 1919

Dear Stan,

Unless all signs fail, I'm beginning to think that we've found *the* spot in all the Highlands. It is true that the river at the foot of the garden produces no fish but that is because there hasn't been any water in it worth speaking of, till today; and it is equally true that one can't get leave to shoot a stag but somehow, I don't think that you and I would be worried by these disabilities. Likewise grouse, blackgame, pheasants and partridges and rabbits and snipe are simply jostling each other all round the landscape but, again, they belong to God and my Lord Ancaster and for my part, I'm content to watch. But never did you imagine such mountains and moors. Glenartney Forest is its name and it's all gentle easy naked slopes running up to 2500 feet, with glens, and corries and rifts in the mountain sides and burns with waterfalls and fairy caves and sweeps of heather and bracken – and an area that wipes the years off your back. Carrie and I went out yesterday and were misled by seeing shelties [ponies] grazing far up the mountainside into the belief they were deer. (The deer are all around the place, anyhow). Whereby we walked about three miles after them and came home, skipping across rocks and stepping stones and disturbing all the game in creation.

It's five miles from a station (which in itself is a miracle) and within an hour and a half motor of all the Trossachs. It's within reach of Aberfeldy, Dunkeld, Pitlochry and the Pass of Killiecrankie etc. etc. and every motor run we took was lovelier than the last. Moreover the house itself rejoices in Conveniences – three of 'em – and a bath with real hot water out of a tap and discreetly arranged bedrooms whereby the Sexes do not cross each other in pursuit of the Obvious. Much better than raw bracken in the face of nature, my cousin. Its provisioning and maintenance – thanks to the opulent and luxurious towns of Comrie (5) and Crieff (12) where they understand food – are direct, simple and easy. It is *not* described by sportsmen since Ancaster reserves all shooting – bird and stag – and the River Ruchell [Ruchill] which I have been flogging for a week only gives sea trout and the *very* occasional strayed salmon. It has a triple garage capable of holding the largest and well-appointed servants offices; the supply of blankets to the beds is beyond the dreams of avarice; and the chamber toilette appliances are abundant and seemly. There is, further, a smoking room. The pictures on the walls though not inspiring are meritorious and the Factor of my Lord Ancaster (he always called him "my Lord") appears to be accommodating and is certainly affable.

I am in hopes of getting it for next August if it can be done without taking it for the season, and our hostess's arrangements permit. (She has a lien on it for the next few years I believe) but *if* the thing works out satisfactorily, I foresee rather a good time for a couple of deserving citizens whereof the most deserving is

Your affectionate cousin,

Rud

Billy: It must've been an awfy dry summer that, a really hot summer; it's funny you never heard o global warmin thae days... We'll need tae ask someone up the glen just where that is, because I think there was mair than one hoose ca'd 'Dalclathic'. There's that hoose in Dalginross ca'd 'Dalclathic' but I dinna think that's it.

Duncan: My Mum an Dad stayed in a cottage called "Dalclathic" – that was the first house they stayed in after the war, their first home after they were married. When Dad was demobbed he came home to Glenartney to work as a shepherd and that was where they lived. The house had no running water, no toilet, no electricity, so I don't think this is the one Kipling rented.

Tom Weir wrote about Dalclathic in one of his articles for *The Scots Magazine* ('The Shepherd of Glen Artney', June 1977) – Dad took him up the glen and he mentions the shooting lodges, which were all staffed in his day. Dalclathic Lodge must be one of them. He has a 'k' on the end of Dalclathic, but it's the same place..... I'll email it to you.

Tom Weir, "My Month: The Shepherd of Glen Artney", June 1977

You're lucky if you can catch a shepherd at home in the middle of the lambing season. I judged my timing so as to arrive when Pat would be finishing his midday meal and I arrived in time to join him in a drink of tea. Stockily-built, red-cheeked, with a merry twinkle in his eye, he grinned, "You've come at the perfect time! It's just fifty years ago since I did my first lambing on Ben Vorlich. It was 1927, and I was 14. I stayed in the old house of Dubh Choirein – you've slept in it so you know it's not much of a place, but it was furnished in those days. It was a hard beginning for a lad, but I had been well trained under my father.

"It's the lower ground we'll be on this afternoon. I want to see the gimmers are right – the young sheep that are having lambs for the first time. It's been a long, hard winter for them, what with snow and floods."

With the dog in the back of the car, off we went to the parks that drop steeply to the rocky ravine where the Ruchill Water foams over the Spout of Dalness. Pat had been over the ground in the early morning. Dog at heel, he moved quietly back and fore across the slopes, eyes everywhere to see that none of the new-born lambs had been deserted. Then, satisfied, he swept his hand towards the river, and told me he would take me to see his bridge, known locally as Pat's Brig, since the one shown on the map was swept away.

The descent to the bridge on a path through gnarled birches was pure charm, past the ruins of a former crofting township, with, above it on the south-facing slope, green rigs of old cultivation encircled by a huge oval of grassy field-dyke enclosing many acres.

"That's all been reseeded and treated with chemicals to get rid of the bracken and make grazing."

Below us was the rocky gorge, and slung across it a wooden bridge supported on twin trunks as long as telegraph poles. "It was some job hauling up the poles and balancing them over to the other side. We had to choose the very highest rocks because of the spates here. The Ruchill rises tremendously fast because of all the burns flowing into it. You see that huge boulder in the dry bit of the river-bed? It was shifted several feet from the bank in the last big flood." We turned down-river now, past the rusted stanchions of the demolished bridge to the spurting white cataract of the Spout of Dalness, the only waterfall on the Ruchill.

To let the salmon up, a rough fish pass has been hewn in the rocks at the side, making it into a sanctuary area where no fishing is permitted. Comrie Angling Club have the rent of the entire river.

Back amongst the gimmers we came immediately upon a lamb soaked in birth fluid which the mother had not licked off. The negligent ewe stood a short distance off, showing little concern. "I'll have to catch her and pen her with the lamb," said Pat and he picked up the shivering wet bundle and moved past the mother who followed slowly. Then, when we had covered the quarter mile to the pen, he opened the gate, dropped the lamb in, and sent off the Border collie who neatly separated the gimmer from its neighbours to be grabbed by Pat who turned her over to squeeze the udder to test for milk. Very little squirted out and he shook his head with concern. "Any lamb can live for 24 hours on what is already inside her at birth. I'll have to come back to this one later." We talked about the effect of weather on the ewes....

"Today is fine. But on the hill four days ago, you couldn't hold up your head for drift. It was a winter blizzard! The problem is the big number of sheep. In my father's time – and he shepherded until he was 78 – a hirsel was 400. Mine is over 800, and I have to do it on my own. I can't handle a number like that and lamb them the careful way he taught me, though I do my best. We have five shepherds for a summer stock of 900 sheep. It goes down to half that number in winter.

"But things are easier for me in some ways than they were for him. We have good medicines and sheep dips. Maggots and disease was a curse in my father's time. In his day, you had to do a lot of doctoring. Of course, we're better paid than ever he was. Wages are high now, changed days from the £27-10s. the half-year I got in Morven in the 1930's...."

Climbing up the hill to Mailerfuar, formerly a gamekeeper's cottage but now a hay barn, we commanded a fine view up and down the glen, from the earthquake centre of Comrie following the swell of the sandstone and conglomerate hills to their apogee on Uamh Mhor at 2181 feet, beyond which are the harder rocks of the Highland

Boundary Fault. There was a severe tremor in 1839, with rumblings like thunder. People in Comrie were terrified and the kirk opened for prayer.

When we dropped down to the school Pat became reflective, remembering that there were 27 on the register in his day, and now it is closed. "It's the only school I ever went to. From April to October we never wore shoes. I didn't notice the two-mile walk to school, for my feet were like leather. In the holidays I was never away from the horses. The estate kept 150 ponies, which they rented out to other shooting lodges at £1 a week. I was horse-daft and helped break them, take them to the smiddy, and go with them to the grouse moors at beating time. Although my father always had a low wage, we wanted for nothing in the way of food. We had grouse, venison, rabbits, everything that was going. My mother kept open house, and nobody went without. For entertainment, there were plenty of fiddlers and accordionists. There was a barn for dancing."

I asked about the population.

"When the shooting lodges were staffed in summer, it could rise to 150. It never gets above two dozen now. I did every kind of job in the glen, from ghillie to killing rabbits, then, in 1938, one of the shooting tenants, a Mr Latilla, offered me a job on his estate at Balcombe, in Sussex. I was to be a gamekeeper, because I knew about grouse and deer, but the main job was rearing pheasants. I got on great. It was there I met my wife, who was a parlour-maid in the big house."

"Upstairs–Downstairs!"

Back at the house, I had a chat with Isobel, who hails from Egremont, in the Lake District, and has a lively sense of humour.

"Upstairs-Downstairs!" she laughed. "And I was back to being a maid after I married Pat in 1940, when I went to work at Drummond Castle, near Crieff, when Pat went off to the R.A.F." Drummond Castle is the seat of the Earl of Ancaster, who owns Glen Artney.

Pat's R.A.F. career lasted six years. Demobbed at last, he came back to shepherd Glen Artney from a cottage called Dalclathick, one mile off the beaten track, without running water or toilet until he made one. Isobel described that convenience.

"It was unusual. It had a square seat, because Pat is no joiner, and didn't know how to make an oval one! I used to carry the clothes down to the burn to wash them.

I think these years at Dalclathick were some of the happiest. We did get a modern house, but Pat was restless, and wanted to move." The move to Lanarkshire was in 1953.

"The year of the Coronation", said Pat. "The bonfire on Tinto was still burning when we got to the house where we were to live, at Parkhall. I knew they had different ways of handling sheep on those hills, and I wanted to learn them. We were away 17 years, and I worked in three different places, finishing up on the Lang Whang. But Glen Artney was always in our minds, and we came back six years ago."

The glen, of course, is very empty compared to what it used to be like.

"We'll go up and look at the head of the glen, and you'll see Dalclathick, the old cottage without water, which we still think of as home."

There it stood in the sun, which it gets from four in the morning until sunset, Pat told me.

"We had a wee Norwegian cart and a pony when we lived there, and when our daughter took pneumonia, it was on the cart we took her to Comrie. Now you would ring for an ambulance. For entertainment, you turn on the television. These things don't make up for the folk who have gone, who rallied round to help you. Folk are very mobile now. My mother made only one trip a year from the glen, and that was to the Rural outing."

Just across from the old cottage, and linked to it by footpath, stood the Auchinner, the house where Pat had been brought up.

"My grandfather died in it, and my uncle left Glen Artney only eight years before my father came to it, so the MacNabs have a long connection with the top of the glen. I've herded every hirsel from top to bottom. My daughter was the first lassie to be married in the wee kirk for 50 years."

I asked him about retirement, knowing that many shepherds over 60 look forward to an easier life, without long hours of walking from dawn to dusk through six weeks of lambing, then the work of marking, clipping, dipping and gathering the sheep from the high tops for the sales.

"I'm a lucky man. I don't know what illness is, not even a headache. I eat well and work a long day. I love to be out and don't look forward to giving up. So long as I don't feel myself a passenger I won't pack it in."

Back at the house and sitting down to a splendid high tea, Isobel and Pat talked enthusiastically about their special delight, fiddle music of the Scott Skinner kind.

"You know, I heard him play in Comrie. I've never forgotten it…"

We looked at family photos. Their two boys and two girls are married now. Three of the four live in England, the fourth [Duncan] is in the Royal Navy at Rosyth. The shepherding link is broken[15].

END

Duncan: My Mum always said that these were their happiest years, when they lived in Dalclathic. That was before they had me, because they'd moved to Lanarkshire by the time I was born. But I've often been down at that cottage – Elizabeth and I were up the glen on Sunday, and we had a walk down there. I'll send you some photos – you can just see the roof of Mum and Dad's first house on the brow of the hill. We saw Alistair Work, Peter Cramb's neighbour – he was down checking on one of the buildings because the estate had been renovating what had been the servants' quarters and had made a new hall for shooting parties. It's been renovated, something like Blairnroar, with a kitchen and dining area. It was finished round the start of the pandemic, but they haven't been able to use it yet. There was no sign of any lodge or big house, but Alistair showed us where Dalclathic Lodge was – apparently it was demolished by the Army; there's nothing left now but a few stones. Alistair remembers it; he'll be able to tell you more, and we're allowed to visit now.

Alistair: When I first came up the Glen to work in the Fifties, Dalclathic Lodge was still standing but there were holes in the roof; it was in a bad state of repair. I'm told that during the war, early Forties, it had been used to house evacuees from Glasgow, though they weren't there very long before they wanted to go home – too isolated for them, miles away from the school or the shops and there was no electricity. After the war the house gradually fell into a derelict state and could have fallen down without major repairs. So the army demolished it – they were still based at Cultybraggan and they did training exercises, using explosives, and they must have been asked to knock it down. But I believe that if Lady Jane had been there, she'd never have allowed that; it would've been saved, whatever state it was in. I mean, this place we're in: in the Fifties there was a family of Gillieses that was in this house but then nobody. And Janet will remember there was an ash tree growing out of this very house, and there was no roof on it, but Lady Jane had that all renovated. Now, Janet can show you an old photo of Dalclathic House, the Lodge – you'll need to show Billy where Rudyard Kipling spent his holiday!

MB: I can't wait! He's been puzzling over this for ages!

Alas it was not to be, as Billy passed away the following evening. His son Sandy, who lived with him, telephoned with the sad news: they had been watching television together and his father fell asleep. Billy died as peacefully as he lived, 7th March 2022. His treasure-trove of memories, local knowledge and sense of humour live on, as does his voice, which can be heard through the recordings.[16]

Endnotes

1   In his book of auto-biographic essays, Fife poet and artist Jim Douglas gives an insightful and detailed account of catching and training a jackdaw which he kept as a pet. 'Jake' in *Run to the Rainbow, pp. 56–60.*

2   Martha Soutar (b. 1923) travelled daily from Auchterarder to Crieff to attend school. Her father was the station-master at Auchterarder, and had photos of the deployment of troops during WW1. Martha later had a career as Station-mistress in Auchterarder then took over at Gleneagles Station after the government closures. Recordings and transcriptions of her discussion on the importance of Strathearn's railways can be accessed at Perth & Kinross Archive, Acc11/52: M. Bennett interviews with Martha Soutar, Feb. 4 and March 11, 2014.

3   When Britain's railway network was nationalised in 1948, the newly formed British Railways Board appointed Dr R. Beeching as Chairman. He prepared a report in which he identified 2,362 railway stations and over 5,000 miles of railway track that should be closed. Rural areas were the hardest hit, and between 1956 and '67 Strathearn was to lose all its stations between Perth and Lochearnhead. By 1964 the busy railway stations in Crieff and Comrie were closed down.

4   Peter Hawthorne tells the story of this pigeon in 'Winkie: The North Sea, 1951' in *The Animal Victoria Cross: The Dicken Medal* (Section 1). In November 2023 (just as this book was going to print), *The Dundee Courier* reported that a bronze statue of 'Winkie' the pigeon had just been unveiled in Broughty Ferry. The same pigeon also features in a 50-minute documentary film about pigeons during the Second World War: 'War of the Birds' by Atlantic Productions for Animal Planet (2005): <https://youtu.be/sZfjbfe5SXM?si=mdI4vrvdFK8SHp-c>.

5   The Dickin Medal was inaugurated in 1943 initially to honour the bravery and service of animals in war. By the end of the Second World War, the medal had been awarded to 32 messenger pigeons serving the Royal Air Force besides 34 dogs and 4 horses serving the Army and a cat serving the Royal Navy. See, <https://www.historic-uk.com/HistoryUK/HistoryofBritain/The-Dickin-Medal/>.

6   The fear of body-snatchers was widespread all over Britain and watch-houses or watch-towers became a feature of many graveyards. (M. Bennett. *Scottish Customs from the Cradle to the Grave*, pp. 228–29, with further references.) There are many examples of watch-towers, such as Edinburgh's New Calton Cemetery Watch-tower (built 1820), which is now included in the city's tourist attractions.

7   *The Statistical Account of Scotland*, Vol. 11, p. 188 and *The New Statistical Account of Scotland*, Vol. 10, pp. 580–81 and 747. See also newspaper reports and oral testimonies in 'Earthquakes and Other Extraordinary Phenomena' in M. Bennett, *In Our Day*, pp.53–62.

8   Perth Railway Station opened in 1848, Crieff Junction opened in 1856, and Comrie Station opened in 1892.

9   P. R. Drummond includes an essays on the Rev. Samuel Gilfillan and his son George Gilfillan in *Perthshire in Bygone Days*, 1879, pp. 160–70.

10   See also, photograph and tribute to Corporal Thomas Gilfillan in A. MacGregor, *The Parish of Comrie's Part in the Great War, 1914–18*, p. 38.

11   Reported in *Glasgow West End Today* (online newspaper), October 27, 2020: "Mitchell Library reopens to the public after lockdown closure… Customers can borrow books and return overdue books without having to pay a fine… Research visits to Special Collections, Archives, General Services and the Business and Intellectual Property (IP) Centre are available through free, pre-booked appointments." <https://www.glasgowwestendtoday.scot/news/news-mitchell-library-reopens-to-the-public-1036/>.

12   Pinney, Thomas (editor). *The Letters of Rudyard Kipling,* Vol 4; 1911-19, Iowa, University of Iowa Press, 1999.

13   The Kiplings bought their Sussex home in 1901. Known as 'Bateman's', the property is now owned by the National Trust. The well-illustrated website includes a photo of Rudyard Kipling's Rolls Royce: <https://www.nationaltrust.org.uk/batemans/features/history-at-batemans> website photos include his study>.

14   From Sir Walter Scott's *Lady of the Lake* (1810), Canto I, stanza 1:

> *The stag at eve had drunk his fill,*
> *Where danced the moon on Monan's rill,*
> *And deep his midnight lair had made*
> *In lone Glenartney's hazel shade.*

15   Tom Weir,. 'My Month' in *The Scots Magazine*, June 1977. In his book *A Stick, Hill Boots and a Good Collie Dog: A Shepherd's Life Fifty Years Ago*, Ben Coutts acknowledges the Glenartney shepherds who taught him as a schoolboy, his 'old companions Pat MacNab and Donald MacPherson who helped with the book". From them, he learned about a 'way of life [that] has all but vanished. See B. Coutts, 1999.

16   Perth & Kinross Archive, Acc11/52; Acc21/12; Acc23/30; M. Bennett Interviews with Billy Gardiner (2015-22).

Chapter 6

Big Hooses, Spare Rooms and Evacuees

Muriel (McGregor) Malloy: I mind the evacuees coming – they were at school with us. There was a lot o them an when they left school they got jobs locally.

Billy Gardiner: The year I left school there was only myself and a lad fae Dunira who were local – the rest were all evacuees.

Muriel: Dunira was turned into a hospital, but that got burned down near the end of the war. It was an awful shame, that lovely house burning down. Some o the nurses and other workers there stayed on and married locals. I was at school when the evacuees came and Nora MacPherson's father was the person in charge of finding homes for them – all these big houses were taken over.

Nora (MacPherson) Hamilton [1920–2015]: There was troops stationed all over the place, Crieff was full of them, the Hydro was full of troops, and the whole of Comrie was full of soldiers, in everybody's house. We had two evacuees and two of our cousins from Edinburgh so we didn't get any soldiers, but we had tank traps at the door there! They were built right across the road there [Burrell Street[1]] and there was guards on them, and at night and we got to know the soldiers. Grandfather would say, "There's no more of those folk coming in here!" And he'd be the one that would invite them in, which was because when they were on duty there, sometimes the tank trap things got knocked down. And if we went along to the farm for milk they had the guard room along at Glasdale and you had to stop: "Halt! Who goes there, friend or foe?" I don't know what they'd have said if you had said 'foe', I mean we used to know them, I'd say, "Oh for goodness sake, you know who I am!"

"It doesn't matter; if you don't answer I'll shoot you!"

And Grandfather was in charge of the evacuees – when the train came into Comrie Station he helped to say where they were going.

Margaret Bennett: And besides your cousins who were evacuated from Edinburgh, where were the other two from?

Nora: Glasgow, Thurso Street – these tenements are all demolished now.[2] Two sisters, Jane and Susan, and when they arrived, they were the two dirtiest, most difficult ones to be evacuated, so he brought them here. We already had four people but he brought these two. There was a big table in the kitchen in those days and also a couch. And the two sisters sat on the couch so Aunt Lou gave them a card table, in front of them and she made the food for them. She made sausages and sandwich kind of things for them, and it just vanished, she couldn't think how it could disappear so fast – they had put it behind the cushions and I said to them "Why did you not eat it?" And they said, "We didnae ken whit it wis, miss."

I said 'Well what do you usually have, Jane?"

"A piece an jeely."

They wet the bed every night for a while. One of them wasn't really mentally stable (maybe she was traumatised), but her sister turned into a nice wee lassie. I always remember her saying, "Hey Nora, take yer bike in or it'll get stealt, so it will!"

And one day I asked them, "Where is your dad?"

"He's in the jail," was the reply.

So that's it, their father was in jail, but when Father got out of jail, he came and took them away because I think they would get some money there if they were at home. And then they wrote and asked if we'd take them back again but Aunt Lou said "No," she'd take Jane but she wasn't going to be responsible for Susan. But they were quite nice wee kids.

Mairi Philp: My mother worked at Dalclathic Lodge when the evacuees were there – that was the big house up the glen. Mum was born in 1926 so she was thirteen when the war started and the school-leaving age was fourteen. So it would have been 1940 when she was of an age when she needed a job and they were looking for help with the evacuees. They lived in the glen anyway, at Auchinner – they were all born at Auchinner because Grandpa went there after the First World War. He was Peter McIntyre and he went to the glen as a pony-man and ploughman. He had been in the Scottish Horse during the First

World War, so he learned all his horse skills there and he became the best trainer of the horses. My Mum was Anna McIntyre, and her mother wasn't one to let anyone not work, as was the work ethic at that time. So, there was a job going at Dalclathic Lodge, Mum was available, so she went to help.

MB: Did she tell you much about it?

Mairi: The only thing she told me was that these kids came from Glasgow and when they arrived they didn't know what a sheep or a cow looked like because they'd never seen any. I don't think they'd seen green grass and trees either, but they brought their own, eh, 'wildlife' and so there was a lot of talk about gentian violet and iodine and clipping of hair.

MB: Oh dear, did she catch any of the wildlife herself?

Mairi: I don't think so.

MB: And did she mention the nit comb?

Mairi: No, they could see the head lice running, so they clipped and shaved the hair and dowsed them all with gentian violet or iodine.

MB: How long did she work at Dalclathic?

Mairi: It would be from when she left the school to the year she got called up, but not quite the four years, because for a short time she went to work at 'Rathlin' [Dundas Street, Comrie] for Dr Watt and Mrs Temple. Then when she turned 18, she was called up, to do National Service and she joined the ATS.[3] She was trained as a cook, and her training as a cook stood her in good stead, because she did that for the rest of her life, working in hotels in Crieff and Comrie.

Muriel: Some of the evacuees didn't stay very long – they went back to Glasgow because they couldnae get used to living in the country. But some of these big houses are pretty isolated.

Helen (Grewar) Gardiner: I can remember Dalchathic House, the Lodge – it was down near the Ruchill.

MB: Where exactly is it?

Helen G: It's about four miles up from Comrie. You know the road out to Cultybraggan? Then you know where the Ruchill flows behind Cultybraggan, well you would go that way. It's quite a narrow road, and it just winds its way along the Water of Ruchill. The other road going up the hill after the sign to Cultybraggan, that's the one that takes you up to Mailermore, where we lived. It's a "You'll tak the high road an I'll tak the low road" kinda thing, and when Dad took the lease of Mailermore Farm we looked down onto the Ruchill, down onto Dalclathic, but I wasn't allowed down there by myself. I'd be in primary school then, and if I had any notion of going down there to play, oh, I got "Now, you're not going down there!" And the finger got pointed at you as much as to say, "Don't even think about it!" The big house used to be rented by shooters and during the wartime it was evacuees from Glasgow.

MB: So when you were in primary school the evacuees were staying in Dalclathic House?

Helen G: Yes, but of course I didn't meet them because they'd be going to Comrie School, and I went to the wee school at Blairnroar.

Jane MacIntyre: You should talk to my Aunt Jane – she was evacuated here during the war. She still comes back on holiday and she's over ninety! Her name's Jean but we call her Aunt Jane.

Jean Parker ('Aunt Jane'): I was born in Glasgow in 1928, on the 28th of June, right in the middle of the city, just a little bit along from the Royal Infirmary in Garngadhill. My father came from Portree in Skye and my Mum was from Garngad and they had a big family – six of us, five girls and one boy. There was Julia and Phamie and I was the third one – I was christened Jean Cameron Matheson, but I get called Jane because there were so many Jeans in the family! Then there was Sybil, then John, and the youngest sister was Lily. I remember in Glasgow when anybody had a baby being christened, if it was a girl, the first boy they met after the christening was given a sandwich with money in it – some folk called it a 'christening piece'. You'd see that after the ceremony. I remember there was a chapel just up the road from where we stayed, and we used to go there with bread for to feed the hens.

MB: Did folk keep hens in Garngad?

Jean P: Back then it was a different life to what we're living now. There was a convent attached to the chapel, and the hens belonged to the nuns in the convent. We were actually

Protestants, and we went to St. Rollox School on Royston Road, and the Catholic school was the school next to it, the two schools together.

MB: *So, what was your introduction to Comrie?*

Jean P: It was the start of the war, 1939. I was eleven when the war broke out and Glasgow was a dangerous place, so children were being evacuated. And if a mother had children under a certain age, then it was quite in order that she would go with the children. There were six of us all together, but the two older than me, Julia and Phamie, worked at MacFarlane-Lang's, the biscuit factory, so they had to work. They both joined the Land Army – they were Land Girls, and they were sent to farms in Perthshire.

Julia and Phamie weren't so far away from us after we were evacuated. When the day came, we younger ones were just collected together and taken to the station, and our mother went with us. I remember we all had our 'tinnies' (tin mugs) with us, and a wee gas mask in a box and a wee case with our clothes. We left from Queen Street Station and we'd never been on a train journey before – well, it was as if you were going on a holiday! We weren't any the wiser about the war at that time. I can remember the journey: it was fantastic being in the train, with a lot of children – mothers with children all mixed up. There were stations in Crieff and Comrie and St Fillans, but there's no such thing now since that railway was taken away in the fifties – it was Dr. Beeching that did that.

When we got to St. Fillans a teacher met us. I can remember it was comical to me that when we arrived, the teacher said, "Well, I have plenty of you to look after with the ones coming off the train." Mum says, "Just learn them how tae talk English!" And we still talk the same way – I just have to talk, and you'll know I'm fae Glasgow.

MB: *What do you remember about St. Fillans?*

Jean P: I remember Loch Earn and the boats at the side of the loch with all the big houses that were there. And I remember the shop that was by the Drummond Arms Hotel – that was where we went.

MB: *And when you got to St. Fillans, where were you accommodated?*

Jean P: There were empty houses, and the evacuee families all had different houses to go to. You were shown to a house where the mothers with a number of children went. And you know where the Drummond Arms Hotel is? Well, there was a big, big house next to the

Drummond Arms Hotel, and I'm not sure if she owned this big, big house, but the Queen of the Netherlands lived there during the war, and we were in the servants' quarters. Queen Wilhelmina was in residence while we were there – she was a big, stout queen, but we wouldn't have been any the wiser who she was, to be quite honest. And we didn't really meet her – you'd see her from time to time but were always kept well apart; that would be quite common in thae days.

MB: *And did you get duties or jobs to do while you were staying in the house?*

Jean P: Well, we had to go to school and Mum got a job in the Drummond Arms Hotel. She was cleaning the hotel, and after the meals she'd have the dishes and the big pots, washing and scrubbing, and working long hours, but she was at home with us at night. She knew we were quite safe in school and so forth, and we were quite well fed. We had our school clothes and we had our 'play clothes'. The girls had a gym slip and a jumper that we had from the Glasgow Corporation before the war, a navy jumper with red through it, and a navy-blue gym slip and a trench coat – we called it a 'trench coat' though I don't know why, and that was navy-blue as well. And in every family it was the case that hand-me-downs were the order of the day. Julia was the oldest and she got the new ones and then Phamie – there was a year and a half between them, and I was a bit younger, so I would get Phamie's. And if there was anything left after I had it, it went to Sybil or Lily, so we never really had anything completely new. Then when you came home from school you would change into old clothes because you had to keep your clothes for the school. Mum would darn our socks or stockings – that's what they throw out nowadays – and she taught all of us to darn and sew.

MB: *Was it a big adjustment for city children moving to the country?*

Jean P: Yes, and they must've have had many a laugh at some of the things we used to say. At first we didn't feel completely welcome, but it was a little village and all of a sudden there were that many children around! So you could picture it, especially as a lot of folk in the village were pretty elderly, and we were all young, and up to all sorts of things. But after a while you got to know them and then you started to do what they did, instead of doing what you used to do, so we fitted in more and we felt more welcome. But then we had a flooding in the house at Drummond Arms Hotel so we moved to another house that was right along the village. 'Lake Cottage' it was called, right beside Loch Earn. And we had a good time there, always out and about. I remember we'd go out in a boat – I don't know if we pinched the boats, but I think if you're a child you'd be up to all you could be up to!

We made a lot of friends in the village, but St. Fillans school was just primary, and no secondary school. So, when it was time to move up the school we moved from St. Fillans to Comrie. We stayed at Drummond Street, along where there used to be a chip shop, we went down this wee lane to go into the house. It was like a cottage – it was lovely, and you could look on to the river. We had lovely times in thae days, though we had strict times, too.

Mum got a job and we went to school in Comrie, and you had a choice of what you wanted to do in the secondary school: you could learn languages, or you could go into 'domestic'. That was quite common when I was at school, so I just chose 'domestic' – classes in laundry, cooking, hygiene – I think they called it 'Home Economics' in later

years. I left school at fourteen – that was the school leaving age at that time. To begin with I got a job where my Mum was working, at Lawers, just between Comrie and Crieff. I was a domestic at this private school for boys that had been evacuated during the war – the school got moved fae Cramond in Edinburgh and they took over Lawers House.[4]

Every morning we got the bus from Comrie, then home again at night. Some of the local people worked there for years – even before it was a school. I can tell you we had plenty to do! I've even got one of the ornaments from one of the chandeliers that was in the school because it fell one time and they couldn't put it together. So the ones that were working, we all got a wee bit of this chandelier fae Lawers House! Although I went into service when I left school, I didn't really like it, so then I got the job at the railway in Comrie – that suited me much better.

MB: *So how did you go about getting the job with the railway?*

Jean P: Well, during the war they were calling up the different ages for the men, and that included men who worked for the railway, like the railway porters. And when a working man got called up and went away to war, they had to take women to do the work, in place of the men who'd been called up. And I knew this girl in Comrie – her name was Nan – and she was working at the railway. She used to stay next to the railway and she had the job of the Signalman. She operated the points, changing where the trains went, so, being pals, we often went up there, I suppose to help her, but I think we would be more of a hindrance than a help!

MB: *Was it a busy station then, Jean?*

Jean P: It was a very busy station, and passengers always had to change there to go further on – in those days there was a train going on to Crieff and then into Perth. And if you were travelling in the other direction, the railway-line went along Loch Earn and then up to Crianlarich, so it was a busy line. So, they needed railway workers.

MB: *Do you remember any exciting things that happened when you were working there?*

Jean P: Oh, quite a lot of things happened. I can remember the SS coming into the Comrie station – the German prisoners of war, who were headed for the Cultybraggan Camp. Oh, I remember noticing that some of them were so young, they were only children, they were really. You'd see them coming off the trains, prisoners, and the SS was very, very strict. We'd see them lined up in order and getting marched from the railway station up to the camp and they were singing all the time. "Hi O, Hi Hee, Hi O" – I don't know what the songs were, German songs, of course, but I get wee bits of it now and again. And there was one man, I've got his photo here, actually, and he worked on the farms. I'm not sure he was an SS man, but he said that if he didn't go into the army in Germany, he would be shot. I can remember these stories.

MB: *When you were working for the railway, did you know, or were you told at the station, that there was a train coming in with German prisoners of war?*

Jean P: No, no, no, no! They just arrived. They looked as though they were just boys, but actually they were 15, 16, 17, and they were all dressed in their army uniform, very smart and well trained. They were ordered to line up in their own way, and kept in order, and the British soldiers were their guards. They were armed with their guns over their shoulders when the prisoners were lined up in order. And as they crossed Dalginross Bridge and marched on to Cultybraggan Camp you could hear them singing, all the way to the camp.

MB: *As far as numbers went, was it a big number?*

Jean P: It was quite a large number.[5] I must admit, a lot went on and you never heard of it, you never saw that.

MB: *Was there any kind of fear in Comrie or did people just simply accept?*

Jean P: No, we didn't feel afraid; you didn't realise there was a war on, to be quite honest. I used to go with a young lad who was in the army, and he was stationed at the Cultybraggan Camp. I met him when I was still working at the big house, Lawers, the boys' school. All of us young folk used to go to the dances, and when I went into the hall this night, one of my friends said, "Oh Jane, you're okay to get a dance tonight." And that's how I met George – that's my husband's name. He was a soldier, a bit older than me, and he was a sergeant in the Catering Corps. He was born in 1919, and he'd been in Dunkirk, but he never talked about the war. And in those days, the soldiers used to go to the dances.

MB: *Where were they held?*

Jean P: They were held in one of the local halls, the one past the church, along the river, and quite often it was Jimmy Shand and his band! Years later he was made a 'Sir' – Sir Jimmy Shand![6] So, when I went to the dance this night and George asked me to dance, at first I was too shy, but then I had a great time. I used to love dancing, and Mum was always waiting at the door when the dance was finished. And after a certain time, when we got to know one another, we got engaged – I must admit George was not a dancer, but I had a great life. He was from Penicuik, and after the war we were married in Penicuik, and that's where we made our home. And although I left Comrie I never lost touch. I've been back to visit lots because my younger sister, Lily, married a local lad and so I've still got family in Comrie. My niece, Jane, who introduced you to me, is a nurse in Dalginross House. She comes to visit me when she has a few days off, and she's a wonderful help.

Peter McNaughton: My family have been in Strathearn for generations – my great-great grandmother was a Gaelic-speaker and she moved from Glen Lyon to Glen Lednock about 1830. Their people were agricultural workers, working for a tenant farmer in the East Ballindalloch, up by Invergeldie. Then part of the family went to Trowan and they worked on that estate and the other part to The Ross in Comrie. That's where my father

was born, in 1912. His name was David Baird McNaughton and the 'Baird' in his name is after Sir David Baird of Seringapatam[7] – you can see the monument on top of the hill.

MB: Yes, I can see it when I look out the front window.

Peter: Sir David Baird wasn't from the area, but he retired to Crieff and he bought the Trowan Estate.[8] He was one of Sir John Moore's generals on the great fighting retreat from Corunna [1809] and he got his arm shot off – it was eventually amputated on a ship going back to England. But years later, after he had bought Trowan, he was out on his horse and he met a number of local men who were mending fences and stone dykes. He stopped and spoke with them and one of them said, "We've met before, Sir David," and Sir David said, "Oh, when did we meet?" And this man who was a McNaughton said, "I was the right-hand man of the regiment at Corunna when you were shot." And from that point on he became the head gamekeeper to Sir David Baird and all the first male children in my family were called David Baird, so my father's name was David Baird McNaughton. He went to Comrie school and then to Morrison's, and afterwards studied history at St. Andrews.

MB: I didn't ever meet your father, but I have his book, Upper Strathearn: From Earliest Times to Today – it's a really interesting history of the area. Did he have a career as a historian?

Peter: When he graduated from university, he became a civil servant. He was with the Department of Customs and Excise, and he was sent down to London in the late 30s, so the family moved to England. I was born in Comrie, but I spent my first five or six years in Bedfordshire. We used to go on holiday to my grandparents in The Ross – my brother was born in The Ross and he's still on the go. I was born during the war, and my mother and father had decided that I should be born in Comrie. But when they arrived in Comrie they had to look for accommodation because my grandparents had several Polish officers staying with them at The Ross. These Polish officers were responsible for Cultybraggan Camp and also for Dunira House, which at that time was a hospital, a convalescence home for war-wounded. They brought in nurses too, and some of them stayed on after the war. For example, Mac Mitchell from the Lechkin [Farm] was out at Dunira and he met his future wife there; she was a nurse from the Black Isle, and they lived for 60 years happily married. This taking over rooms and big houses was a requisition type of thing from the military; people were told that so many soldiers or officers or whatever are going to be there next Monday, you know, make your own arrangements. Same with the Royal Hotel, it was all packed up you know, so when I was born, like Jesus there was no room at the inn, and that's why I was born on Drummond Street. [laughter] My parents rented the house next to Donaldson's the painters and McNab's Garage – it isn't there now because it was full of dry rot and they knocked it down, but they left the lintel round the fireplace. So that's the only sign that was left of my birth [laughter].

MB: *Was your father in active service during the war?*

Peter: He joined the army, and he was at Normandy on D-Day plus 1 [June 1944]. He was the Disembarkation Officer involved in the Mulberry Harbour schemes[9] and then he was sent up for de-mining in Antwerp. Then, from Antwerp, he was sent out to Java and Sumatra and ended up his war, with his men, looking after 15,000 armed Japanese soldiers. His brother went through the Western Desert, the whole shooting match, and then up into Italy. When he had leave to go home, he got to Crieff and he was told he could get a lift to Comrie because it would be easy, as there was so much military traffic. But all of the military traffic was coming *from* Comrie and not going *to* Comrie so he had to walk home with his full pack, and his rifle, and the whole shebang.

MB: *Did your father ever come back to live in Comrie?*

Peter: Yes, he moved back in 1974 after he retired, but by that time we'd grown up and left home, and I emigrated to Canada. When we were young, almost all our summer holidays were spent in The Ross as well as in Glen Lednock at the Balloch. We went to The Ross until my grandparents died, and then my father bought a caravan and we put that on the Lechkin Farm with the Mitchells. The Lechkin Farm was owned by Mac Mitchell, John Mitchell, Jimmy Mitchell – my family have known their family for years and years. I still come 'home on holiday' and I can only recall two or three *other* family holidays: one was to Rothesay, and it rained every day, and another time we spent two months down in Ayr – I have a very fond spot for Ayr.

Mildred Logan: My family are from Ayrshire. Dad was a minister and, when I was born, 1933, our family lived in Dailly in Ayrshire. I still have wee pictures of the place in my mind – there was a little dairy opposite the manse and Mum used to go there for milk. She gave me a tiny wee jug and I went with her, and I remember there were cobbles down to it. I remember going carefully down the cobbles with my wee jug and bringing milk back. And I remember Dad taking a hedgehog out of the dog's mouth! The dog had got it, and he came to Dad, and I remember him wearing his gardening gloves and removing this hedgehog.

Then, in 1938, when I was four, we moved to Glasgow when Dad became minister in Bluevale Church in Dennistoun. The manse was in a tenement in Mount Vernon, a beautiful place, just beyond Tollcross, and I remember there was a flight of stone steps up to the front door. That was the main floor, then there was another floor above that, but there was also a flight of stone stairs that went down to the basement, to the maid's room and Dad's study. It looked out on the wee front garden and it was lovely. And that's where we lived when war was declared.

MB: What do you remember about the years?

Mildred: Dad joined the British Army of Occupation, and he was a fire warden for a while – Glasgow was quite spectacular at the beginning of the war with bombs and air-raid sirens and shelters, and I remember being carried down the stone stairs into the basement into what we called the maid's room. Then Dad became a Padre with the Cameronians and the regiment was based in Comrie for a time. My brother and I were in Glasgow with my Mum, and Dad wrote to say "This is the most beautiful place. Bring the children and come up to the Royal Hotel". In those days it was run by two old sisters called Campbell, not the posh place it is now, but it was lovely. And I can remember we came up by train from Glasgow, and I can still see my father walking along from the train station, wearing his khaki army uniform and carrying our cases.

After that we often came to Comrie and we stayed at the Comrie Hotel. We walked about Comrie and we just loved it. We came back in the springtime, and people got to know us and they'd say "It's just as beautiful in the Autumn". I don't remember how long Dad was there, probably only a year or two years or something like that, but he never was in the midst of the fighting. Then, at the end of the war, the Cameronians were posted to Germany and he went with them as the regiment's chaplain in Germany.

If it hadn't been for the war. I might never have come to live in Comrie. Most of our holidays were spent in Comrie because we really loved it. When I left school, I went to The Atheneum, now the Royal Conservatoire of Scotland, and I trained as a music teacher. I taught at Mary Erskine's School in Edinburgh, and in the holidays Mum and I used to come up to Comrie – we never tired of it, and I decided I would come and live here when I retired. That's over twenty years ago now, and it's still the most beautiful place – I just love it.

Mollie MacCallum: When I first began to teach in Crieff in the Sixties, I went to Crieff Parish Church, which was the St. Michael's building. It was full of children – a lot were from

Morrison's, but there were also Seymour Lodge girls going to church then. Seymour Lodge was a private girls' school in Dundee, and during the war they were evacuated to Ochtertyre. Then after the war, they continued as a boarding school in Ochtertyre House for many, many years.[10] I'm not sure when Seymour Lodge closed, but some time after they left Ochtertyre, Sir William Murray started the theatre. It was held in what had been the school gymnasium. It wasn't within the house, it was a separate building – a typical school gym with no windows.[11] A friend and I went to see 'Private Lives' by Noël Coward – but I remember being disappointed when I went to the theatre because it wasn't in the house. So I've never been in the house.

Doli Maclennan: I sang in Ochtertyre Theatre twice: the first occasion was their opening night [July 1972] with Scottish Ballet who were on an Arts Council tour performing *An Clò Mòr*. That was opening night of Ochtertyre Theatre.[12] Sir William Murray was a total devotee of the arts – he was open-hearted and welcoming.

MB: What a fantastic choice for an opening night! Was the theme of the ballet about the making of clò mòr, or about the weavers of Harris tweed?

Doli: No, it was nothing to do with that. The tweed was a prop for the dancers. The ballet was a love story, a ghost story, and the tweed was held by the dancers and used as waves of the sea. We didn't actually use Harris Tweed as there was too much fluff, so it was Border Tweed and there were five lengths of cloth in different shades, colours and shades, like waves of the sea. And I sang for the entire ballet, on stage with the dancers. The storyline was by George Reid – he wrote the scenario and it was choreographed by Stuart Hopps, who was Assistant Director of Scottish Theatre Ballet, as it was known then .[13] Morag MacLeod at the School of Scottish Studies and I chose Gaelic songs that went with the storyline, and the whole performance was rehearsed in Glasgow at Scottish Ballet. It was a big tour – we opened in the Citizens' Theatre in Glasgow, then Dundee Rep – we went to Orkney and other major theatres and Ochtertyre was part of a long tour.[14]

MB: Were you involved in any other performances at Ochtertyre?

Doli: Yes, I was there with 'The Heretics' – Donald Campbell, David Campbell, Norman McCaig were all part of the group and Adam McNaughtan was with us that night.[15] But there was no audience because they forgot to advertise. So we went into the bar and joined the herds down from the hill on a Friday night – one of them had us all in stitches with his stories.

Adam: The Heretics were Edinburgh and I'm a Glasgow person, but I was called on to be the singer for some of The Heretics meetings and this was part of a weekend tour – I remember that no audience turned up at Ochtertyre [laughter] but Sir William Murray was very apologetic.

David Campbell: As it turned out, it was a rather amusing evening, because, when there was no one there, Doli, being very resourceful, said, "Well, we'll just adjourn to the local hostelry," which we did. And there was an old fella in there whose name I forget, and he was the one to tell a story or to sing a song. And he told a story about this lad who worked on farms, in the bothies, and he said, "When I was a loon, I gaed oot wi a lassie caa'd Maggie, and he said, eh, the ither loons in the bothy said, "Whit wye are ye gaun oot wi Maggie?" Because they knew that ither loons in the bothy had pit a leg ower her. So they said tae him, "Whit wye are ye gaun tae play second fiddle?" and he says, "Right, I'll tell her, 'I'm no gaun tae play second fiddle tae onyone.' And whit did she say? She said, "Jockie, wi an instrument like yours, you're lucky tae be in the band at all!"

Adam McNaughtan: But what was interesting was when we retired to the kitchen, the rest of the staff kept hounding him to tell stories. But he wouldnae, because he said his stories 'werenae 'Parlour'! Being an outside worker, he was accustomed to the bothy rather than the big hoose, but he eventually did tell a couple of jokes and he sang. And there was a song I got off him – I'd seen the words (in a book), but I'd not known a tune for it until he sang it, so I sang that song thereafter.

Doli: There was a beautiful big drawing room with a huge fireplace and log fire. And then we all stayed overnight – Sir Willie Murray was enormously hospitable. I remember when Adam came down to breakfast, he said to Sir William, "You could sublet my wardrobe!"

Adam: Well, the bedroom I was in was very spacious and it had a huge 'walk-in' wardrobe.

MB: Was it a dressing room?

Adam: Aye. And what I remember saying when I came down to breakfast was that they could house a Gorbals family in the wardrobe in my room! We went into the dining room for breakfast and there was this big sideboard with dishes of food. Till then, I never realised that is what a sideboard was for! Porridge, kippers, the whole lot, and it was all on the sideboard, ready for us.

MB: *Was that the first – or the only – time you met Sir William Murray?*

Adam: Yes, that was the only time, yes.

David: Hospitality is the cardinal virtue of the Gael, and being there, as guests of Sir Willie Murray, put me in mind of that old Celtic blessing:

> "Yestreen a stranger was at my door.
> I put food in the eating place,
> drink in the drinking place,
> story, music and song in the listening place."

Endnotes

1   The street is part of the A85, the main road from Perth to Lochearnhead.

2   Student residences were built on the site.

3   The Auxiliary Territorial Service, commonly known as the ATS, was the women's branch of the British army.

4   Lawers became the home of Cargilfield Preparatory School from 1939 to 1947 when the school was evacuated from Edinburgh to Perthshire during WW2. In 1948 Perth and Kinross Council opened Lawers Agricultural College on 300 acres of arable land. Students enrolled in a year-long residential course which trained them in all aspects of farming. The college closed in 1978 and Lawers reverted to a private residence.

5   Officially known as Camp 21, Cultybraggan Camp housed 4,000 prisoners of war. See <https://comriedevelopmenttrust.org.uk/>.

6   Ian Cameron and Robbie Shepherd document Jimmy Shand's long career in touring and broadcasting in The Jimmy Shand Story.

7   The Siege of Seringapatam (April 5 to May 4, 1799) was the final battle of the conflict between the British East India Company and the Kingdom of Mysore. The British army was under the command of Major General David Baird.

8   P. R. Drummond includes three essays on Sir David Baird in *Perthshire in Bygone Days*, pp. 39–147.

9   'Mulberry' was the code-name for two prefabricated harbours designed and constructed in Britain, then secretly towed in sections across the English Channel to create two harbours for the ships that would transfer thousands of troops and military equipment during the D-Day operations, June 1944.

10 Seymour Lodge School closed in 1966 after the Head Mistress, Mrs. Sturrock, died. In 2016 the 'Old Girls Association' held a Fiftieth Anniversary visit to Ochtertyre House and exchanged memories and photographs; see <http://seymourlodge.co.uk/>.

11 The Ochtertyre Theatre brochure (Introduction, 1974) notes that Sir William Murray had previously been involved in documentary film production and "he is, in addition, an acknowledged

theatre lighting expert." See, The National Library of Scotland archive collection, *Ochtertyre Theatre Crieff Theatre Programmes Playbills Posters Etc.,* [NLS Shelfmark: PB9.217.26/10.]

12 The Scottish Ballet performance was acknowledged in subsequent brochures for Ochtertyre Theatre: "From the time it first opened – with a performance by Scottish Ballet in July 1972 – Ochtertyre Theatre has maintained an enviable reputation for the consistently high quality of its productions and the wide diversity of its activities. This miniature showcase in the Perthshire hills has hosted many of the best-known faces in Scottish theatre – among them Russell Hunter, Iain Cuthbertson, and John Cairney. The dramatic presentations have ranged from Strindberg and Pinter to Noël Coward and Neil Simon, and the total flexibility seating arrangements have been exploited with productions done end-stage, thrust-stage, and in the round."

13 In her book, *Scottish Ballet: Forty Years.* Mary Brennan includes *An Clò Mòr* (The Big Cloth) in her chronological record of the 1972 choreographic workshops and theatre performances (including Ochtertyre).

14 In their *Annual Report, 1971–72,* the Arts Council of Great Britain notes, " Scottish Theatre Ballet's *An Clò Mòr,* deserves special mention" [p. 25] ... "The company's new associate director, Stuart Hopps, also scored a hit with *An Clò Mòr,* a new ballet with a vocal accompaniment sung in Gaelic by Dolina Maclennan, which the Council also toured to the Highlands." [p. 34].

15 Co-founded in Edinburgh in 1970 by poets and cultural activists Stuart MacGregor and Willie Neal, 'The Heretics' held regular events to give a platform to poets, playwrights and singers to promote the "poetry and music of Scotland's living tradition". (Trevor Royle, 'The Watcher by the Threshold: John Herdman and the Scottish Literary Tradition' in *Not Dark Yet,* p. 215.) The performing artists included Gaelic singer and actor Dolina (Doli) Maclennan, playwright and poet Donald Campbell, BBC radio-producer and storyteller David Campbell, and poet Norman McCaig were all regular performers with The Heretics. Song-maker and singer Adam McNaughtan was invited to join them on several occasions as were other guests including Hamish Henderson, Sorley MacLean, Robert Garioch, Derick Thomson, Hugh MacDiarmid, Billy Connolly, Aly Bain and others. In her memoirs, *An Island Girl's Journey,* Doli gives an inside view of the emergence of the Heretics which shines light on Scotland's cultural 'scene' at the time. She also includes photographs and a And did youer from the Edinburgh Festival Fringe – the ticket price is 55 pence! (Photo section following p. 84.) See also, David Campbell's autobiography, *Minstrel Heart* (2021), 'The Heretics' (Chapt. 11, pp. 139–149) and photograph (after p. 128).

OCHTERTYRE THEATRE
1974 FESTIVAL

DIRECTED BY SIR WILLIAM MURRAY, BT.
LIVE THEATRE IN ONE OF SCOTLAND'S STATELY HOMES.

APRIL — SEPTEMBER

Plays, Folk, Jazz, Poetry-Readings, Opera, Ballet, Music.

Plays include 'RELATIVELY SPEAKING', 'THE LION IN WINTER', 'BOEING-BOEING'. 'THE ONLY STREET'. Artistes appearing include David Kossof, Edith Macarthur, Scottish Opera, Scottish Theatre Ballet.

—— Performances begin 8.15 p.m. ——

Students and Children 75p. — Special terms for Parties of 10 and over. Special Menus arranged in Ochtertyre Theatre's Restaurant, The Grouse Grill, for parties of 25 and over.

Full details of Season from Box-Office, James Square, Crieff. Advance Booking — Crieff 2218.

Chapter 7

Wartime Memories, 1939–45

Listening to reports on the pandemic reminded elderly folk of how, during the Second World War, everyone used to tune in to the 'wireless' (radio) to listen to the daily broadcasts. It brought back memories of what it was like, especially for young people, whose lives were to be affected for many years. The date became fixed in their minds – September the third, 1939, and, regardless of the passing of the decades, they would remember what they were doing and where they were when they heard the declaration of war.

Cathie McPhail was born and brought up near Inverness, though she retired to Comrie more than 20 years ago. At the age of 99, during a visit from her friend Mairi Philp, Cathie recalled the BBC broadcast just three weeks before her eighteenth birthday:

Cathie: I was at home, not far from Inverness. My father was a sheep-farmer, and he farmed up the hill about eight miles out of Inverness – it was called 'Farrmains'. It was a big farm, and my father had bought a car, though he himself didn't drive – he had a driver. So I had a few lessons and then passed my test. When war broke, they urgently needed drivers – there were posters everywhere, asking women to volunteer. Men were called up almost immediately, but there wasn't any conscription for women until December 1941. So, I volunteered as an ambulance driver and then joined up. A few of my friends also joined up – some joined the ATS, one went into the Navy, and another girl and I joined the RAF. We went by train from Inverness down to Watton, the training grounds, where we were stationed for a while. We got our uniforms there, a skirt and jacket, and they issued you with shoes as well, so everyone looked smart. Since we were training as ambulance drivers, we had to take a lot of First Aid classes and we also had to learn how to maintain the vehicle and deal with emergencies, so we were prepared for the job. Drivers were always on call, and there were a lot of call-outs so there were different shifts all round the clock, ready for the minute an ambulance was needed. Sometimes you had to stay up all night, and as soon as there was a call-out the ambulance would be sent from the RAF station. There would be no warning about what had happened or where you were going or what you would find, but you had to get there. During daylight driving wasn't too bad, but after dark there was the blackout, so you had to put a kind of mask over the headlights, it had a slit in it – there was just a little beam of light shining downwards from the ambulance, maybe two feet in front of me. We were often called out during the night, and sometimes it could be really difficult, especially if there was fog – you could hardly see the road ahead. You didn't think about the danger, so I don't remember feeling frightened – you had to get there as quickly as possible. There was terrible bombing over that area, and a lot of the casualties were military – poor souls, some of them, and I remember some were very young. There were some very sad situations. We did what we could, and somebody would help you carry the stretcher into the ambulance so we'd get them to hospital as fast as we could. Ely was one of the hospitals for the RAF, and of course Cambridge Hospital.

Margaret Bennett: You must have been quite exhausted when you got back to the base after these emergencies.

Cathie: Yes, but I didn't really feel it. We were young!

MB: Did you get some time off?

Cathie: Oh yes. We'd maybe go to Norwich for a day out. On some evenings there were dances. Popular dances were the foxtrot and the quickstep and we'd do the 'Hokey Cokey!'[1]

MB: Oh, that was great fun! Mairi knows that one, and she's a really good singer!

Mairi Philp: (singing) "You put your right hand in, and you shake it all about!" Come on, Cathie – we'll all sing it!

> You put your right hand in,
> You put your right hand out
> You put your right hand in
> And you shake it all about
>
> You do the hokey-cokey
> And you turn about
> And that's what it's all about   Woooo!
>
> Oh, hokey-cokey-cokey!
> Oh, hokey-cokey-cokey!
> Oh, hokey-cokey-cokey!
> And that's what it's all about.   Woooo!

You put your left hand in,
You put your left hand out
You put your left hand in
And you shake it all about

You do the hokey-cokey
And you turn about
And that's what it's all about   Woooo!

Oh, hokey-cokey-cokey!
Oh, hokey-cokey-cokey!
Oh, hokey-cokey-cokey!
And that's what it's all about.   Woooo!

You put your right leg in ...

You put your left leg in ...

You put your whole self in ...

Cathie: [laughing] Oh dear! We had plenty fun too.

MB: Did you have any favourite singers in those days, like Gracie Fields? Or Vera Lynn?

Cathie: Vera Lynn, yes, oh yes.

Mairi: Robert Wilson?

Cathie: Yes, yes. I loved to hear him singing 'Down in The Glen' – that was my favourite song. He was lovely.

MB: And did you spend all your war service time in Watton?

Cathie: Almost all, yes, then I got posted near Chester, but not to drive ambulances. I had to drive a staff car, driving RAF personnel around, fairly important folk. It could be quite a distance, sometimes about 100 miles – and then you had to go all the way back again, which was usually after it got dark, and you had the blackout. But I didn't stay until the end of the war because my mother got ill and so I returned to Inverness, where I then got married. So I was in Inverness on VE Day[2] and by that time I also had my son.

Ann Thomson was still in her teens in 1941 when the War Office announced that women were to be called up. At the age of 98 she decided to write down her memories, when her friend Austin O'Toole told her about our project. Austin delivered the letter and explained, "She doesn't hear too well, especially on the phone, so she asked me to drop this off:"

Ann Thomson War Memories

In 1941, I was a young woman of nineteen living with my parents in Selkirk in the Scottish Borders. Women were called up, I think in 1941, when you could be forced into anything necessary, such as forestry, nursing, land, munitions etc., which prompted me to enlist in the Women's Royal Navy Service, the Wrens. About two weeks later I was notified to report to the Assembly Rooms, George Street, Edinburgh, for a medical, which I did, and about two weeks after that I received instructions etc. to report in London where I would be picked up to go to quarters. There were quite a few of us and we were taken to a place called Mill Hill, where I was for two weeks. I was given a sort of overall to wear and a small piece of coloured ribbon which we pinned on to this overall. This was quite important as this showed when we went for meals. During my time there we were only allowed out for two hours at a time. I was told that this base was built as a hospital, so our sleeping quarters were quite large. I think there would be about 20 of us in the one cabin. At the end of the two weeks, we boarded transport and were taken to New College Finchley Road, Hampstead, where we were issued with our uniform – great – and then instructed to send home our civvies.

We were delighted to get our uniform and the next problem was to learn how to put your collar on – we needed two studs, a front and back, and we had to learn how to attach them. You soon learned, especially when we were to muster for a kit inspection. Next lesson was to learn to muster, to raise the flag certain times daily. You feared you might be raising it the wrong way round. Two of you had to do this and lower it again in the evening. You were meant to salute this flag every time you passed, and you breathed a sigh of relief when all formalities were past and your turn was over. We learned how to use nautical terms – decks, bunks, galleys. We went to classes twice daily to learn morse code, and every Friday we sat exams to see how we were progressing. At this time there was a clear-out as some did not meet the standard expected and they were taken off the course and transferred to another category. After that was when I met Mary Hampson and we became very good friends and continued to be so for many years. In peacetime Mary worked on the Manchester Guardian newspaper and was, I think, about the last person to interview Ruth Ellis who was hanged for murder.

Back to the WRNS: After three months we were drafted to a place called Soberton Towers near Droxford in Hampshire. Completely isolated. I think there was one shop but nothing else. We were given leave to visit Portsmouth once a month and we had to board a boat to get there. Portsmouth was very busy with troops from all over the world. By the end of our time there we had been trained to accept morse at over 30 words a minute. After three months of intensive training, we went back to London. We were now wireless telegraphists, fully trained to intercept messages from German shores to German ships and we now had category badges which we wore on our right arm. Ours was a streak of lightning through a pair of wings. Most people in the forces would know we were wireless operators. We were then given the choice of either going to Winchester or Scarborough. Mary and I chose Scarborough as it was nearer transport for getting home. We were put into private billets and were unlucky as we got the most miserable landlady possible. I think she had about five of us, plus an evacuee. A real professional landlady.

Our base was a few minutes' walk away and this was where we went for our meals. We were put into what were termed 'watches' and we were in Watch 2, and this determined what time we would go on our shifts. The wireless station was situated out in the wilds of the Yorkshire moors, and off the beaten track, and we were transported there by bus. To get into the watch-room we required a pass, and a soldier with an Alsatian dog boarded the bus and inspected the pass before reaching the station, which was underground.

The watchroom where we worked from must have been huge, as along with us Wrens there were sailors and a lot of men who were all ex-naval, but we never made contact with any of them. By this time, we were put into quarters which became ours for the rest of our naval life and we were quite comfortable. There were ten of us all put into this room, all doing the same work and shifts, five bunk beds, a small chest of drawers, a rail with a few coat hangers, a chair and I think that was our lot. The cabin was large and had two full length windows – this might have been a hotel in peace time. We had quite a good social life, there were lots of troops stationed in Scarborough and they would put on dances and invite us. I remember a lot of the airmen were in very good hotels on the sea front and these men were recovering from air accidents, and they ran a club named the Caterpillar Club and they wore tiny caterpillar brooches and the colour of the caterpillar's eyes told you how they were rescued.[3] I became friendly with one and his caterpillar badge had blue eyes as he was rescued from the sea.

We soon fell into a routine in the watchroom and changed wireless frequency every month, this was to make sure we did not become careless and let any morse messages go by. We were expected to receive messages at thirty words per minute and the Germans sent beautiful morse at a speed of 28 words per minute. A word was four letters, this we could cope with.

On the notice board would be dress for the day. Raincoats, great coats, etc., depending on the weather. One day it said exams would be taking place and to apply if we wanted to sit them. We all did, and we all passed. This meant an increase in pay, and we now had rank, we were Leading Wrens and had an extra badge to be worn on our sleeve. Apart from that, life was the same. A list would go round, and you would put your name down when you wanted to be relieved and that Wren would make the cocoa, which I hated. When you received messages you placed them on top of the set – these would be collected frequently, and you would take them to the teleprinter part and someone there sent them to Bletchley Park, but we did not know this at the time.

When the D-Day invasion took place we were kept very busy, but when peace was declared we were redundant and were all spare.[4] Somebody had the bright idea that we would tune in to Japanese but that never took off as nobody knew how to write it down, so we were demobbed quite quickly.

We all exchanged addresses but lost touch through time, but not Mary and I, but we're no longer in touch and she was a lovely person. Murray (my nephew) met her in London with his Uncle John. In 2019 I received a medal in recognition of wartime services at Bletchley Park, and letter signed by Boris Johnson.

THE GOVERNMENT CODE AND CYPHER SCHOOL

Ann Murray Thomson

*The Government wishes to express
to you its deepest gratitude
for the vital service you performed
during World War II*

Rt Hon Boris Johnson MP
Prime Minister

July 2019

Austin O'Toole: Ann asked me to show you the letter and the medal – she'd tell you herself, "At least Boris got something right!"[5]

Tam Kettle: I was only four year-auld when the war started – too young to understand, but I remember the tanks and the big Bren Gun Carriers. I remember seeing them goin aboot in the Bankfoot area – that's where we were when war was declared, and these tanks appeared. Oh, it was exciting, I thought it was good! They'd be training and they'd possibly be attached tae a regiment. I was just a wee boy so we wouldn't realise the danger, but I remember hearing bombs drop, near Almondbank, round that area, near Bankfoot in what they called the Five Mile Wood. There was a big long stretch of wood and they dropped bombs in there, but there were no injuries.

MB: What they were trying to hit?

Tam: There was a big naval base hidden by the woods at Almondbank, The Royal Naval Stores Depot. It served the base at Rosyth – it was a repair yard and stores depot for aircraft carriers. The estate workers were in 'reserved occupations' so they were all working through the war – ma faither was on the agricultural side of it all and not long after that we moved near Crieff – I was ten when the war ended.

Billy Gardiner: It'll soon be the anniversary o the Clydebank Blitz – I just heard on The News they've tae postpone the eightieth anniversary plans. They're no goin tae cancel, but it's to be postponed till after aw the Lockdowns. I was still at school, but I mind the bombers coming over, March 1941. You knew the German planes from the noise of their engines, an when the Jerrys went over this area ma mother couldnae stay in the hoose; she walked round the gairden. I wrote it in my Notebook: A land mine was dropped behind the Aberuchill Hills, 4 bombs fell at the field near the Shakey bridge and 4 at Dunira; this was the Clydebank Blitz. The sky was lit up with search lights away over Glenartney. We heard the bombs and the land mines.

Margaret Motherwell: I hear on The News there won't be any Remembrance Day parades this year. Not allowed because of the Lockdowns. That was always a special day at BLESMA (British Limbless Ex-Servicemen's Association), all the old veterans, most of them gone now.[6] I remember Nan McPhail and Irene Addison – they always used to sit together in the lounge; Irene was from Clydebank, and she and Nan used to talk about the Blitz. D'you remember them?

MB: Yes, I used to visit them.

Nan McPhail [1918–2016]: I was born the year the first war ended, 1918. When I finished school in Gartmore and got my Leaving Certificates, I went to Glasgow to train as a nurse. I went to the Southern General – I did my general training in that huge place and afterwards my midwifery. When I started as a student nurse I was in a nurses' residence in the hospital grounds; we had single rooms most of the time, tiny little rooms, and a large bathroom area along the corridor. Then it got a bit crowded, and some of us had to get lodgings close by, so I lived in a bedsit, just about ten minutes' walk from Southern General. It was very basic indeed and it belonged to a lady called Mrs Lamb, and on a Sunday afternoon she would say, "Now we'll just have a little chat and I'll read you some stories from *The People's Friend*," and I probably had an exam to do and wanted to study! But she was lonely, and she wanted to read from *The People's Friend*! And the Minister in Govan used to call and see us, the Reverend John Brown – he was Gordon Brown's father and I used to sing in his choir.

MB: Was there more than one student nurse staying there?

Nan: No, she just had me, and I slept in a bed in her sitting room. She'd give me a cup of tea when I got off duty, but we got our food in the hospital. During the war there was rationing, and we weren't terribly well fed. Every morning the patients used to get porridge and when we were on night duty we'd bring it to them before we went off duty. But some of them wouldn't eat it and we were hungry after working all night – we were all young of course, just students. So we students on night duty used to steal some of the porridge that would have been thrown down the drain. One of us watched out for the Sister coming round and the other would eat their porridge and then we'd swap places.

We didn't bother whether it was hot or cold or what, we were so hungry we ate a bowlful of that. After we came off duty, we would go back to the nurses' home and be given a little breakfast, but that might have been two hours later, and then we went to a lecture. We didn't go straight to bed and go to sleep; you had to go and have a lecture that lasted about an hour. When I finished my General Nursing, I went on to do Midwifery and they were still bombing and we would put as many pregnant mothers under the bed as we had time to do before the bombs fell.

MB: Oh my word, how you would put a pregnant mother under the bed?

Nan: Well, the beds were quite high in those days and we got as many in [under the bed] as a place of safety. Just on the floor, no mattresses, we hadn't time for that we just got them underneath. We just looked after them till things quietened down again, and sometimes the baby was delivered on the floor.

But one morning I was sent out on an ambulance to bring in a woman who was pregnant and I said to the driver "Hurry up as much as you can," because I was holding the [baby's] head but the woman just raised her shoulders and she pushed me and I fell on my back on the ambulance corridor and the baby was born on the floor. She was having her tenth baby, so she knew she was about to give birth. But pity the poor women who went into labour during the Clydebank blitz.

MB: *Irene, where were you during the blitz?*[7]

Irene Addison [1934–2016]: In Clydebank, in my house in Parkhall. I wasn't quite seven, but I can remember it as if it was just yesterday. We lived in Ash Road – the four-in-a-block cottage flats, with back and front gardens, and the flat we had was upstairs. So when the air-raid siren went, calling you to the shelters, we had to come down the outside stair and up the garden to the Anderson shelter. I can't remember being frightened but I suppose I must have been. It started just before nine o'clock, so I was in bed when the siren went, but my Mum and Dad were still up. So we went down to our Anderson shelter in the back garden, and there were two wee benches inside it so I sat beside my mum on one side and Dad sat on the other. But the door of our shelter wasn't fixed on properly, so Dad held up a piece of wood against it, and we sat there for the night, just on these wooden benches. I can always remember the sound of the aeroplanes, the drone, the drone, drone, drones of the heavy aeroplanes with the bombs in them. You knew they were full of bombs.

MB: *Can you remember what you were wearing?*

Irene: I had on my pyjamas and a raincoat and a scarf and that's all I can remember.

MB: *Did you have your shoes or your slippers?*

Irene: Wellingtons! You could put them on in a hurry. And I remember the people in the house behind us, we could hear them screaming – they had all stayed in their house because the grandmother was so old and stout that she couldn't get down the steps into the shelter, so they all decided to wait with her. Then we heard whistling bombs coming, and we all bent down, put our heads down – that's the dangerous period. We sat and listened to them whistle, whistle, whistle, and when the whistle stopped you knew – we cringed, because that's when they were about to hit the ground. I remember landmines coming down into the back garden or into the front garden of the house behind us and suddenly there was a terrific explosion, and we were blown up into the air.

MB: *So the landmine blasted the shelter out of the ground?*

Irene: Yes, and it landed back down again – it had a wee wooden floor and it landed back in its own dugout. We were all unconscious, and when I came round my mouth was full of dirt and splinters of wood. Mum and Dad were still unconscious, and Mum had landed down on top of me and I started to scream – my mouth was full of dirt and all the rest, then Mum and Dad came round. I don't know whether Dad dislocated his shoulder or hurt it badly, but he couldn't use his right arm, although, when the door was blown off he had to hold up a piece of wood for the rest of the night to keep any blast from us. Then an air-raid warden came round and says, "Are you alright in there?" I remember his voice and he asked Dad if he could go to a First Aid centre with a man who had hurt his head. Dad said, "I'll go, but I've got a young child in here." So the warden said, "That's alright then, we're not taking anybody with young children." So he stayed, and in the morning, after we heard the 'All-clear', when we come out we had to climb over the rubble of our house – the neighbours had all been killed with this bomb, this landmine that dropped on them, and there was nothing left of our house but a gable end; that was all. But when we got down to the garden gate – we'd lovely hedges all round – there, sitting in the middle of the hedge was a doll of mine, she was sitting up quite straight, looking around, not a scratch on her! She was called Bubbles and in those days we had the porcelain dolls, you know, and the least wee bit shattered them. But there was Bubbles, sitting up and not a scratch on her! So I was really quite glad of that.

MB: *Had you lost everything you owned?*

Irene: Yes. Everything. Except Bubbles. We'd nowhere to go for the night, the rest of the day or the night, but my uncle had a small-holding around Drumchapel. Not the Drumchapel we have nowadays – it was all fields and farms then, and he had a small-holding, so we walked along as we called it the Boulevard, the Great Western Road, and we were walking around holes – I can remember going around holes all the way along the road. Then on the second night we were at my uncle's small-holding up in Drumchapel, and it started all over again, and we all went to the shelter, but we were alright the second night; we just heard all the bombing and everything. Then when we tried to get back home the next day to see what was left of the place, the Boulevard was all roped off because these holes were all unexploded mines – we had walked in the minefield, but we didn't know it at the time. You'd never forget it, March 13th and 14th, 1941.[8]

Nan: Yes, I was on duty during the blitz – I'd finished my General Nursing and I was doing my Midwifery training. I remember all the ambulances arriving at the Southern General, and we were going out to the car park and bringing them in, but they were so blackened by everything we didn't know whether they were men or women. We didn't bother writing up admissions, we just brought them straight inside, put drips up where that was appropriate and one nurse would stay with maybe four people, trying to comfort them, it was terrible.

MB: Did you ever feel in danger yourself?

Nan: No, danger doesn't hit you at the time, you're not thinking about yourself … but the poignant thing was that relatives would come in the morning, they'd be coming all night long if they could, and they would come and say, "Have you got so-and-so here?". And we would say, "Well we don't know who's here, you'll have to look at every patient in the ward, see if you can find them". They were looking for their relatives. And when I went off duty the next day, on my way home I could see this tenement in Govan that had been bombed, blown apart, and away up, about three flights of stairs up, I could see two ladies in their beds and they were just suspended there, waiting for the fire brigade to come and rescue them. You could see them, still in a room, away, way up.

MB: Oh they must have been terrified out their wits!

Nan: Well, yes, then the fire brigade came, with the big, long ladders, and a fireman came and took them down from that position and rescued them. The rest of the building collapsed but there they were, in what remained of the tenement – with no exterior wall. And that was on Govan Road.

Irene: There was a lot of that in Clydebank: for a year so afterwards you could look up and see the whole house, the inside of the house, but there was no gable wall or anything, but you could look up and see each room with all the furniture and everything set. It was quite frightening to think there'd be people in there, you know. Now, I don't know whether this is true or not but the Government kept the Clydebank Blitz very quiet, they didn't advertise it very much because they wanted, that was their plan, they didn't want people to know how badly a city had been bombed … Well, Clydebank got it so bad because of John Brown's [shipyard] and Singer's factory[9] and they thought the Boulevard, where we lived you know, they thought it was the River Clyde cause it's a long straight sort of road and that night the moon was shining and it made the road look kind of silverishy, like water, and that's why they bombed us in that area. They wanted to bomb Singer's Factory, and they got Singer's wood-yard – it went up in smoke and it burned for four days I think, and it gave them the light for the next night.

MB: And did your family live quite close to Singer's?

Irene: Oh yes, we lived right on the Boulevard, Parkhall, and my father worked in Singer's. He was a storeman in the wood-yard.

MB: So that was his livelihood up in smoke.

Irene: Oh exactly, and he was called into the army just after that, so Mum and I went to live with an aunt in Biggar in Lanarkshire. I had to travel in the bus in a pair of wellingtons and an old school coat, my pyjamas, that was all I had. Well even to this day, when I hear a siren I begin to tremble you know; I don't like it at all. I remember all the banging, the explosions, the sirens and all the rest of it.[10] The all-clears were alright but whenever I hear the siren, even in these old films, oh dear –

MB: Do you have happy memories of being in Biggar?

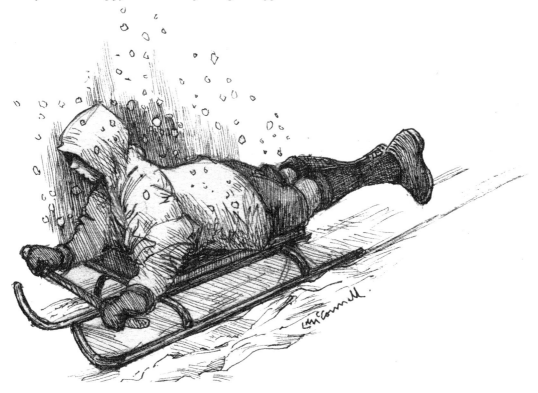

Irene: Oh yes! I've got very, very happy childhood memories, living in Biggar with my mother. I went to school there until Primary 7, and we used to sing in the playground, skipping, cawing the ropes, just playing around, and there was one song you just make actions with your hands [Irene sings]:

> Underneath the spreading chestnut tree
> Mr Churchill said to me
> If you want a gas mask don't ask me
> Ask the blooming ARP![11]

I remember at a certain time of year, March, I think, we used to set the Burnbraes on fire every year. It's a big grassy area and I used to run in and out, in and out, and when I came in at night my mother used to give me a row because I'd be smelling of smoke. But it was great fun!

MB: *Did you sense there was a real community spirit in Biggar?*

Irene: Oh, yes, it wasn't just children that joined in games, the adults used to join in with us. I remember in the winter they used to have a lot of snow in Biggar and we all went out sledging – it wasn't just the children that went, the whole village went out. And one of the times Dad was home on leave and he was on the sledge with me, and I remember him saying something about "Oh, where I've been the last two or three years you get a lot of snow in the winter but not the whole village goes out sledging, just the children." But he didn't talk about the war.

MB: *Did you get news of the war?*

Irene: Yes, the BBC News. Everyone listened to the nine o'clock news on the wireless. We weren't allowed to speak; we'd to sit quietly and listen and nobody dared come to the door or anything. The nine o'clock News shushed everything; everything went quiet, and it was the same at Uncle Bob's in Drumchapel. Oh dear, you daren't blow your nose, or sneeze, or anything – he was terrible! But you just did as you were told. And when Mum and I were in Biggar I used to have to take the [accumulator] battery down every month to get charged, to a shop.

MB: *That was pretty heavy for a child to carry.*

Irene: Yes, you're telling me it was!

MB: *What kind of entertainment was there, or did you make your own?*

Irene: Well, we had the pictures; we had a Corn Exchange building which was used as a picture house at the weekends. The benches at the front were fourpence [about 1.5p] and they didn't have any backs to them, just a seat; and the ones behind them were sevenpence [about 3p], and these benches had a back to them, so you could lean back. And my mother gave me fourpence for the pictures, so I used to sit in the back row of the fourpenny ones and my boyfriend would go in the front row of the sevenpenny seats, and spread his elbows and legs out to keep a place for me, then when the lights went out I'd get down on the floor and crawl under the bench and up on to his bench so we could sit together. I wasn't even a teenager – when you had a boyfriend in these days it was just a *friend*, you know, a *boy* friend, and I was a tomboy, so I enjoyed playing with the boys better than the girls. And the picture always used to break down, but when you were given your tickets at the door you'd be told to keep your half because if it broke down you'd get in free another night. Sometimes you'd be waiting for an exciting bit to happen and suddenly, Wham! It would break and we'd have to wait another week to come back and see the end.

MB: *Did you have any favourite films you saw in those days or actors?*

Irene: Errol Flynn – I loved the swashbuckling type, and he was always my favourite. And I liked Brigadoon ...

MB: *When your dad came home on leave, do you remember those leaves as being happy times?*

Irene: Oh yes, very. I remember, funnily enough, I only once in all my life saw my dad kiss my mother! [laughs] It was one year when he arrived home on leave unexpectedly and the two of them met in the kitchen and they kissed each other and I can remember sitting at the side of the fire saying to myself, "My goodness me! Look at that, my mother and father kiss each other!" *[laughter]* I was shocked, so I've always remembered that. Mum used to write to him regularly, every week, and Dad wrote to my mother a lot and at the bottom of the letter they used to put a line of a love song, like 'My heart cries for you' or 'Will you be my sweetheart?' or things like that, they used to write that along the bottom of the letter.

MB: *So, they obviously had a good marriage?*

Irene: Oh yes, very. They were married for over fifty years. I was an only child until after the war.

MB: *Can you remember the end of the war?*

Irene: Yes, we had we had a bonfire in Biggar, on the Burnbraes, to celebrate the soldiers coming home. But some didn't have a home to go to, and Dad was back for about two years before our house was rebuilt, so after the war Mum and I carried on staying in Biggar and Dad came at the weekends. He had to go back to work in Clydebank and so he boarded with a woman who took lodgers.

MB: *When the houses were finally rebuilt, can you remember being told you were going to go back home to Clydebank?*

Irene: Yes, but I wasn't very pleased about that. I wanted to stay in Biggar even though my Dad had come out of the army and got his old job back in Singer's. But of course, you settle down and make new friends.

MB: *And I hear you had a career as a school-teacher.*

Irene: Yes, and I retired to Crieff because my son worked here, so I'd be near family.

Endnotes

1   A 78 r.p.m. record of an up-beat boogie-woogie version of 'Hokey Cokey' rocketed into the hit parade in 1941 and soon became part of the entertainment at dances and social gatherings. Based on an older party-game (variants, R. Chambers, 1826, pp. 137–139) the popular version is credited to music-hall song-writer Jimmy Kennedy who wrote the English version of 'Lili Marlene' and several other wartime favourites.

2   VE Day, Victory in Europe, was declared on May 8, 1945.

3   The 'Caterpillar Club' is an informal association of RAF personnel who have successfully used a parachute to bail out of a disabled aircraft. After authentication by the parachute maker, applicants receive a membership certificate and a distinctive lapel pin, such as the caterpillar with blue eyes indicating a rescue at sea.

4   D-Day was June 6, 1944, which marked the start of the Normandy Landings, involving 150,000 allied troops (soldiers, sailors and airmen) and thousands of ships and landing crafts. The operation led to the surrender of Germany (VE Day) and the liberation of Europe. The end of the war was August 14, 1945, which is remembered as VJ Day, Victory in Japan.

5   On April 12, 2021, Ann suddenly passed away – she had kept her mind active until the end, and she not only realised how important it is to record memories for new generations but also picked up her pen to do so.

6   Margaret was a former staff-member of Crieff's care-home for war veterans, BLESMA, the British Limbless Ex-Servicemen's Association. It was built on Alligan Road in Crieff, on land donated by the Ancaster Estate, and was opened in 1963 by the Duchess of Gloucester. Although BLESMA was closed down in 2013, the building (Ancaster House) was taken over by a private company and continued as a care-home (currently closed for refurbishment).

7   I.M.M. MacPhail, *Clydebank Blitz* (1974)

8   Members of a creative writing group at Clydebank College were encouraged to write personal memories of the blitz, and their collection of stories give a moving account of experiences during the blitz. Clydebank Life Story Group, *Untold Stories: Remembering Clydebank in Wartime*.

9   Memorabilia, oral history collections and photographs of the blitz (including the Singer Archive) can be accessed at West Dunbartonshire Council's Archive in Dumbarton Heritage Centre. During

the Second World War, Singer's Sewing Machine Factory's precision engineers in Clydebank manufactured aircraft parts, Sten guns, machine gun bullets and other weaponry. Singer sewing machines were also used to make army uniforms.

10   In 2005, to mark the 60th anniversary of VE Day, I recorded a group of women in Glasgow who lived through the blitz. They recounted their experiences as young women, when they worked in munitions factories and other wartime services. Transcriptions of the project include their vivid and heart-breaking memories of the Clydebank blitz, the air-raids and the bombing as well as the aftermath. M. Bennett, *"See, When You Look Back": Clydeside Reminiscences of the Home Front, 1939-45.*

11   The Civil Defence Service recruited and trained civilians as wardens of the ARP (Air Raid Precautions), responsible for enforcing the wartime blackouts and duty-bound to warn and protect people during air raids, when enemy planes dropped bombs. Children at play became familiar with their local ARP wardens as they reminded them to wear their gas-masks and to rush to an Anderson shelter as soon as they heard the air-raid sirens. The Imperial War Museum's display of their role during the blitz is a stark reminder of the dangers they faced: <https://www.iwm.org.uk/history/8-objects-used-by-air-raid-wardens-during-the-blitz>.

A page from Billy Gardiner's notebook

DURING THE WAR
A BATTLION OF SOLDIERS WERE BILLETED IN
GLASGOW HIGHLANDERS   THE VILLAGE
CAMERONIANS THE BUFFS POLES FRENCH CANADIAN E.T.C
SHERWOOD FORESTERS
WAR FOOD RATIONING WENT ON TO 1954.
WAR NO ORANGES NO BANANAS.

MY MOTHER DID NOT HAVE THE VOTE
WHEN I WAS BORN IN 1927.

IN 1918 ALL MEN OVER 21 HAD THE VOTE
WOMEN GOT THE AGE 30 AND OVER
IN 1928? ALL WOMEN GOT THE VOTE
A WORKING WOMAN HAD TO LEAVE HER
WORK WHEN SHE MARRIED.
WOMEN NEVER WENT TO FUNERALS (CEMETERY)
WOMEN STAYED IN THE HOUSE (HOME SERVICE)
10 MIN. HOUSE 10 MIN CEMETERY
A WOMAN ALLWAYS WORE A HAT GOING TO CHURCH
MY MOTHER OR NONE OF MY MOTHERS FRIENDS
MOTHERS WORKED
WOMEN WORE HATS IN CHURCH
GRAVE STONES FACED THE EAST,
OR RISING SUN, SOME OF THESE THINGS
GO BACK TO THE MIDDLE EAST

Chapter 8

Life in the Army and Home Again

Margaret Bennett: Were you called up when you were eighteen?

Billy Gardiner: I should have been called up in 1945 but it was actually '46. My call up papers arrived at the end of February 1946. I was 18 years of age an I got a letter saying to report to Hadrian's Staging Camp at Carlisle. Although the war was finished, we were told to take our gas masks, an a train warrant was included wi the letter. I went doon wi another boy fae Comrie, Stan Sinclair – he got his papers on the same day an we went together. Call-ups were on Thursdays, so on the 4th of March 1946 – that was a Thursday – we set off from Comrie Station. We had to change at Gleneagles an got the London train to Carlisle. Steam trains at this time were usually late an crowded, an neither Stan nor I had ever been past Glasgow. In fact, Stan had been born in Glasgow an had been evacuated to Comrie in 1939, with his mother an siblings. Many of the evacuees had wandered back to Glasgow over the years but the Sinclairs had stayed.

We were standing on the station at Carlisle an we saw this Sergeant, an officer, an N.C.O.[1] waiting to welcome us, or at least herd us all into this lorry. So away we went, through the darkening streets an were taken to Hadrian's posting camp. By the time we got there it was nearly dark an we were taken to a dining hall an given something to eat then shown into huts – I don't remember much about the layout of the huts, but they were Nissen type huts. Inside there wis beds, but there was nothing on the beds. Although it was around 10 o'clock at night the beds had no palliasses or blankets, just the bare springs, an we were wondering what's the game here. Then an old soldier came in carrying a raffia mat – I remember it to this day, green an black squares! An thinking we were green, he was selling raffle tickets for it, at tuppence a ticket or something, an we didnae ken what was going on! We didnae even ken where or when the draw would be taking place. Later, we found out that the army issued what they called 'biscuits' to put on the beds. Then towards midnight this Army Officer came in, "Now," he says, "you're going on a long journey, so put on all the warm clothes you can get." Warm clothes? We just had the clothes we stood in, an our gas masks. Then this boy who'd just been to the toilet tells us, "It says on the graffiti on the toilet walls "Next stop Ballykinler." The next stop was Northern Ireland, you ken!

Doubts began to form in my mind about the way our British Army was managed, an I decided tae write hame, because afore I left, my Mother had given me a wallet, a fountain pen an some bits of paper an stamps. So I wrote a letter hame saying we're going tae Ballykinler – the post was quick in thae days, an my Mother had the letter the next day. And when my Faither cam hame she was greetin, an she says "They've sent him to Northern Ireland." And my dad says "A lot of damn nonsense! That's the Army for you! Just a lot of stories, dinnae believe a word o it!" But the next day she got another letter from me fae Northern Ireland! What had happened was, after we were told tae put on all oor warm claes, before we knew it, we were at Carlisle Station an boarding a very crowded troop train, an I was surprised to hear some of the lads from the West of England saying they had never been on a train before being called up. I think some might have been from the Fens. At no time where we ever told where we were going, but we just accepted this, 'you're going on a long journey,' an we finished up in Stranraer at the harbour station. By this time, we realised we were making for Northern Ireland, an before long we were on the early morning boat for Larne.

In Larne we were taken to another hutted camp an given sausages an mash an I broke a tooth on a hard sausage – the first tooth I had ever managed to break. Then we were then taken to the station an went down to Ballykinler, a camp in County Down that had been built around the time of the First War – corrugated huts in threes, joined at the back by an ablution block. There was a big modern brick building nearby, but we were never in it. The camp had no hot water but some of the lads used to get hot water for shaving, from where I don't know. The most of us were young an we didn't bother about just having cold water, but some of the lads were a bit older than the rest o us; they'd been in jobs which had been reserved during the war, an got called up later, maybe in their early twenties – we thought they were ancient! The rest o us were conscripts with demob numbers – mine was 73 – an we didnae ken when we were getting oot. It wasn't till 1949 that the National Service Act came in, requiring 18 months service, an later on it was reduced to a year.

MB: *What were the huts like inside?*

Billy: Each hut held 32 men, double decker beds, bunks wi plywood bottoms an no springs. We were each given three 'biscuits' as they called them, like hard cushions about 30-

inch square. Every morning they were piled on top of the bed an the bedding folded inside one of the blankets.

Some camps had different ways, but the kit was always laid out on the bed. We kept on asking the Sergeant in charge about the gas masks: "What are we gaun tae dae wi this gas mask in Northern Ireland?"

"Oh, I dinnae ken," he says, so we young fellas went out one night when it was dark an we dumped them all in a big rubbish dump behind the cookhoose.

Our camp commander was a colonel in the Irish Guards; he wasn't very tall – quite a number o the men in the Guards were under 6 foot. His idea of showing what training would do was to get us on the range in our civvy clothes. So we were taken to the range out in the sand dunes, given a rifle, a 303 an two rounds each, an told to lie down an fire at the target. That was our initiation to army drill, then the same with the Bren gun. After that it was back to the camp stores where we were kitted out in uniforms an boots – we were given two pairs, wi 13 studs in the soles. Once you had your uniform, you got two sheets o brown paper an some string, an you had to wrap up all your civvies, an you got a label an addressed them to your Mother, so they were sent back home. An then we got a terrible haircut! There was this Irish barber, an the boy in front o me got an awfu scalpin, an he says to the Irish boy, "Paddy, what did you do in civvy street?" An Paddy says, "I cut hedges for the cooncil." [laughter]

One evening not long after we got there, we were exploring the camp; it was quite late an starting tae get cauld, so we had our great coat collars turned up against the wind. An officer or N.C.O. bawled at us to get our collars down at once. You had to do everything their way.

When we were in Northern Ireland, 1946, there was nae trouble – it wisnae like they speak o the 'Troubles' that started in the Sixties. The only thing was that, in the barracks we had to take the bolts oot our rifles at night. There wis metal pillars in the middle of the huts, an there was a chain, an aw the rifles was put in the middle o the room, an the chain went through the trigger guards. An then you slept with the bolt o your rifle in below your pillow – well, we didn't hae pillows, it was biscuits we had. Come to think of it, we had no sheets either, an we didnae hae pyjamas – the RAF got pyjamas, but in the army ye just slept in yer sark-tail.

Every night you put the bolt of your rifle in below one of the biscuits an then in the morning you got up an all your blankets had to be folded right round the biscuits an all your kit laid out in front, same routine every morning, your boots turned up, thirteen studs all polished – all this kind of stuff

Our sergeant was in the Ulster Rifles, an all the rifle regiments marched very quickly. He had charge of the hut of 32 men an he had a room at the end. There was an office, headquarters for the Sergeant Major, Quartermaster Sergeant, an two A.T.S. clerks[2].

MB: How long was the training?

Billy: That training was for eight weeks, with drill, shooting, P.T. an route marches, an we had hut inspections every day an a weekly competition among all the huts. All our gear would be out on the beds, boots no just polished, but we had to get them smooth, with the toecaps shining like glass – when the boots were new they were rough, dimpled leather; I cannae remember the correct name, but we had various methods to get them smooth. I used a candle an the handle of a spoon. You got the leather hot an rubbed it smooth wi the spoon handle, then used polish with heat an so on. An for this inspection, they were that strict we'd be down on our hands an knees picking up matchsticks, bits of dead grass, small leaves on the small area of grass outside the hut.

MB: Was there any entertainment?

Billy: Once a month a brass band would come from the depot o one o the Irish Regiments an they played on the drill square while we marched round to the

music. The camp was built near the sea beside a huge area of sand dunes with a shooting range, an there was also a football field. Many years later someone told me that Stanley Matthews played a game here during his army service an he claimed it was the best pitch he'd ever come across. But we werena allowed to go near the seashore, because the whole of this area was full of mines an fenced off.

One lad hated the whole show so much that he managed to get a round of ammunition from the shooting range. Having read stories about men in the First War, he put the round in his rifle an blew his index finger aff – the idea was he'd be unfit for service. Unfortunately, the bullet went through the old huts an hit another lad in the chest. The last I heard he was ok but the doctors had to leave the bullet where it was.

After we'd been in the army for 12 weeks, an we'd passed the drill, shooting an all the tests, we were ready for postin to another camp, an to be assigned to our regiments. We were then given aptitude tests, but this turned out to involve another farce. They'd take six of us at a time, an we were given various articles that had been dismantled or disconnected, broken down in pieces. The idea was to see if we could put them together again. They were all simple except two. The gear wheel off a bike an an old type electric ceiling light, a lamp holder. The bike was easy for me because we aye had bikes although some o the lads had never ridden a bike, far less taken a free wheel to bits. Sos I was alright with that, but when it came to the other thing, one o thae brass fittings off an electric light lamp, I didnae ken anything about that because we didnae hae electric light at hame – we only had paraffin lamps, so I made a muck of that! Anyway, we all had to go for an interview afterwards, an got asked various questions, an the young officer, a toff, told me, "Oh, your aptitude's very good, you might get sent to the REME."[3] But what actually happened was, there was thirty-two in the hut, an half went to the Ordnance Corps in Portsmouth an half went to the Catering Corps in Aldershot, including me. So, this aptitude test was just a farce because they had already marked doon some o us for the Catering Corps, an wi me being in the bake-hoose in Comrie I automatically got sent to the catering corps.

MB: So you went down to Aldershot?

Billy: Aye, doon to Aldershot via Larne an Stranraer an then by train. The billets at Aldershot were timber 'spider huts', so-called because the wash room, baths, showers etc. were in a centre block an there were passages, like spider's legs, leading off to the sleeping huts.

We got 12 weeks there including two weeks' drill. And the Catering Corps had two weeks baking, two weeks sweets, two weeks cookhoose work, two weeks field kitchen, an so on.

When we were stationed in Aldershot we went to the pictures an we also got one weekend leave, so we went to London an went round all the usual sights, the Zoo, the Palace, the Waxworks, etc. At Stockwell, on the Waterloo Line, the Underground, a new station had been getting built before the start of the war, but when the war began it was used as an air raid shelter. The whole thing was long but very low an after the war it still had rows of double decker beds, an that's where we slept, for a nominal sum. Looking back, it was very dangerous, for at weekends it was very crowded, an a real fire hazard because the only entrance was a circular stair. Another snag was that through the wall you could hear the trains on another line. Not the best place to sleep!

After training at Aldershot, we all sat an exam, an a few, who had fair writing an spelling with full stops in the right place, were kept back on an N.C.O.'s course. My pals all went on embarkation leave an they landed in the Far East, while I was stuck in Aldershot. When I was finished this course, I was posted to the Isle o Wight and stationed at Golden Hill Fort at Freshwater, near the Needles – it's on the top of the hill, an looks down on Yarmouth Town, the port where ferries crossed from the Isle o Wight to Lymington, Hampshire.

The barracks at Golden Hill Fort look very impressive, like a big hexagon defence on the top of the hill. The fort had been built in the mid-1800s when Britain was under threat from a French invasion. There was another one down by the shore near Yarmouth called Fort Victoria, a different type. Out in the Solent there were several Martello Towers, round and fortified at one time. When I went there one of the lads took me to see the Needles and as we got to the edge of a cliff path, a woman and a small child appeared. She was carrying a basket full of small oranges. It turned out that a Greek cargo ship had drifted on to the rocks at the Needles lighthoose during a really stormy night, January the 5th, 1947. The engines failed so the ship was a total wreck – the name of the vessel was SS Varvassi, and she was carrying a cargo of wine in huge wooden casks, an oranges. There was a camp near at hand where German POW work gangs were billeted. Some of them went down with pails from the cookhoose an helped themselves to the wine. They finished up in the army hospital at Netley, Southampton. Customs & Excise soon sealed all the casks before any more was taken.

Our sergeant-major at Golden Hill was called Burma Joe, though I never found out why, but some of the men who had been with the unit for some years were certain he had never been near Burma. We had an R.S.M.[4] at Aldershot who was called 'Big Tony'; he was big, but his proper name wasn't Tony.

The unit on the Isle of Wight was called the Waterborne Training Wing. This was special training for waterborne army troops, because the army had ex-tank landing craft for dumping duff ammunition, and they worked from Cairnryan. They trained on MFVs, ex-fishing boats, an also had boats working in the Western Isles an on the Thames at Woolwich.[5] Dunoon had been their base for many years until the policy for moving everything to the south of England came in.

When I was stationed in the Isle of Wight, the catering staff were the only ones in the camp who really had to work at that time – by then I was a Corporal in charge of the cookhoose. We only had two old coal burning cookers, one was a Green's Steamer an we had an early start an late finish. We tried to work shifts, but we had too few men to do this properly, so we had long hours. Meanwhile, the rest of the unit worked short hours, five days a week.

The Sergeant Major seemed to think I was too easy with the men, and he started niggling me, asking me how long I had been an N.C.O. etc. And before this he had wanted my men to whitewash the stones at the side of the road leading to the camp, this on a Sunday, because they had word that some big shot was coming on the Monday! "Whitewash stones on the Lord's Day?" I said, very indignant. "You can't mean it!" He hummed an hawed an cleared off, but never forgave me. On more than one occasion when we had had lambs' kidneys, his favourite dish, he'd get some from the cookhoose, so he couldnae say very much. But I'd had enough o him an I told him I wanted an overseas posting.

About a month later I was sent on embarkation leave, 14 days, and posted back to Aldershot, to Blenheim Barracks, a new one to me. Then after 10 days we were trucked to the station at Aldershot, got on the train to Southampton an onto a troopship 'The Otranto'. Our lot were all corporals an the next day we sailed out to the Channel an we didnae ken where we were going. Aboard ship we were down in what had been the cargo hold when the ship was a liner. We were supposed to sleep in hammocks, but that wisnae for me – I fell out an so did some of the rest o the boys, so we slept on the floor, on deck. Then the Bay of Biscay was very rough an I was sick for two days. We went through the Mediterranean an passed Gibraltar at night. We called at Benghazi an spent a day in

Malta, the Grand Harbour of Valetta. We got shore leave an we saw the masons working on stone to repair the bomb damage – Malta suffered terrible bomb damage during WW2. The sandstone is like hard cheese, easy to carve but I've been told it hardens with the air. When we were ashore most o us didnae hae any money, but there was one boy had money an went intae the shop an bought chocolate. When he opened it, the blinking thing was very near white! It must hae been the heat.

Next, we landed in Egypt at Port Said, an from there we were taken to a camp at El Ballah, between the Suez Canal an the Sweet Water Canal. Nothing but sand and gravel, an very cold at night. When we were there, after the war, the British were oot o Egypt except for the Suez Canal, or 'The Canal Zone' they called it – that was a nominal twenty-one mile up each side of the Canal, but it wisnae that at all, it was zigzag you ken. I was at El Ballah at the beginning – between the Sweet Water Canal an the Suez Canal, an where we were stationed, with the sand dunes around us, you could just see the funnels of the boats an the masts going past. An then we were sent up to Fayed – that's on the Great Bitter Lake. The Canal goes through the Great Bitter Lake, the Little Bitter Lake an what was in my time was Lake Timsah but seemingly has got another name now, beside the Great Bitter Lake.

The camp had a big fence right round it, an guards on, an there wis a lot o German prisoners there – they got horse meat, an they were always mooching for tea or coffee to send home. It was all tents, except the cookhoose, which was a big place with a corrugated iron roof. But we lived in tents there, an I was a Corporal, an they had was what was called the 'English shift' – they mean 'British' but they called it the 'English shift' an you couldnae do anything aboot it – so there was the English shift an the German shift, an the head man, a Navyman, told us what shift to take. An there was this fellow senior to me, an he says to me, "I've been picked for the football team," an I says, "You've only been here two days!" An he says, "Can you take the other shift?" He wanted to swap shifts, so I took the German shift, but then I could see where my bread was buttered there, because there was a German in charge of the German shift, an ex-Navy man, perfect English, an he was bossing them all about, an I just had to stand an do nothing. So, when this boy come back fae the football I says to him "Would you mind just sticking with the English shift?" cause I knew they were a clarty[6] lot, you ken, an the Germans were a smart lot.

All the labour at the camp, the cleaning etc. was done by local hires. We had a Sudanese with us wi cut marks on his cheeks, a nice lad. When we were abroad, on pay day we all got 50 cigarettes, whether you smoked or not. I didnae smoke an I think it did a lot o harm, especially tae the ones who started smoking because o the army's free cigarettes.

After about a year, two of us corporals were told we were going home. We got the train to Port Said, a train wi no windows an wooden spars on the seats. Then crossed the canal to a transit camp at Port Fuad where we were awoken at an unearthly hour by the call to prayer from a high minaret close by – we'd been sound asleep so you could hear all the names under the sun from the ones who werenae pleased to be wakened up. At the end of our National Service we came back on the 'Georgia', a big ship, an we were all in the hold, sleeping on standee bunks, three high; they were like folding shelves, put up during the day. The ship headed straight to Port Said then to Haifa in Israel. We passed Gibraltar in darkness comin an goin, an we sailed back tae Southampton again.

MB: How many years did you serve?

Billy: Two an a half years. When we landed at Southampton we were sent up tae York an demobbed at York.

MB: Did you get a demob suit at the end?

Billy: Aye, an they were all saying if you slip the boy behind the counter a fiver he'll give you a navy blue suit, but I wasnae carin what suit I got, so I got a broon suit, a braw felt hat, an a raincoat.

MB: Tam, did you get called up for National Service?

Tam Kettle: Aye, I was working on the farms till 1953 then I got called up, and I did my National Service

MB: And where did that take you?

Tam: Well, down to England for a start. The training was down at Catterick camp and I was in The 14th/20th King's Hussars – that's a cavalry regiment. I asked to go in the REME but I was put in the Hussars. And they'd changed from horse to tanks at that time, so we had the big tanks. And after Catterick I got posted to Tripoli for my two years National Service. I mind it was very warm there.

MB: How did you travel out there?

Tam: We went by plane to France, then the plane from France to Malta. It was just an old army plane, it was nae luxuries, it wis mair like a cargo plane.

MB: Was that the first time you flew anywhere?

Tam: Aye, and in fact it was my first time away from home.

MB: And how long did you stop in Malta?

Tam: About four weeks, aye, a month, something like that. It was a nice place though you could see all the damage done during the war, wi the bombing. But it was a good time in Malta, then from Malta we sailed to Tripoli.

MB: Did you sail from Valetta?

Tam: Aye, an I remember I was as sick as a dog – that was my first ever trip on a boat. The weeks spent in Malta probably didnae help that – I should've stuck tae a wee cup o tea! In my younger days I used to like a dram – too much, too much, though I huvnae touched it in a while. But I got through it all and straightened out by the time we got to Tripoli. Well, the thing helped me most, was one o the Navy guys says, "Come wi me." So we went down the bottom o the boat, the middle o the boat and he gave us a good dram o rum. [laughter] I had quite a few rums an that settled me out [laughter]. Oh, they were good lads.

MB: Was that the Merchant Navy or the Royal Navy?

Tam: The Royal Navy, aye. And when we landed in Tripoli, I can remember the heat just hit me. Really warm, really hot, but you got used to it. We were young and hardy!

MB: And what was the accommodation in Tripoli?

Tam: We had a barrack room. Then most o our time was spent in the desert, training in the desert, wi Centurion Tanks, but we were never in active service. I was a gunner, training to use a big gun, practising in different situations. You needed to aim accurately, and there was a team of engineers with us – oh, it was good training.

MB: And how long were you in Tripoli, training in the desert?

Tam: Altogether, eighteen month. And after a while you got really accurate, really accurate. Eighteen months o practicing, and most o the time we'd tae fire. But they had a diminished range that a small gun, a 22, a .22, that was strapped to the big gun. And it was just everything worked the same as you're firing a big gun. That was just for the sake o expense more than anything else. It was just the same accuracy an everything as the big gun. We did have the big machine guns and we'd use them more than the other guns.

MB: And did you have to learn navigating skills and all that kind of stuff?

Tam: Well, there was a navigator in the tank, that was his job. There were four crew-members in the tank: the driver, the gunner, he was there, navigator and gunner, then the commander, then another gunner.

MB: Any idea where these tanks were made?

Tam: Oh, they'd been made in England. They had Rolls Royce engines in them.

MB: And you had a good team.

Tam: Oh yes! There wis four Scots boys – they'd the good sense to put the four Scotsmen in the one tank. [laughs] Well, we could understand each other, especially the language. I remember one, Jock Comrie was his name, he was a farmer's son fae near Stirling. And one of them was from one o the islands, he was a Gaelic speaker and when he got a good dram he was fair speirin[7] the Gaelic. [laughs] He didn't sing very much, but I mind he got called Ginger Smith.

MB: And did you ever keep in touch afterwards?

Tam: I met the guy from near Stirling, Jock Comrie, when I was cuttin trees in that area. Aye, I made a point I'd go in to see him.

MB: And after you finished your National Service, how did you get home? Was that straightforward enough?

Tam: Not really – we went by airplane from Tripoli to the south o England and then motor transport up to Edinburgh. But then I think the railway workers were striking at that time, so, we were told if we could find our own way, just to go. I said, "I'll just go, I'll find ma own way," and I thumbed a lift back to Auchterarder. But in those days you could thumb a lot easier than you can now. People are frightened to stop now because they don't know who they're going to get in their car. But back then, you never had any trouble. So, I got back hame again in '55.

MB: Were you glad to be home?

Tam: Oh aye, aye. But looking back on my National Service, it was good. Your first six weeks, your basic training, that was the worst times. It got much easier, once you went abroad in your regiment, life was a lot easier. You got into the way of life, and it was good – an experience you wouldn't have missed.

MB: My Dad was in the army during the war, '39–45, but for years and years afterwards, if he saw or read about teenagers up to no good, he'd say, "Two years in the army would sort him out!" [laughter] Did you ever hear people say that?

Tam: Oh, many a time, aye! You need to have the discipline, I would think so, aye. Never done me any harm, that's for sure. We had a lot of discipline when we were training, aye that's right. So, when I got back home, 1955, I was just twenty and I was back to the same farm, but not for very long. The fairmer an I didnae get on too good at Netherforden, so I decided to part company. I'd itchy feet [laughs], and I'd had enough o workin on fairms, so I went to work at the sawmill, near Dunning.

MB: What was your job in the sawmill?

Tam: It was what they called 'tailsman'. When I started off in the woods, cutting, it was always wi a chainsaw – we didnae use axes much, everything was done wi chainsaw. Then you'd take the sawed wood away an put the sawn wood in one pile an the waste in another. The wood was all manhandled then, there was none o these huge machines they have now.

MB: What kind of wood was it?

Tam: Topwood, mainly. Scots pine, spruce, and larch. The larch was for fencing posts.

MB: That's the one that's very sparky in the fire – I used to buy offcuts from a sawmill, just to burn it in the woodstove, but never on an open fire.

Tam: Aye, it's too sparky for an open fire. In the sawmill we cut them into lengths; we used to call them 'lorry lengths', then they used the lengths they wanted, for various orders. We didn't square them off, we used round trees, and sometimes we used to roll them on by hand, on a pair o skids up the side o the lorry.

MB: *You must have had a good strong back!*

Tam: Aye that's right. An I done it every day, an I worked for thirty three year in Dunning. Oh, aye, it was a good place to be.

MB: *And where did you live all those years?*

Tam: I still bade near Auchterarder. We were in Dunpatrick Ford – that was the name of the farm my father was on. There was eight of a family of us, and there was a bothy at the side of the farm cottage, used as part of the hoose. My brother was workin at the fencin then, an we slept in the bothy – when you got home in at night and it was late, they wouldnae hear you in the rest o the hoose. [laughs]

MB: *Dunpatrick Ford's a bit of a distance from Dunning, is it not?*

Tam: Oh, I traivelled by car every day, in my own car. After I quit the army, I had a bob or two, so I bought a wee car. Oh, well we used to go up to Comrie to the dances. All the villages had dances, and they were really good. Every evening there was a dance somewhere, and they had really good bands as well. Jimmy Shand was one of them. And Ian Powrie was there – I knew Ian quite well, because he had a farm in Auchterarder. He was a really good fiddler. And we used to have Bobby MacLeod and his dance-band, and Jim Cameron. And there was a woman used to have a band – her name'll come back tae me ... I remember the fiddler who played with her, Kevin Brown, he was one o my neighbours. 'Fiddler Brown' they called him. He moved to Bridge of Earn, an he was staying in Bridge of Earn a long time. I suppose Jimmy Shand was the favourite, he was kent to be one o the best at that time. He never smiled much at all. He was a dour man, though he'd a good sense o humour. And we used to go to some of the barn dances. After the dance we'd get home about fower in the mornin, and we'd be up at half past six! Put the kettle on for a cup o tea, then through the hoose, get the clothes and back out again! You didn't know what tiredness was in those days! [Laughs] We were young and we enjoyed ourselves. Great fun, though it wasnae all clean fun![8]

MB: *Did you have a favourite dance, Tam?*

Tam: Oh aye! We aw hud a favourite dance!

MB: So what was that?

Tam: [laughing] The favourite dance ? That was the Squirrel Waltz.

MB: Tam, are you saying the 'Squirrel Waltz'? Like the wee animal, a squirrel?

Tam: Aye. [Laughing]

MB: Oh, you've lost me now – I've never come across that dance anywhere. So, tell me, how did that one go?

Tam: [still laughing] That was just twice roun the hall and then oot for your nuts! [laughter]

MB: You're an awfu man, Tam! Now I'm scared to ask if your brother was as wild as you?

Tam: Well, he wouldnae be far away! [laughter]. But he's in a home in Auchterarder now, and I've been in Dalginross nearly a year now. I came in to Comrie when I had a stroke; it wasnae a bad one, so I was lucky. And it's very nice here, it's very good, an everyone is very helpful, and very patient. They'd have tae be wi me!

Endnotes

1   A non-commissioned officer is usually referred to as an NCO.

2   Shortly after Billy was conscripted, the women's branch of the army, the ATS, or Auxiliary Territorial Service, was disbanded and the troops transferred to the newly formed Women's Royal Army Corps.

3   The REME: The Royal Electrical and Mechanical Engineers, set up to maintain, repair and manufacture equipment and aircraft.

4   R.S.M. is the Regimental Sergeant-Major.

5   M.F.V. refers to Motor Fishing Vessels.

6   clarty (Scots): dirty.

7   speirin (Scots): speaking, questioning.

8   David Kerr Cameron discusses 'The bothy lads' and their 'social hour' in The Ballad and the Plough p.76 ff. In Bothy Nichts and Days, David G. Adams includes a chapter on 'Fun and Games' recounting the range of pastimes in the bothies (pp. 42–46) and also some of the practical jokes and pranks played by farm workers. (p. 52).

Chapter 9

A Fraternity of Hill-folk

Alistair Work: Dalclathic Lodge used to be let out to various fly-fishing parties during the salmon season.[1]

Margaret Bennett: Apparently the summer that Kipling was there, 1919, the water was so low there was virtually no salmon.

Alistair: That's right – once in a while you'd get a hot, dry summer. It'll all be recorded in the game books. There was one year they got about 500 salmon. When I came here in the fifties there was sea trout and salmon a-plenty, but there's nothing like that now; the salmon are still coming up, but they're struggling. And we didnae have a very good season for the pheasants this year [2022] and neither did a lot of other estates. We didn't have much snow, so the pheasants could just go where they liked. They know the place we feed them, but when there's no snow the pheasants seem to think, "Och we're not going in there, we can go all over the place," so they were a bugger to hold this year, out on the road and everywhere. At one time anyone driving along country roads would draw up and let the pheasant cross, but not now, they're just right over the top of them – they don't care what they kill; not just stunned, but completely flattened.

MB: Does a successful season depend on the weather?

Alistair: Definitely. You'll mind the 'Beast from the East'?

MB: Oh, who could forget it? [February, March, 2018] Completely snowed in.

Alistair: Well, we lost about fifteen hundred stags and hinds; they all died, all the way out to Ardvorlich, along the loch side. And when something like that happens you can do nothing with the carcasses; they just lie there, then the foxes and crows might have a go at them, and they just deteriorate. But that sort of thing wouldn't have happened years and years ago when the estate had the deer forest. In a bad, bad storm the stags would come out of Glenartney and walk right through to Dundurn over towards Ardtrostan. That was the wintering ground for the stags and it was the only place for them to go, and then when the storm was passed, back they came, up the glen. When I started work on the Drummond Estate I remember the wee white cottage this side of the farm, Ardtrostan Cottage. Well, that's where Archie McNaughton used to stay.

MB: *Was that the fellow that Pat MacNab occasionally saw when he was trapping rabbits up Glen Ghòinean?*

Alistair: Yes, that would be Archie. I remember going out there with a surveyor for the last job I had with the Forestry Commission. I mind going out with him and marking out a wood for the Forestry Commission on the Drummond estate. It was around that time they sold Ardtrostan and the farm with the lovely big house along the loch side. Up until then, all that land had been the wintering ground for our stags off the deer forest – and then it was all sold to the Forestry Commission, so the stags have nowhere to shelter.

MB: *Why in the world did they sell that?*

Alistair: After World War 1, when there were no jobs and all these men were on the dole, the government set up the Forestry Commission and big estates were obliged to sell land for planting timber. The country needed timber and the men needed jobs, so it was a case of "you can give us that bit, and that bit, and that bit," and the big land-owners were obliged to sell to the Forestry Commission because it was another man off the dole, you know. That went on for years and years and now they're the biggest landowners in Britain.

MB: *What did the stalkers and game-keepers do between the different sporting seasons, when there was no shooting or fly-fishing?*

Alistair: Whenever the season finished, you maintain the fences. There's sixty miles of deer fence right round the deer forest, and the stalkers maintained all that. They didn't have any vehicles then, just the ponies, and you were walking all the time. Fit? I wish I was that age again! There's 22 miles of fence from St Fillans to Callander, and then there was a part of the deer fence right at the top of Ben Vorlich, and in the snow that gets damaged and even the iron stanchions can be just pushed over with the weight of the snow. So all that, posts and everything, used to be carried up with the horses. There's a special saddle for carrying these posts; you put the posts along each side of the horse and carry them out. Yes, 60 miles o fence, right round.

MB: *What a distance! So did you get to know the estate workers and shepherds over as far as Ben Vorlich and right down to Callander?*

Alistair: Oh yes, you got to know the hill folk for miles and miles around.

MB: You'll mind Jimmy Stewart who was at Locherlour for years? That's where Jimmy was from, near the Falls o Lennie, but he went shepherding in Glen Buckie when he was still in his teens.

Jimmy Stewart [1921–2011]: I started workin on small farms near Callander, milking cows, doing some agricultural work, ploughing – I was working a pair of horses when I

was fifteen year-auld. But sheep was my thing – so in 1936, I got the chance to go to Balquhidder to a Mr and Mrs MacIntyre on a hill farm by the name of 'Immeroin'. It's up Glen Buckie – the glen runs from the bottom of Loch Voil, right up to the top end of Immeroin Farm. I started out in what they called Glen Sionnach, a small hirsel[2] of sheep, then after three years the boss said to me, "I'm puttin ye onto the big hirsel, the Grachler [?]" – that's "green hill" in English. So I was there for a good while. Oh, we were well fed and looked after at Immeroin. The lady of the house, Mrs MacIntyre, was a tremendous cook and when there was a sheep slaughtered for the house there was not a thing missed. Tripe was a regular thing; she made sheep's head broth; the blood was used for puddings – the marags – she cooked the kidneys, it was all used, everything. None wasted.[3] She used to make hare soup, and I'd be sent away up the hill with the gun to get a pair of hares, and that would be quite enough. And they were hung for a few days and then she boiled the hare with the soup, took the hare off the bones, all in parts and then made the pie with onions, vegetables and a crust on top of it. She roasted it in the oven, and oh, it was beautiful, you know, with that crust on it. We grew our own potatoes and everything, Kerr's Pink and Golden Wonder. They kept two cows and when they were heavy with milk, butter was made just about twice a week. Oh, we were never hungry!

In those days there was quite a few Gaelic speakers in the area – you'll know the Fergussons?[4] All the Fergussons had Gaelic. Jimmy Fergusson at Muirlaggan for one, had very good Gaelic. Alan Ferguson at Gartnafuaran was a very good speaker and a lot of the

shepherds were Gaelic-speakers. And even over at the Braes of Balquhidder, old John MacNaughton at Inverlochlarig, it was all Highlanders he had as shepherds, so it was Gaelic all the way.

You got to know them for miles around. And every year they used to have a night at Stronvar with all the horsemen, shepherds, and the cattlemen an whoever, and this night Lady Carnegie asked one of the shepherds, "Where's my friend Scott tonight?" This was another shepherd by the name of Will Scott and he was a real character. And this fellow told her, "He's got a sore foot – I think he's got foot rot." [laughter] You know, like a sheep! You had to live among them to find it out!

MB: *And who was Lady Carnegie?*[5]

Jimmy: Mrs Carnegie? The Carnegies were up at Stronvar in that big house[6] – they had Stronslanie as a farm, and they owned Gartnafuaran, Immeroin, Ballimore, Tulloch, Kirkton, Auchleskine – the Glenbuckie Estate belonged to the Carnegies. She was an awfy, awfy nice buddy, Mrs Carnegie. When they were painting the rooms in Stronvar House, the Carnegies came up to Immeroin and they stayed with the MacIntyres until the painting was finished. That's where I was shepherding, Immeroin, and the MacIntyres had plenty of room in the farmhouse. During the fishing season, Mrs MacIntyre used to run a guest house – she did that kind of thing, and one time we had Lord MacMillan up there and I got orders in the morning to be sure my hair was combed properly! He was Prime Minister for a while, in later years [1957–67].

MB: *Harold MacMillan?*

Jimmy: Yes. [laughter]

Being in the glen like that, it was a community and you knew everyone. Mrs Moir at the Post Office was one of the old 'glenners'. She was the Post Mistress and oh, she was a topper of a lady altogether. Many's a ceilidh we had in the house. She sold cigarettes and tobacco in the Post Office, and I've seen us going down late at night, maybe after lambing, for a packet of cigarettes or something. She'd say, "Oh just come away in, you better have a dram before you go up that bad road again." You know, people in the glens were so welcoming, you were just at home with them. I've seen us leaving Gartnafuaran at 11 o clock at night after playing 'Catch the Ten! [card-game] and oh, the drams flowing of course! [Laughter] Then afterwards we had the two and a half mile walk home, sometimes up to the knee in snow. Oh, ye never thought anything about it. Just young and daft!

When I started in Balquhidder they used to sell all the sheep in Perth at the Mart, and I used to be sent away with a drove of sheep over the hill, *Beinn-an t-Sithean* (Ben Shian), that's the hill of the fairies, and all the way to a field just above the railway station at Strathyre. And they were taken on to the waggons there. In my day they went by train but I think it was lorries after that.

I was in Balquhidder for ten years and that's where I met my wife, Mary – her people were from Balquhidder; her grandfather was the precentor in the kirk before our time.

After we were married, we went way up to Glen Isla, above Alyth. There was three shepherds in the place, a nice hirsel, nice sheep and everything, but Kirriemuir was the nearest for shopping (11 miles away) so if you wanted to go and do a big shop you had to hire a car. A married man in a house was only getting £3 15s a week [£3.75 today], so you can imagine we couldnae save very much. Then when we got cut off by the snow in 1947, that finished it, so I left in the November and we came to Corriemucadh, just about a mile from Amulree, on the Crieff side.[7] I think I told you I was shepherding there for five years then I came to Glenturret. We used to keep a pig – we'd buy a piglet, about eight weeks old, from a man from Dunkeld – it cost a couple of quid (£2), then we'd buy the feeding, but we always finished them off with bruised corn and apples if you could get them.

MB: Oh, yes, quite a few folk have apple trees and there's always the wind-falls.

Jimmy: It was the best o meat and Mary was a braw cook – she even used to make potted head. One of the keepers at Amulree used to come doon and help us when we cut up the pig for salting and started taking the stuff oot and getting pieces rolled up.

MB: Did you slaughter it yourselves?

Jimmy: No. There was a man who was good at that, and he came and did it. Afterwards it was straight into the – like a tub, for the boiling water until you felt the hair was going off it, then it was put onto an old clipping stool and everybody had a knife going like hell, scraping off the bristles.

MB: No word of abattoirs back then?

Pat MacNab [1912–2011]: In Glenartney when it was time to slaughter the pig they'd send for my father [Peter MacNab]. And whether it was a pig or a sheep, they made maragan [puddings], marag dhubh, marag geal [black pudding, white pudding], tripe and everything. And even the tripe of the deer, I'd take them home from the hill and my mother used to scrape them and wash them in the burn and clean them, and cook them for the family, with plenty onions!

And Father castrated all the lambs for miles around – nobody else was allowed to do it. Even Cultybraggan Farm at the bottom of the glen, the arable boys came with a machine (a horse and gig) for my father to cut their cross lambs. And that's eight-mile doon the glen and they came for him in the gig and took him back down again. It was all done with the teeth in these days, no fancy gadgets then, no wee rubber rings and stuff like that, no, no, no. Everything was done with the teeth, and before ever you started to castrate at all, you took a glass o whisky, you washed out your mouth with a glass o whisky! And spat it out!

MB: My mother told me that's how they did it in Skye, before these wee rubber rings came in. But I never heard of them spitting out whisky! I was in Dornoch not so long ago, and a man from Rogart, Alec Campbell, asked me if I knew Pat MacNab. I could scarcely believe it, a crofter from Sutherland knowing shepherds from so far south. But Alec told me he has more neighbours in the hills than he'd have in a village – he and his wife used to stay with Pat and Isobel when they went to the Lanark sheep sales.

Duncan McNab: The shepherds went to the market several times a year, the sales – my Dad would be away to the Perth Mart, down to Lanark or over to Dalmally, and that way they all got to know one another. They walked around the holding pens talking with the other shepherds and buyers, waiting for their turn to put their sheep through the ring. That was how they got to know folks. And of course they'd all be looking to see what kind of sheep were getting the best prices, to see what other breeders were going for. All the markets had a Herd's Bar and they'd get together in there after the sale. Dad had a friend called Bob Black, who ran a farm called Caolasnacon up near Kinlochleven. Dad went up there three times a year to help with the gathering. Bob was blind in one eye after an accident at the clipping – a sheep knocked the shears out of his hand and the point caught him in the eye. So Bob wasn't very confident about his balance going along the Aonach Eagach Ridge[8]. The steep drops never bothered Dad and he did that three times a year to help Bob out. There would be other neighbouring shepherds there to help as well, and so Dad got to know them. Mum and Dad didn't take a holiday very often but when they did, Dad would put his shears and his dungarees in the boot, and when they'd be driving through the Highlands if he saw a fank, he'd park the car up, then on with the overalls and the next thing it'd be "Hello lads, can I give you a hand?" He got to know shepherds and keepers all over the place – shepherding was his life, and all these people that he got to know, they all spoke the same language.

Mervyn Browne, Lochtayside: There's this free masonry of shepherds, stalkers and farmers all through these hills, it's a federation if you like, a fraternity. From a very young age I just wanted to be working on the hills. We used to have sheep in Tyrone, and I used to spend a lot of my youth with Tommy, the shepherd. My uncle who ran the place was a disciple of 'Jimmy Muirlaggan' in Perthshire, but due to the uncle's, ehm, 'entry into the

world of distilling' (fondness for whisky) my father had to take over. But Father wasn't really in good health and hadn't any training for that. I was in the Black Watch at the time, [stationed in Edinburgh] and by that time I had become disenchanted with the family's way of life. I didn't want to go about like a stuffed shirt and a figure-head in Aughentaine Castle [County Tyrone].[9] I knew that once I left there I was going to plough my own furrow, literally. So, I left the army in 1949 and went to work as a shepherd at Muirlaggan in Balquhidder. My boss there was Jimmy Fergusson – that's with a double 's' – and he was known as Jimmy Muirlaggan.[10] He was a great friend of Fisher Ferguson, the manager of Glenartney Estate – everybody knew Fisher because he used to judge

the Highland ponies at the Show. And Jimmy Muirlaggan was quite a character too – I remember one time when they had calves right at the head of Balquhidder Glen and the calves bolted and ran away down the opposite side of the glen, and Jimmy, off with the trousers, you see, went across the river, which is quite deep, and he couldn't turn them and he was right down at the kirk in Balquhidder, about eight miles down the loch before he got them turned – and him in his shirt tail. Oh, Jimmy Muirlaggan was a complete character and he became like a second father to me – a far more approachable one than my actual father, I would say.

Then 1953, 54 I was shepherding at the head of Glen Lyon, a place called *Tom na Chaorainn* – that's the knoll of the rowans. There was two of us at the very head of the glen: there was one shepherd, Jimmy, who was herding up *Beinn Mhanach* – that's hill of the monks – and there was myself herding *Tom na Chaorainn*, and the house I was in, you had to either walk up the side of the loch to reach it or row up in a boat.[11]

MB: Was this part of an estate?

Mervyn: Yes. In those days it was owned by the Wills, the cigarette people. When myself and Jimmy were shepherding up Glen Lyon, the Wills had about 200,000 acres, and they had about 10,000 ewes on it. And we had the whole summer gathering, clipping, gathering, clipping. Sir Ernest Wills bought the whole Meggernie Estate around 1920, so he became The Laird of Meggernie Castle.[12]

The castle is about halfway up Glen Lyon, by the River Lyon, just before it joins the River Tay, so there were a lot of estate workers. Wills was the owner till he died (1958), then his son inherited the estate, and had it for about 20 years. The rivers are famous for salmon, and there were quite a few stories there. One I remember about the late Sir Ernest Wills of Meggernie, he was fishing his favourite salmon pool and he saw a poacher on the other side of the river. So, he says in a very stern voice, "Who are you?" And this fella, a character called Craig Errol shouts back, "I'm nae bad, foos yersel?"

When we were shepherding in the glen, it was before the big hydro-electric scheme, so there was no electricity in the estate workers houses. But we were used to that.

MB: What was the accommodation like?

Mervyn: The house I was in wasn't actually in *Tom na Chaorainn* because when the managers got word there was going to be a dam for hydro-electric on the Wills Estate they didn't

do anything to maintain the houses. I didn't have the whole house, but just the bit over the kitchen and one room – the part of the house where the roof was OK. But the roof over the other side of it was just falling through. Not much of a house – I just had my dogs, a frying pan and a teapot, a place to sleep and that's about it. There was a fire, and I used to take a four-ton tractor up on the old, old track with a load of coal and put so much off at each shepherd's house on the way up and we had the last of it. If the loch was low enough, you could go along the side of the loch in the tractor. Otherwise you had to just use sticks or peat – I used to cut a bit of peat too.

MB: *And what about water supply?*

Mervyn: Oh, there was a [large] bottle for the water, but when the bottle froze up, you had to go down and break the ice on the loch! [laughter]

MB: And did you have to carry in paraffin or kerosene for a lamp?

Mervyn: Oh yes, we used to do that, myself and Jimmy, who was up at the top, used to walk down to nearly Meggernie every week. And we carried lambing bags with a cardboard box on them and you'd fill them with your groceries – ten shillings worth, and that did you all week. And on one occasion, I remember it had been snowing for a long time, and hard frost, and Loch Lyon was frozen. And all these wee springs that you'd see rising, they were freezing too, and the ice was going down and meeting the loch ice, and the loch was already covered by snow. And on this occasion, Jimmy and I were going back up the Glen and we had a torch, but the battery was nearly finished. And it was so slippery, as well as pouring rain, freezing on top of the ice. It was too dark to see the whole situation, and it was only the next day I realized that, had we slipped, we would have slid down the ice onto the loch ice, and the loch had dropped because of the frost; there was a slope right into the centre, so if you'd hit your head – that would've been it! So, these are the things we remember.[13]

The hydro-electric scheme came in the Fifties, and the work started when I was there. By the time I left Glen Lyon, the dam was being finally filled in and it took about two years to fill. [It was completed in 1958.] And now Loch Lyon is about nine miles long and it's got two arms; the old original one going up *Meal an glas* and the other one going up Glen Meuran, and the houses that we were in, all the shepherds and estate workers, are now ninety to a hundred feet under the water. My old friend Bob Bisset of great repute was the keeper in my time, a real character – he was the Head Stalker for over forty years, and he also made shoes, he made fiddles, he made leather telescope cases, clocks.[14] Bob and his wife Peggy were there for years and years and we kept in touch after I moved to Ardtalnaig on the other side of Loch Tay. And in 1984, which was a very dry summer, the water level in Loch Lyon fell so that all these old buildings began to reappear. And Bob told me later he was going to Invermearan, the old original headquarters of the Invermearan Estate, and he'd been poking about through the ruins and he said, "What did I find but a last for making shoes for the cattle!" Bob made everything – so he'd know at once that was for the cattle, as opposed to the horses. So, they would be around still I suppose.

MB: Drowned under all that water, beside the houses and other buildings. So, the map has changed for the Glen Lyon area?

Mervyn: Oh yes, yes. You see the shift of the names. For example, on the old map you'll see Invermearan, so-named because it was the confluence of the two rivers, the Mearan and the Lyon – that used to be the estate headquarters where all the clippings where done, beside the Head Stalker's house, and there was a school there at one time.[15] But when the hydro scheme was constructed, all the buildings in Invermearan were demolished, as were the old shepherds' houses right up the Glen. But they kept the name and moved it to the bottom of the dam, so now what they call Invermearan is a complete misnomer.

MB: *So the hydro-electric schemes changed the landscape as well as the way of life. But despite the spartan conditions when you lived there, you still have good memories of Glen Lyon – you returned again and again.*

Mervyn: I'd say my experience of Glen Lyon ranks very highly, shepherding in the hills, working on Meggernie, Loch Tayside and a lot farther than that. I remember one summer going gathering with Jimmy, and we went right out across *Carn Dearg* [Strathspey] then right down to the Blackwater Reservoir [Lochaber]. We'd drum up [make tea] in a syrup tin with the piece of wire [to hold it over a fire], and we had pieces [sandwiches] with us. And after I got my own place at Ardtalnaig [Lochtayside], I used to drive up to a hill-farm up near Keith [in the Grampians] to get a load of hay and then to winter the hogs up there. I had an old Commer lorry and it took me five hours with a load, then four without, and I would always get a meal and tea and scones with 'the Strathdees'. Donnie Wilson in Laggan had the same kind of lorry as me – I got mine in 1960 and I put it to the museum at Kittochside, East Kilbride in 2000.[16] Many a load we took into Perth, and up to Banffshire, to Oban, Fort William, up through Dalwhinnie and over to Laggan. Last time I was there I stayed with Campbell Slimon and his wife Sheena – he was telling us they didn't get the hydro power till 1963 and I was telling them about my first recollections of Dalwhinnie. It was the late Forties and Campbell's father had the hill-farm then. I was still in the army and I was stationed in Edinburgh and the commanding officer wanted to get all these fellows out of the Midlands of England to see the hills. So because I was of the hills, he asked me would I take these boys up every now and then. They had one of the Newfoundlanders' huts at Dalwhinnie and we'd stay in this hut and I would take them right out – you know where *Carn na Caim* is, up on the other side here, and the Farra and up to *Creagan Mòr*, and oh, they'd never seen anything like this before in their lives![17] I always wanted to be among the hills and I spent the happiest years of my life among shepherds, stalkers and hill farmers.

Endnotes

1   The 'to let' column in the *Stratheam Herald* carried advertisements for the seasonal rental (e.g. Aug. 31, 1929): 'PERTHSHIRE, Glenartney, 8 Miles from Comrie Dalclathic Lodge (Furnished), and Fishing to Sub-Let or Lease for Season. 2 Public Rooms, 8 Bedrooms, Bath-Room, 3 Servants' Bedrooms; good offices; garage; men's rooms, Grounds, 12 Acres. (Enquire by Telephone).' The men's room may refer to a smoking room and a billiard room, which were common features of 'big houses'. The telephone was in the estate office.

2   A 'hirsel' refers to an allotted area of pasturage to be grazed by a flock of sheep and is also used to refer to a flock of sheep amounting to the number looked after by one shepherd or the flock on one small farm. *Glen Sionnach* is Gaelic, the glen of the fox.

3   'Marags' is the Anglicised plural of the Gaelic, *marag,* a pudding, and the plural, puddings, is *maragan.*

4   Both spellings are used by different families in Balquhidder, Fergusson (Muirlaggan) and Ferguson (Gartnafuaran).

5   The Balquhidder landowner was David Carnegie [1830–1890] whose grandfather emigrated to Sweden where he set up a brewing company, 'Carnegie Porter' (Founded in 1817, it is now part of the Carlsberg Group.) Having decided to use his inherited wealth to return in his homeland, David Carnegie purchased the Glenbuckie Estate, which included the 'big house' of Stronvar, and several hill farms to the north shore of Loch Voil, Balquhidder.

6   University of St Andrews Libraries and Museums Photographic Collections, Stronvar House, Balquhidder, 1911, (Ref. ID: JV-70662-A).

7   The OS maps have the Anglicized rendition 'Corrymuckloch'.

8   Famously the narrowest mountain ridge in Britain, the *Aonach Eagach Ridge* (the notched ridge) runs along the northern edge of Glen Coe, stretching east–west and including two Munros, *Sgùrr nam Fiannaidh* (the peak of the Fingalians) and *Meall Dearg* (the red hill). Pat's son Duncan recalled that on his father's 80th birthday, December 5, 1992, "in the middle o winter, we donned our hill-boots to walk in single file along the *Aonach Eagach Ridge* – just one last time and a dram by the fireside at the end o the day."

9   Davies, O. 'Aughentaine Castle' in *Ulster Journal of Archaeology* 2 (1939), pp. 72–82.

10   James Fergusson (Jimmy Mùirlaggan) was recorded in 1958 by Gaelic folklorist Calum Maclean of the School of Scottish Studies. See, https://www.tobarandualchais.co.uk/person/2382?l=en See also the local magazine, *The Belfry*, Winter, 2018, memories of Jimmy Muirlaggan; online <https://issuu.com/lochearntourism/docs/thebelfrywinter2018_9_lo_res/6>.

11   Photographs in University of St Andrews Libraries and Museums Photographic Collections, Glenlyon, Perthshire, 2011 (Ref. ID: ALB-12-25-1 and ALB-12-37-1).

12   The Wills family (from Bristol), amassed considerable wealth from the tobacco trade. Sir Ernest Wills, who took over the family company, was a very keen sportsman and fly-fishing enthusiast so he bought the Highland Perthshire estate, which covered over 250 square miles and included deer forests, hill sheep farms, the River Lyon, stretches of the River Tay and other salmon rivers. *Perth and Kinross Fabian Society, 'The Acreocracy of Perthshire, p. 8.*

13   The condition of the house allocated to Mervyn and other estate workers was not unusual in his day. Perthshire forester John McEwen recalled his childhood in Glen Lyon when his father was a shepherd-forester on Garth Castle estate, owned by millionaire Sir Donald Currie, of Currie Shipping Lines. Living conditions for estate workers were Spartan and "every drop of water had to be carried up a very steep slope" from the Rannoch Burn to the house. The family moved to an estate in Argyllshire where they were allocated a dilapidated, rat-ridden 'but-and-ben', more like a hovel than a house, with a run-down garden. It took over two years to get rid of the rats and longer to cultivate the garden. John McEwen, 'Introduction' (p. 1-9) *Who Owns Scotland?*

14   In 1964, Anne Ross of the School of Scottish Studies recorded Bob Bisset talking about Glen Lyon traditions; see <https://www.tobarandualchais.co.uk/person/3795?l=en>. See also, the online *Stalking Magazine*, 'A Very Special Character', <https://www.thestalkingdirectory.co.uk/threads/a-very-special-character.175095/>.

15   In her autobiographic account of life in Glen Lyon, Alexandra Stewart remembers Glen Lyon School, see *The Glen that Was,* pp 47–48. Her family settled in Glen Lyon in the 1600s and her father, shoemaker Alexander Stewart (1852–1941) described life in the glen in his book *A Highland Parish* (1928).

16   The National Museum of Rural Life, East Kilbride. The lorry is on display on Level 1, described as "Four-wheeled lorry with Mervyn K. Browne, Milton of Ardtalnaig painted on each door, made by Commer, 1956". The Museum reference is W.2000.41.1. See <https://www.nms.ac.uk/explore-our-collections/collection-search-results/lorry/419009>.

17   See Ordnance Survey maps OS25: 050 (Ben Alder, Loch Ericht & Loch Laggan); OS25: 393 (Ben Alder, Loch Ericht & Loch Laggan); OS50: 042 (Glen Garry & Loch Rannoch)

CHAPTER 10

Lighting Up the Glens and Villages

Nan Doig [1912–2014]: When we moved to Glen Lednock in 1929 and took the lease of Balmuick, we had a good double-burner paraffin lamp. It was on a long stand that stood about a foot high and in 1953, when we farmed in Blairnroar at the Straid, we had a Tilley for the kitchen and for the rest of the house it was just the little paraffin lamps. We thought nothing of it. We had a good, warm stove in the kitchen and the Straid was a nice place to live – it had a square in front of the house with the buildings at the sides of it. Along one side was the barn, the cart shed, the stable and then the loft and the barn, and down the other side was the byre and the turnip shed, then another shed, and there was the bothy down in the far end.

Bobby Thomson: I mind the cat used to sleep in the bothy – it could come into the house during the day or in the evening, but at night it went to the bothy.

ND: Oh, we had many happy days at the Straid. We were just two field breadths from where the Blairnroar Hall was built, and that was just across the road from the school, so that people using the hall for a dance or anything, could go across and use the school toilets – well the ladies went, the gents didn't bother. They were very homely [welcoming and friendly] dances we had up there – everyone felt at home.

George Carson [1930–2014]: Hamish Reid used to play for the dances and he played for the Blairnroar Burns Supper for years and years. The old hall's not there now, but it was at the crossroads as you go up towards Braco from Comrie, where the telephone box is – the Blairnroar Hall was along there. And Isabel, Pat MacNab's wife, was a stalwart in the Blairnroar Hall, and so was my wife, Mamie – oh, the whole lot of them! It was a great place, with great dances![1]

ND: And at the end of the hall there was a sort of kitchen bit, and we made the tea in there. We took along the water for the tea and boiled it in an urn on a paraffin stove. It was the Rural [WRI] committee that would usually do this, and if you had the paraffin stove on

about six o' clock then it was ready for the tea about half past nine or something. We had some great nights there. The electricity came along to Blairnroar whilst we were there.

Helen (Grewar) Gardiner: I mind at Mailermore we had the Tilley in the kitchen, and there was also one in Mum and Dad's room – they had a spacious bedroom, and there was a couple of sofas there, so we generally sat there in the winter evenings with the fire on. The cat got to sit at the fire till about ten, then it went into the shed for the night. So, we had a Tilley in that room too, and for the other rooms we had paraffin lamps, wee glass lamps, the ones with the wick. And oh, and I remember the "Toby long" [ornamental paraffin lamp]! I haven't seen one of these for a long time.

Margaret Bennett: And where did you get the paraffin?

Helen G: There was a firm down in Comrie used to come round with a van, because a lot of people were on paraffin at the time. If you'd a paraffin heater in the bathroom that would keep it nice and warm, and it would keep the pipes from freezing in the winter.

Billy Gardiner: There was a lot o vans at one time. When we were young it was a pony and float came round, wi the likes o Campbell Fruit Merchants fae Muthill, and when vans became common you'd see Lipton's an the Co-op vans fae Crieff. Miller in Comrie had a very big area selling paraffin and lamp fittings, up the glens, over to Blackford and that way. Dishy Miller sold a huge amount o paraffin.

MB: Dishy Miller?

Pat MacNab [1912–2011]: Aye, Dishy Miller's was a china shop and she sold everything. Mrs Miller was the agent for the rabbit skins and when I'd have them at home, I would fill them with newspaper and she always gave me top price. She would pay eight pence a skin for them, so you could make a few bob. And you could buy your paraffin there.

Muriel (McGregor) Malloy: And we sold paraffin at Jenny's when I worked in the shop. It came in a big drum with a spigot on it, and folk would bring in their paraffin can, a gallon can, or a half-gallon, and we'd fill it. A lot o folk had paraffin heaters. But it was the gas lighting in Comrie when we were young, and the shops were lit with gas lamps. At home we just had the one lamp in the living room – it was on the wall above the fireplace, and it came out like a wee bracket. It had a glass globe on it, with a kind of mantle inside it, and you'd to be careful lighting it because it was very fragile. There was a wee knob you turned on the gas to light it, then after it was lit you could turn it up to be brighter or down if you didn't need much light.

MB: Was there street lighting?

Billy: There was a gas lamp at the end of that lane oot there an a man came an lit it at night, Colin Gillies, an then he put it out in the morning. Mind, I told you there was a gas-works in Comrie?

Muriel: There were two gas lamps at the school, one at each end of the building, to light up that area at night. They were on iron brackets, and I think it was the janitor who put on the lights at the school. I cannae mind teachers lighting gas lamps in the classroom. Uncle Willie had a gas lamp outside the smiddy across from the library there; sometimes it'd be getting dark when he was shoeing horses. I remember when we used to go to the dances, it was gas lamps on the walls of the village hall.

Sarah Black: On the farm we always made sure we had candles and matches handy.

Muriel: There used to be people in the village made candles. They had a mink farm [Dalchonzie] and when they stopped that they started making these candles. They must have made a lot o them because a friend of mine used to take boxes of candles all the way down to England to sell them. But dinna ask me how they made them!

Jean Innes 'Jean the Braes' [1900–97] [2]: We made our own candles down the Braes [of Balquhidder]. In November they killed a fat sheep. People wouldn't want that now, but it had to be *fat,* and father used to go in and look at it, and if the sheep wasn't fat enough [he'd ask] "Who chose this one?". And there'd be an awful row! So they chose the fattest sheep they could get. And the fat (suet) that wasn't used in the white puddings and haggis and different things, that fat was all boiled down for candles. And it was put in great big pots and sat on the grate to melt, then that was sieved into basins and left. And then when it got hard you scraped the foot [of the block of lard to remove unwanted matter] and that was done three times till it came out all pure. And when that solidified it was rolled in paper and put in a wooden barrel. And that was the candle fat.

And then late in November, or the beginning of December, on a day when there wasn't much wind [to affect the temperature of the kitchen stove] there'd be a huge, big pot sitting on the grate to melt this big block of fat. And when all the fat melted, the floor was covered with newspaper and then another great big pot was placed on that, in the middle of the floor. And then there was a trestle went from one end of the pot to the other end, and two bits of stick placed over it, and we'd cut up the wicks to hang down over the pot. We'd prepared all this the night before we made the candles, because it took the whole day to make them. There were eight wicks on each stick, about that much [**2** inches] apart, hanging over the sticks, and they were placed so you could reach from a chair in the middle. And somebody made a wee chair for me at the end, and I had two wee sticks for my candles – that was when I was very wee!

And when everything was ready, with the melted fat in the pot on the stove, the other big pot was filled with boiling water then the boiling grease from the stove was lifted in a scoop and into a pail to top up the pot on the floor. Then you lifted one of the sticks with the wicks and you dipped these in and out, and in and out, and in and out, and so the candles grew. And you see you would have eight eights, that's sixty-four, so you would have a lot of candles. And they were left hanging over the sticks to harden for a day, then another day, because they had to be really hard. Then they were stored in a box like this [about a foot square] with newspaper at the bottom, all round the sides, and newspaper put on top of every row until you got up to the top and the whole thing was covered – if you put newspaper the mice didn't go for them because they didn't like the print, the ink. And that box of candles went up into the loft – we'd an attic upstairs, a big loft, and the candles were kept there; I remember the very place.

MB: *Did that sort of a candle have a smell to it?*

Jean: Well, it had a pleasant smell. Oh, they were good candles. Of course there was no electricity in those days.

Billy: Doon at Lawers they made their own electricity. Away back, ye ken, aw thae estates had electricity, an Sir Robert Dundas had what they called a belting machine, for the electricity at Dunira.[3] It's made o brass, copper plates, copper discs that went roon an roon, driven by a belt. I mind it was beside the river there doon there – it's water-driven an it's reckoned tae be one of the earliest in Scotland. As far as I know it's still there yet, generating electricity.

MB: *So that's a long, long time before the hydro schemes.*

Billy: Oh aye, that was way back. The Hydro didn't come here till the Fifties, but there wis engineers here for maybe two or three years before they built that dam in Glen Lednock and they used to bore down into the stone, you ken, in preparation.

MB: *They'd maybe survey the rivers and lochs too?*

Billy: We had some very, very dry summers during the war, in fact you could walk across the Ruchill with dry feet, walking on the stones, and yet that Milntuim Burn never went dry. I wondered how did they know that that burn wouldnae dry up? When they built Cultybraggan camp in 1941, they needed water for four thousand prisoners and maybe five or six hundred auxiliary staff, guards, office workers, and all that water came aff the Milntuim Burn.[4] So when they were starting the Hydro schemes, I asked a civil engineer how they'd know there would be enough water for the camp, or for the hydro-scheme. He told me, in cases like that they would monitor that flow for at least two years. But you'd think that if they'd been up there putting poles in the burn an all that, you'd think the farmers an everybody would ken. That's a big mystery to me, that.

Arthur Allen (civil engineer): In 1947 I was asked if I would come to Comrie and start some initial surveying and supervise some drilling into the rocks. This is necessary to see what is underneath where your dam is going. Another thing was to take measurements in some of the rivers and streams, especially if we could manage to catch them at very low water time.

MB: How did you get involved in hydro dams and hydro engineering?

Arthur: When I was a student, I prepared a paper which was called 'Power from Water' and I delivered it in London and in Edinburgh, and the Institution of Civil Engineers awarded me its Miller Prize for my paper.

MB: Where did you study?

Arthur: In Loughborough. In those days, the Engineering Department of the university awarded a Diploma in Engineering and so I also took an external B.Sc. (Eng.) degree from London University. And I had a friend who was with a firm of consultant engineers in London, Sir M. MacDonald & Partners, and he said, "You should come here because there's some interesting work going on – we've got some hydro-electric work". My friend convinced me to apply for a job, so I went to Victoria Street in London – a construction engineers' mecca – and after a very short interview they asked me if I would come up to Scotland.

MB: Sir M. MacDonald? Did you know what the M stood for or where he was from?

Arthur: Yes, Murdoch. He was from Inverness.

MB: With a name like Murdoch, I wonder if he was a Gaelic speaker?

Arthur: Yes, I think he was.[5] There's an interesting story about why he never used the name 'Murdoch' – when he was in Egypt it was confused with the name Mordecai, so that's why it was Sir M. MacDonald & Partners.

MB: What was he doing in Egypt?

Arthur: He worked on some big civil engineering projects – the construction of the Aswan Dam and some big canals.[6] He was the resident engineer on the heightening of the Aswan Dam and he designed irrigation schemes and the Sennar Dam on the Blue Nile, and major engineering improvements to Alexandria Harbour.

He became director-general of irrigation for the Egyptian Government, and he's remembered for his design and construction of the head works of the Menoufia Canal and other waterways. He was knighted in Egypt, and when he came back to Britain, he formed his company. When I started working for the firm, he was up in years and was easing himself out of the firm, and his son Roderick was becoming the senior partner.

MB: So when you joined them in the Forties, this would have been in the hey-day of Tom Johnston's proposal for all those hydro-electric schemes?[7]

Arthur: Yes. There are more than seventy hydro dams in Scotland and over fifty hydro schemes.

MB: I used to hear about Tom Johnston from my dad – he was the resident engineer on the Nostie Bridge power station (Lochalsh) and then on the one at Storr Lochs (Skye).

Arthur: Oh yes, they were part of the North of Scotland Hydro-Electric Board. That changed into Scottish Hydro-Electric, and Scottish and Southern.

MB: I was too young to remember Nostie Bridge (1948)[8], but I remember when they switched on the power in Skye – 1952. While they were working on that scheme there was a cable railway to the top of the hill for carrying bags of cement and equipment, and one Sunday my dad took us there for a family picnic – no doubt he wanted to inspect the job, but nobody in Skye dared work on Sunday. Anyway, he rolled up his donkey jacket like a cushion and put it on the bottom of the wee railway wagon, and he lifted me inside, so I rode to the top of the hill in the wagon while Mummy and Daddy and my three sisters walked up the 647 steps[9] – I'll never forget it! [laughter]

Arthur: Two of the schemes were allocated to Sir M. MacDonald & Partners. The one I worked on was the Lednock-Earn Scheme, which is part of the Breadalbane Scheme,[10] and the other one was the Shin Scheme up in Sutherland.

MB: You were a very young engineer to be tackling this, were you not?

Arthur: I think that's right. I came to Scotland first in 1947 and that means I was 21. I remember I took the mainline London-Inverness train to Gleneagles, where I waited on another platform until a local train, Stirling to Crieff, caught up with me. It stopped in Crieff station for about an hour, until it could take the school children to Comrie – and I got off at Comrie Station, which was near the school. So I arrived in Comrie for the first time on August the 2nd, 1947.

MB: Up until then, had there been no electricity supply whatsoever?

Arthur: There was a very early hydro scheme at the Turret, without a dam – not the one they have now. There was just a small weir across the river, and that provided electricity to Crieff, and I think it might have come out towards Comrie as well.

MB: Maybe as far as Ochtertyre House or some of the other big houses on the road to Comrie.

Billy: The big estates made their own electricity, Lawers, Dunira an up at Invergeldie, they made their own electricity [for the Lodge, c. 1.5 miles south of Loch Lednock and over 4 miles north of Comrie]. An the Miss Coates had a big hoose in St Fillans – St. Serf's they caa'd it, but it's the Four Seasons Hotel noo – an the two ladies had a big bit o grun at the back, wi hens , an there was a man who fed the hens an done the gairden, an he looked after the heating an lights an things like that.[11] But it was gas lights we had in the ordinary hooses in the village. I mind later on, when they built thae wooden hooses in Earn Place – they were for the engineers.

Arthur: There were three other engineers from the firm came up with me to the Comrie area.

MB: Four engineers?

Arthur: Yes – each one had a particular project: I was to look after everything to do with the Lednock dam; another engineer would look after the power station at St Fillans; another was to be responsible for the aqueducts and tunnels we have over to Glenalmond; and the fourth engineer took care of the Dalchonzie scheme from St Fillans to Dalchonzie. The catchment area in total is 90 square miles, and the levels of water needed are all decided. So, during heavy rainfalls, when there's a lot of water in that 90 square miles, the plan is to devise a way it will flow back in to Glen Lednock and be there for use during a drought in the summer. The preliminary surveys are needed in the calculations to decide how much you need to have in storage, and how high your dam has to be in the valley chosen for it. Obviously, Glen Lednock was a prime candidate for the dam – it had been a reservoir of some sort before. If we think about the last glaciation, which was about 10,000 years ago, the ice from the north came over Scotland and travelled south, and there was quite a depth or height of ice over Glen Lednock and places of that height. The glacier, being pushed down and up at Glen Lednock, scoured out the softer material upstream from Spout Rolla. And looking at the geology, there is a ridge of very resistant rock that the glaciation couldn't tear away, and it had left behind a basin.

MB: Were you involved in the design of Lednock dam?

Arthur: Yes. It's a diamond-head buttress dam.[12]

MB: Do the buttresses have a particular purpose?

Arthur: Yes. I decided on buttresses because the rock was sound enough to take high stresses. You don't get that with more common massive gravity dams (such as Pitlochry); they're really like a huge block of cheese spread across the valley.

MB: Was the fact that the dam is in an area known for earthquake tremor a consideration in your planning?

Arthur: Yes, it was. Comrie was noted for its earthquakes; the 10 years in which most occurred was 1870 to 1880, but anyway, because of that, I felt there should be some recognition of that made in the planning. The result of an earthquake, assuming that the dam stays perfectly ok, is that the dam tries to move with the shock, and therefore the water drops. And then the dam comes back and it rises again, so there is this undulating pressure on the dam and the shock on the base of the dam when the earthquake passes through. In the case of Lednock (working out the calculations before the construction) the assumption was made that, instead of it storing water, it was storing an imaginary fluid that was 15% heavier than water. So, the mobility in an earthquake was accounted for by imagining the dam to hold a heavier liquid.

MB: And do the buttresses have a function in that, in the bigger picture?

Arthur: No, they were a fundamental choice of a more economical design: much less concrete needed than on the massive gravity dams I mentioned. During the actual construction, some engineers thought I was being a bit daring as I opted for a process which had been used in the United States a lot – it's a waste product from coal-fired power stations, known as 'fly ash' and I was the instigator of using it in Lednock dam. The dam was constructed with 20% of fly ash and 80% of cement...[13] The diamond-head buttresses are capable of taking a load that's 15% more than water. Some of the pressure on the upstream face is squeezed down into the buttress – that's where the concentration of stress comes. Concrete nowadays can withstand much higher stresses than just holding [the weight of] water, so if you trim down the [volume of] concrete a little bit that's economical, and we also have an economy in substituting 20% of the cement with fly ash. The buttresses are over 70 years old now, so they are getting old and tired now, not quite as pretty as they once were.

MB: Once the dam had been designed, plans drawn, and estimates submitted, how long did it take before the contractors moved in and the work started? A year or so?

Arthur: Longer than that. Part of that length of time was political – somebody in the politician system said, "We haven't got any more money to build anymore hydro-electric schemes...", something of that sort.[14] A lot of dams and hydro schemes were being built, and I think we were one of the last. So, we had a gap of six or seven years, where the firm had to find something else for us to do. Sir M. MacDonald & Partners had taken on design-work in London, so we were involved in that and, once that had been done, many of the young engineers wanted to continue and get the construction experience. But they had to hang around, and another large scheme that the firm was involved in was a Grade 2 flood protection scheme from Bedford down to Kings Lynn ... fen country, with a lot of flooding. Sir Murdoch MacDonald worked on a design to bring that into the 20th century, but the war delayed that. Then in 1949 he took on the contract for the Great Ouse Flood Protection Scheme, which he designed, so I had some experience on that. The delay in starting on Lednock needn't have been that long, and even when we did start, there was further delay. One time, when I was having to kill time with junior engineers, we did some initial surveying, stream measurements, river flow, for a [proposed] scheme on the River Ruchill ... it has since been developed into the local government pattern of measuring river flows right across the board.[15]

When the work eventually started, the contracts were divided between the firm called Taylor Woodrow – the contractors for the dam – and Mitchell Construction, who were contractors for all the rest of the work, the tunnels, the aqueducts, the power station and such like.

MB: When the work begins, does the resident engineer continue with the job to the end?

Arthur: He's there right through the job, and when it's finished, there's a maintenance period after that. I forget exactly what it was in Lednock's case, it may have only been a year, so that if any faults come to light in that time there would be an investigation and every detail had to be right or fixed.

MB: And when the contractors and the workforce moved in, where did they come from and where did they all live?

Arthur: Of the 125 workers on the dam, roughly one-third of the manpower was Scottish, one-third of the workers were Polish, and one-third were Irish. They lived in a construction camp very close to the dam. There is a flattish area at the side of the waterfall, Spout Rolla, and a hutted camp was built there. All of their food was cooked there, and that provided employment for some of Comrie's ladies and men. Comrie, as a community, was very glad to have the extra business in the village. One small illustration was that a newsagent in Comrie would take newspapers up to the dam at the lunch break time, and the 125 or so workers up there would get their newspapers at lunch time. I think he also provided a service of 'could you manage to bring me a so-and-so?' and that would be done. That was commendable on the part of the shopkeeper.

MB: Was it a very noisy site?

Arthur: It was certainly noisy during the excavation of the site where the concrete buttresses and diamond heads were going on to the rock. Before that work started, all the earth had to be cleared away from the rock surface, and then the top 5 feet of rock had to be taken out, because that is what we would have called 'weathered'. And after we went down 5 feet, we were on to the bedrock, to provide a good, solid foundation. In a valley, the excavation involved more than 5 feet, because if you think of going up the side of the valley, if it's 5 feet at one end it will be a lot more than 5 feet at the other end. I should mention that there were thirteen buttresses, though I'm not superstitious! And on either side of the buttresses, at each end of the dam, was what we called the 'east gravity section' and the 'west gravity section': these were the solid wedges because it wasn't worthwhile cutting down into buttresses and hammerheads, where it wasn't high enough to justify it.

MB: When they were excavating, how did all that crushed rock or fallen rock impact on the site – was it trucked away by lorries?

Arthur: Yes, and a lot went into building up the ground around Dalchonzie [dam] where the land was low. The topsoil at Dalchonzie was removed and rock was put in, then the topsoil was put back on the top.

MB: So the engineers worked out the efficiency of moving rock between the sites?

Arthur: Yes, that's right. A lot of collaboration between the engineers and the other sites.

MB: When the Hydro work started how did it affect Comrie?

Billy: Well, there was two bobbies in the place for a start [laughs]. Aye, two bobbies – I don't know whether the second bobby was just on duty or what. They had a camp up there, ken where the caravan site is along there on the A85? That was a big camp for the workers – the single men or men without their families stayed in the camp.

Muriel: I can remember all the ones that came in, all the English people and the Irish, they were in digs all over the place, and Mitchell Construction built places for them to stay at the Twenty Shilling Wood: that was Mitchell Construction's camp.[16]

John F. O'Donnell ('Big John'): A lot o men came over from Ireland particularly from Donegal and Mayo to work on the hydro dams. A tunnel tiger could basically earn three times what a farm labourer could earn, so the money was the magnet.

Billy: There was a Pole up there who knew my brother, an he worked in the tunnels ...The camp was in the Twenty Pence wood, well of course it's the Twenty Shilling Wood now you ken.[17] Then the Taylors whatever they're called, the firm who had the contract for the actual dam, they built thae timber hooses doon in the Glebe an they were for all their surveyors an engineers.

Muriel: Comrie was thriving – the shops, the hotels, the garage, everything. It was a big way of doing construction work, big lorries and dumpers and a lot of the vans and lorries came into MacNab's Garage for petrol – that was on the main street where that car park is now. My cousin married Bill Pratt; he was from England, and he worked as a 'tea boy' and he drove up to the camp in an old Trojan truck and got all the things from the shop for all the men. I was working at Jenny MacGregor's shop and there was another tea boy called Alec MacArthur who used to come into the shop for stuff and he'd make Jenny blush like naebudy's business – she was a spinster, and he used to make her blush wi the things he'd say! You should've heard him!

And Geordie Watt who had the newsagents in the village had another paper-shop in a wee hut up at the dam. It was for the men, and it opened every lunchtime and stayed open till the evening. My sister Agnes went up to work in the shop with Geordie Watt, then I remember one night she wasnae very well, so I went up in her place, and this wee German man said, "and where is Agnes tonight?" I says, "she's no very well tonight, but I'm her sister". "No, no, no," he said, "Same mother, different father!"

That Alec MacArthur also had a Scottish Dance band, and we had dances in Comrie every weekend up in the public hall – that's all flats now, but that was the dance hall. And we had all the bands every Friday and Saturday night, Jimmy Shand, Ian Powrie, all these bands, it was wonderful. And back then in Comrie they used to hold the Farmers' Ball and the Masons' Ball every year, and then there was the Mitchell's Ball. and all the local girls went, with long gowns on.

MB: Did you even wear long evening gloves with the ball gowns?

Muriel: Oh yes! It was the same when the Cultybraggan Camp was on – all the shop girls got invited to the officers' mess for a dance so the army officers and staff would have someone to dance with. They took us up on a lorry, and brought us all back in the lorry and it was a great night. It was held in one of the Nissen huts but there was no proper ladies loo – and when you went to the loo it was just a room wi buckets in the middle of the floor! And we had the long frocks on and you're sitting on this bucket with a big frock, it was hilarious! But Comrie was a great place to stay when we were young.

MB: Did the workers up at the Taylor Woodrow camp come down to Comrie on a Friday or Saturday night?

Arthur: Certainly at the weekends they would come down to Comrie. Taylor Woodrow, the contractor on the dam, had a passenger-carrying vehicle and it always had its own driver. I think at the weekends he might well've driven down the Glen Lednock to the village, then at 10.30 it would pick them up again. If anyone missed it, well too bad.

MB: That's a long walk home after a dance – over seven miles! Did the work cease on a Sunday?

Arthur: Yes, in those days nobody worked on Sunday. Oh, I still think it's very sensible. They were off for a half-day Saturday and all-day Sunday.

MB: Nowadays when you look on a construction site the place is covered in bright yellow and orange jackets and waistcoats. In your day, what did the engineers wear?

Arthur: All we had were protective hats – just a hard hat.

MB: Photographs in the Fifties and Sixties taken on building sites show men with their donkey jackets.

Arthur: You don't hear the word these days, but yes, we'd all have donkey jackets. They were warm though they weren't luminous, and they weren't waterproof. In an emergency, if you had to go out in the wet, there would be a heavy raincoat you could put on, a navy-blue one.

MB: What about the men, the labourers, the tunnel workers, the cement workers, how were they attired?

Arthur: They certainly went to work in their own clothes. They may have had some waterproof clothing, but nowhere near entire outfits you see now.

MB: 'Big John' O'Donnell in Muthill has quite a few photographs from the Donegal workers. His father was one of the men who came to work on the Turret dam. But the men who worked on the tunnels were labouring in fairly grim conditions, with clouds of dust.

Arthur: Tunnelling was the more hazardous job, although we did have one fatality on the dam, someone falling from a height. George Carson's wife, Mamie, was the nurse on the site with the tunnel contractors, Mitchells.

Muriel: I mind when Mamie nursed up at the camp – Mamie MacPherson she was then, before she married George, and some of the local folk used to work there too.

George Carson [1930–2014]: Mamie had been a nurse at the scheme when they were building the dam and all the tunnels for all the water. There was a medical station, like a hospital, at the Twenty Shilling Wood, in Mitchell's Construction camp. There were 500 men living there and they had to have a policeman in the camp. He and his wife hadn't been married long, and his wife was expecting – she and Mamie were the only two women in the camp and there was not a word out of place amongst all the men. Hard, hard men.

The men did 12-hour shifts and Mamie was the only nurse there, so she was on duty 24/7. She'd often go out in the middle of the night if there had been a rockfall and somebody got hurt. She ran the sick bay with a rod of iron, in that none of the bosses were allowed in the sick bay because they'd say, "That man could be working." But that was her domain, and Mamie would say, "No, he's not fit to work" She got on very well with the men and they'd have done anything for her. There was never a bad word or anything. The only thing then was the culture of smoking. Everybody smoked, all the men smoked, and they'd be lying in bed and no matter how ill they were they'd still have their fags beside them. That's the way it was away back then, and Mamie smoked – it didn't do any of them any good.

Big John: My father was among the men from Donegal and Mayo came to Scotland to work on the Hydro dams in the 1950s. It was dangerous work, full of dust and noise. Well, the danger went hand in hand with the money and it was torture working inside these tunnels – they were young at the time, and you wouldnae think about the long-term effects. For a lot of the men, their lungs were knackered – emphysema and everything so a lot o them died way before their time, in their forties and fifties, just way too soon, and back then there was no compensation. My dad was seventy when he died, but he mainly worked on the exterior of the dams doing cement work and such like. They still had all that cement dust and no mask or anything – a cloth cap doesn't really do it!

MB: *I can't imagine the amount of cement needed or how many cement mixers! Arthur was saying that the Lednock dam was constructed with 80% cement and 20% fly ash.*

Arthur: That's one thing that we haven't covered as far as the dam is concerned: concrete. When it hardens it shrinks a little bit, but the hammerheads of the buttresses were 50 feet from one end to the other, so you might get half an inch to an inch shrinkage.

MB: *Were you pouring concrete into wooden shuttering?*

Arthur: Yes, it was wooden shuttering. And because concrete shrinks, you have to have something there in the gap that will not shrink when the buttresses are shrinking. When they were casting concrete there was a mould put in at each end of the hammerhead, and that was referred to as a 'key'; it was a little bit wider at the join with the next buttress than it was on the inside. The buttresses are all the same shape and size, so the same shape of shuttering was used for the whole lot. Then, when pouring the concrete, it had to be done in stages; you brought it up 5 feet at a time, and the wooden boxes were such that you could slide a piece out from the middle and break them off and they would come up, and you are left with this hole, roughly 6 inches by a foot in each head as it comes together. The filling of that was left for a long time, say half the total height of the dam before bitumen was poured into it.

MB: How high is the dam?

Arthur: Just over 130 feet high, 40 meters. So [when the dam had reached a height of c. 75 feet] we poured the bitumen in the gaps, because if you are pouring in longer lengths of bitumen the stuff at the bottom may harden before you have got it up to the top. To keep that from happening before it was completely filled, a very lengthy U-tube was put in this gap, right from the top of the dam to the bottom. For this enormous U-tube we were using piping for gas, and that has a screwed connection between two lengths of pipe. The connector is screwed on to the bottom one, it goes halfway down, and then you screw-in the top pipe on the other half. The idea was that we would have a boiler at the top producing steam, and we would just pass it in one side of the U-tube, and it would come out the other side a lot colder, but it would have melted the bitumen or softened it. The difficulty that wasn't anticipated was these joints in the tube were not steam-tight, so steam came out and into the bitumen and bubbled through up at the top. I got a new pair of trousers out of the insurance company! [laughter] So, we had to rethink this stage.

MB: To solve the question of expansion in the concrete, did you choose bitumen for the gaps because it's got 'give', whereas concrete doesn't?

Arthur: Yes. A lot of thinking, with a big firm in Dundee that dealt with bitumen and bitumen products ... There is a standard test for bitumen, and the one that was chosen for the dam was Penetration 70. Thankfully, what was also available was narrow copper tubing; the inner diameter would be about a quarter of an inch or something like that, and we threaded electric cable into that, and pushed it round the bottom, connected it up, and it heated the bitumen.

MB: Did it heat it slowly?

Arthur: Yes, heated it slowly, and we didn't have any mishaps at the top of the dam. That is engineering: you learn by pushing the limits a bit too far. But that bitumen is still there, and it is still quite watertight; there is a little bit of leakage but not significant.

MB: I've been looking at the surface of the dam – when shuttering is removed you sometimes see the sharp edge of a join, where the cement has seeped through. Is the Lednock dam exactly the way it was when you removed the shuttering, or did it have to be refinished?

Arthur: Sometimes when you take off the shuttering it's a bit rough, so if there were little fins, or little porous pieces, open pieces, where the cement had not come through, we would go up afterwards, filling in pieces and rubbing rough pieces off. I can remember I was laughed at by a party of visiting Russians because [when they saw what we were doing] the Russians who came round said "Ah, you are finishing the dam as a bride for her wedding!" [laughter]

MB: He recognised there was a touch of the perfectionist about the engineer who didn't want to see blemishes on this massive piece of magnificent work. When you were pouring the cement, I imagine you could only pour so much at a time and had to wait for that to dry before pouring in more?

Arthur: It was all done in 5-foot lifts.

MB: And how long would it take for a 5-foot lift to dry and be ready for the next one?

Arthur: I think we allowed a week. But before there was any such thing as concrete, dams were built with great big stones together with mortar joints. Nevertheless, as a precaution against cracks, it was decided not to concrete more than a certain length at a time.

MB: You had squads of men working – labourers, foremen, etc. How many would you have had building the dam?

Arthur: It was about 125; probably a little bit less, because there may have been a few supervisors and people in the laboratory at the dam. Every so often a sample of concrete would be taken away and made into a tube in an iron mould, and there was a crushing machine in the laboratory. After 28 days the concrete had to take a certain load before it suddenly cracked.

MB: Was this to test the pressure it could withstand?

Arthur: Yes, and another precaution we took because we didn't have that test result for 28 days, and we could have been two or three lifts higher up when we would discover that was a bad one down there. So, we had a preliminary test at seven days to see if we were getting round about the stress we would expect at that earlier stage. [18]

MB: Looking at a map of the tunnels and the connections across the whole scheme it's remarkable how they were all planned and how calculations were worked out – it's so ingenious.[19]

Big John: And there's miles o tunnels.

Arthur: Yes. And at certain locations there are big shafts from the surface into the tunnels – maybe 30 feet in diameter at a guess. The reason is, say there is a thunderstorm in the area while the scheme is working, it may stop the transition system from working, which then automatically stops the turbine. If that stops suddenly the water coming towards the turbine would have no place to go, and it would just burst out all of the rocks. So, by providing this large shaft up to a level above Lednock dam, the water rushing towards the power station changes and goes up the shaft until it is higher than the level in Lednock dam, and it will gradually stop the water rising – it will fluctuate up and down for a mile, but gradually less and less fluctuation, and it will settle at the level of the water in Lednock dam. The power station at St Fillans is underground – it's excavated into the rock, just upstream from the third shaft, as we call it. Then from the power station level, there's further excavation up to a level very high above Lednock dam.

Big John: The men who worked on one of the tunnels above St Fillan's power station broke the world record for tunnelling.[20] Dynamite, explosives, massive machines, picks, shovels, you name it, in 1955 they tunnelled through 557 feet of rock in a week . They finished it on October 27, 1955 and they're in the Guinness Book of Records! It was a big cause for celebration at the time, but a lot of them developed lung diseases that shortened their lives.[21] They called them the 'Tunnel Tigers' so I wrote a song to remember them.

The Tunnel Tiger Boys'
by John F. O'Donnell

Chorus:
> They came from Arranmore and all o'er Donegal
> From lovely Achill Island and all around Mayo
> They made their way to Scotland to build the Hydro dams
> Oh, we always will remember them, the Tunnel Tiger boys.

These men they worked at the Lednock Dam when the world record broke
They dug for seven days solid right through the Scottish rock
Five hundred and fifty-seven feet down the tunnel dark and low
And when they made the break-through, boys, the beer it sure did flow.

Chorus:
>   They came from Arranmore ...

So when you're in the Scottish hills and see the mighty dams
Think of the men who built them and tunnelled underground.
Take a moment now to pray, to remember those who died,
For we always should remember them, the tunnel tiger boys. [22]

Arthur: There was a tremendous effort to break the record. That was Mitchell Construction; the tunnels are out of my sphere really. The smaller tunnels are not the fastest to get through because if you're tunnelling a larger one you can have two lines of railway tracks instead of one. Then when you've got a *huge* tunnel it takes longer because you have scaffolding, and ranks of people drilling holes, and blasting. Dangerous work.

MB: Do you have photographs of any of it, or of building the dam?

Arthur: There were official photographs taken at the dam, A4 size in black albums. And I presume they would be the same at the tunnels, all went back to the North of Scotland Hydro-Electric Board in Edinburgh, that changed into Scottish Hydro-Electric, and Scottish and Southern. They will be in an archive. [23]

MB: What an achievement – the whole project, start to finish. How long did it take to complete, to the point where they finally switched on the power?

Arthur: In June 1958 the Secretary of State for Scotland opened the scheme at the power station to let the water start running. I'd gone up in '47 to start the surveying, so that's eleven years.[24]

Muriel: I remember when the dam opened, Taylor Woodrow had a big reception, a dinner, in the George Hotel in Crieff – that's the old hotel that's just been demolished.[25] I was married by then and I moved to Crieff, so I worked in the George Hotel. It was a busy, busy place with a restaurant, they did bed and breakfast, and they did bus tours. Scottish

Brewers had the hotel then, and I was there for years and years, but it's been sold several times over and now it's gone. But I remember the big celebration when the dam opened, Princess Alexandra was the special guest and when they all came to the 'do' in Crieff my mother-in-law and I went up to wait at the tables for all the guests. I mind Arthur – I got to know Arthur and his family quite well because I used to baby-sit for them in Comrie.

Arthur: My family finally moved to Comrie in 1958, when we bought the house in Dalginross. To start with my wife wasn't too keen to move from London, but after a few years of living here, nothing would drag her away from Comrie – she loved it and Comrie has been my home ever since.

Endnotes

1   Perth & Kinross Archive, Acc11/52: M. Bennett interview with George Carson (2010).

2   Mrs Jean Innes (née MacNaughton, known as 'Jean the Braes') was recorded in her home in Inverlochlarig, Balquhidder, March 18, 1990 SA 1990/10. See also M. Bennett, 'A Balquhidder Farm with Mrs. Jean Innes' in *Tocher* 46, pp. 209–215.

3   In 1824 Sir Robert Dundas of Beechwood bought the Dunira Estate from his second cousin, Robert Dundas, who had inherited it from his father, the controversial Sir Henry Dundas [1742–1811].

4   The burn supplied the water-power for the Milntuim Corn Mill. The Milntuim Mill Dam and the mill are shown on the OS map (1st edition, 1843-80). See the National Library of Scotland "Scottish Water Mills Project': (https://maps.nls.uk/projects/mills/) and (direct link) <https://maps.nls.uk/projects/mills/#zoom=16&lat=56.3452&lon=-4.0045>.

5   Murdoch MacDonald [1866–1957] was born and brought up in Inverness where his father was a carter. His mother was from Lochalsh. Following a 5-year apprenticeship with the Highland Railway Company he was appointed assistant civil engineer on the Black Isle line and then main line from Dalnaspidal to Blair Atholl.

6   Smith, Norman. *The Centenary of the Aswan Dam, 1902-2002*. London: Thomas Telford, 2002. See also <https://www.ambaile.org.uk/asset/387/>.

7   Tom Johnston was Secretary of State for Scotland during Churchill's Government (1941–45). In 1943 he introduced a Bill to set up the North of Scotland Hydro-Electric Board to supply electricity to the remoter areas of the Highlands and Islands. He proposed this would not only be a commercial undertaking but would also develop industries, improve conditions and prevent depopulation. I am indebted to my father, civil engineer George Bennett [1917–2009] for taking me on site visits and explaining the background to the development of the hydro schemes. (He had been site engineer on Nostie Power Station, Lochalsh and Storr Lochs Power Station, Skye.)

8   <https://canmore.org.uk/event/882030 >.

9   The funicular railway, see photo: <https://canmore.org.uk/site/283211/skye-storr-lochs-dam>.

10   The Breadalbane Scheme includes six dams and seven power stations, with storage reservoirs linked via tunnels to Loch Earn, Loch Tay, Loch Daimh, and Loch Lyon. Power stations were built at Lednock, St Fillans, Dalchonzie, Finlarig, Lochay, Cashlie and Lubreoch.

11 An advertisement for the 'winter let' of the MacLaggan's house in Comrie confirms an electrical supply in the 1930s. See, *The Strathearn Herald,* Dec. 10, 1938, classified ads (p. 1): Winter let of 'Earnhope', Comrie, 2 public rooms, 5 bedrooms, Bathroom, Electric Light. Telephone Miss MacLaggan.

12 See photos and further details: https://canmore.org.uk/site/164397/loch-lednock-reservoir-and-dam. Also, P. L. Payne, *The Hydro: A Study of the Development of the Major hydro-electric Schemes Undertaken by the North of Scotland Hydro-Electric Board*, 1988 (Aberdeen), pp 24, 161-2;164;168-9;314.

13 See Arthur Charles Allen, B.Sc.(Eng.), A.M.I.C.E. 'Features of Lednock Dam, Including the Use of Fly Ash' in *Proceedings of the Institution of Civil Engineers,* Vol. 13 (2): 179–196, Jan. 1959.

14 Parliamentary debates, see *<https://hansard.parliament.uk/ >* Relevant debates include those held on 4 May 1949; 17 April 1951; 15 Dec. 1952; 2 Oct. 1953.

15 Recording and full transcription, Perth & Kinross Archive, Acc21/12: M. Bennett interview with Arthur Allen, 2014.

16 The camp had accommodation for 500 men as well as a canteen, boiler-house, cinema and hospital. It was in use from 1954 to 57 and later demolished, but in 1963 the site became a caravan park, retaining the concrete bases for Mitchell's bunkhouses as stances for caravans. See, Hall, M and Lowe, A (2002) 'Twenty Shilling Wood, Comrie, Perth and Kinross, Construction Workers' Camp, Temporary Cinema' in *Discovery and Excavation in Scotland* 3, p. 92. < https://archaeologydataservice.ac.uk/archiveDS/archiveDownload?t=arch-753-1/dissemination/pdf/2000/2002.pdf>.

17 The valued rental of land was reckoned in terms of the old Scots mark (or merk), which was equivalent to 13 shillings and 4 pence, hence the terms 'merkland', 'shillingland' and 'pennyland'.

18 ELECTRICITY GENERATING STATION TESTS, 1949. Film (16mm) at NLS by Sir Edward 'Electricity' MacColl, see <https://movingimage.nls.uk/film/6731>.

19 The plans, drawings, pictures, and photographs of the Breadalbane Scheme can be seen at the Perth and Kinross Archive at the A.K. Bell Library. See Mott MacDonald, ref. GB/252/MS140.

20 <https://www.bbc.co.uk/news/world-europe-34934795>.

21   Edward Bramley, whose father was the General Foreman on the tunnel, recounted his memories for the SSE archives. Photos and transcriptions, see <https://www.sserenewables.com/news-and-views/2020/10/a-world-tunnelling-record-65-years-on/ >.

22   <https://youtu.be/hlDeDM9WxyY >.

23   They are now held by Perth and Kinross Council Archive; see: <http://archivecatalogue.pkc.gov.uk/Record.aspx?src=CalmView.Catalog&id=MS140&pos=1>.

24   Newspaper report of the project, 'Hydro-Electric Station at St Fillans' in *Stratearn Herald, July 5, 1957, p. 2.*

25   Newspaper report of the opening, 'Power Station Deep Under Perthshire Hill: St Fillan's Project will be started up today' in *Perthshire Advertiser, June 28, 1958, p. 3.*

Chapter 11

Tourism in the 'Forties and 'Fifties

The BBC "News at One" is a regular talking point, and Billy is quick to pick up on discussion points: "They're aw talkin aboot 'staycations' noo – is this supposed to be something new?"

The word 'staycation' may have been new to most folk at the start of the pandemic, but by December 2020 it was common currency.[1] Yet holiday-makers and tourists have been visiting Strathearn's glens and villages for centuries – memorably, Robert Burns in 1787, Sir Walter Scott in the late 1820s, Queen Victoria and Prince Albert in 1842, and Rudyard Kipling in 1919.[2] For local children, however, the idea of a holiday meant freedom from school, perhaps a week or two with grandparents or a special aunt, a family visit to the city, or a 'day out' at an agricultural show. Looking back on her long summer holidays in Glenartney, Helen Gardiner remembered they were 'a lot o hard work.'

Helen (Grewar) Gardiner: After my Dad died, it wasn't easy to keep it all going and earn a living. So Mum and her sister decided that maybe we should try for summer boarders. People might like to come up the glen and they could be free to wander anywhere they wanted, and they got fed, and got a picnic to take if they wanted, maybe down by the river. So that's what they did, and the visitors came back again and again, every year.

Margaret Bennett: How many rooms did they rent out?

Helen G: Oh, it was quite a big house, and it just depended how many were in the family that came. I think one year we had about ten people – I had to give up my bedroom, of course, but that was quite common wi folk who kept summer visitors. It was a lot o work, and a lot o cooking; breakfast was usually egg and sausages and there was always a lot o dishes for me to wash.

MB: And so did you keep hens so you'd have your own fresh eggs?

Helen G: Yes, we had hens and we had two and a half dozen ducks. We had quite a bit of marshy ground up above the farm so the ducks used to go out there every day, but then they had to be brought home again at night, otherwise the foxes would get them. So one

of my jobs was to go and get the ducks! [laughter] Sometimes when I'd call them they ran the opposite way – eventually they'd head home again and I'd shut them in for the night.

Billy Gardiner: I like tae go doon the gairden in the mornin to let the ducks oot every day. My legs arenae very good noo [at the age of 94] but it aye gets me oot the hoose in this lockdoon. I like the Indian Runners; they stand up very, very straight, an they kinda run, you ken – I just like watchin them, but since that damn fox got two of them, I've only got the two left. Two drakes, but I didnae keep them for the eggs. A lot o the Highlan folk wouldnae eat duck eggs – ma granny wouldnae eat a duck egg and ma grandfaither, he wouldnae eat duck eggs. Ma faither's folk came here generations ago, an none o *his* faimily would eat a duck egg, an ma mother, being fae the Black Isle, she wouldnae eat a duck egg. That's going back to Judaism; there's a lot of these things go back to the Middle East, but that's how a lot o thae older families werenae keen on duck eggs.

MB: I hear that ducks' eggs are very good for baking with. Did your mum bake, Helen?

Helen G: Bake? Nonstop, nonstop! Although I don't remember her baking on a Sunday; maybe at that time there was some sort of 'Thou shalt not bake on Sundays' kinda thing... I'm not sure.

MB: And did you have to serve at the breakfast tables every morning?

Helen G: No, I didn't want to do that, but guess who had to do all the shopping for the summer visitors? Going away down to Comrie with the bike and the big basket on it, then having to cycle back up with it full. All these steep hills – oh dear, I can't say I enjoyed that

bit! We did have vans up the glen, but again it was just once a week they came. Then of course, there was no refrigeration, just the dairy, with a stone floor, a window that was sort of facing outside. The dairy was big enough and cold enough for these big milk basins – after the milking we'd set out the milk for the cream, and then you made the butter.

MB: And who did the churning?

Helen G: I'll give you one guess! [laughter] We had a wooden churn, you know the kind, it stands on end, and it's got wooden paddles inside, and a swivel lid? And it was my job to wind the handle.

MB: And with so many visitors there would be an awful lot of cleaning to do.

Helen G: There was, although that didn't seem so bad because Auntie had been a housemaid at Ochtertyre; she was working for the Murrays in that big house on the hill. She was good at all that and she loved it – she'd quite happily have stayed at Ochtertyre, but she was needed on the farm and that was it.

MB: She probably knew that Burns and Sir Walter Scott also visited the Murrays, not to mention Queen Victoria – it's changed a lot over the years. Did you keep in touch with any of the summer visitors?

Helen G: Oh, it's such a long time ago now, but only two or three months ago I was looking at the obituaries in the *Courier* and I saw the death of one of the ladies. She and her husband and son always used to come, and I thought, my goodness, they've been around a long time! But looking back, I enjoyed the summer visitors. Though mind you, I think I was glad to get back to school!

Muriel (McGregor) Malloy: Oh, that's right enough, it was always a busy time. There was always jobs needing done. We'd a big family so even when we were in primary school there was jobs you'd get. My brothers were all message boys in the village. Children could help buy the school clothes or shoes and we'd get a little pocket-money on a Saturday. We were never bored – we didnae ken the meaning o the word! I would have been 14 or 15, still at school, and I used to work at the weekends for Mrs Doig – she kept a bed-and-breakfast house at Ardtrostan, just above St Fillans.

Helen Doig: I remember when we moved there! My Dad was working on Locherlour Farm when a lease became vacant for Ardtrostan Farm. It was a hill farm on the Ancaster Estate, not far from St Fillans, on the south side of Loch Earn, about 6 miles from Lochearnhead. My father obtained the lease of the farm in 1941 and we were there for twenty years. It had a huge, big house, a *beautiful* house, and I'll never forget the first day I saw it. There were five bedrooms, a big dining room and a most beautiful drawing room with high ceilings and three big windows overlooking the loch. And best of all (or so I thought), the house had a bathroom. I remember when we first saw Ardtrostan I said to Mum, "Come and see this lovely room!". I thought it was the best room in the house, because before that we didn't have a bathroom – in fact when we moved into the Quoigs there was no running water. There was a tap in the middle of the yard and a dry lavatory round the back of the sheds, and we lived with it. What would they do now without their "mod cons" and everything?

So, when I saw Ardtrostan I thought it was wonderful because there was a real bathroom with a bath, a washbasin, and a flush toilet! There were bells in every room, with a bell-board in the downstairs quarters, on a wall in the kitchen. And next to the kitchen was the scullery, the maid's bedroom and the dairy – that area alone was bigger than my whole house now, at Dykehead [Lanarkshire]!

Moving to Ardtrostan was a big change for us – when we first moved there I still got a bus to Crieff High School every day and my two brothers went to Morrison's, and of course we all helped at home. The farm had 2,000 acres, but a huge area was all rocks and bracken – my father had about 200 sheep, Blackface; that's about all that kind of hill farm could support. Mum kept summer visitors who'd come for their annual holiday – I'm still friendly with some of these people yet.

MB: Where were your visitors coming from?

Helen D: Everywhere! Even America, but mostly England, Wales, Edinburgh, Glasgow and in between. In the school holidays, when we were younger, we'd go to Auntie Nan's for a few weeks, so Mum wouldn't have us under her feet, and we'd all have a great time with Auntie Nan. She was in Fife for a few years.

Bobby Thomson: She was keeping house for her father and her brother Duncan who worked on a farm near Lower Largo.

Helen D: Our cousins also spent holidays there too, so we'd see Elma and her brother Norman – their mother was my father's sister. And we'd see our cousin Muriel.

Elma Cunningham: We'd go for a whole month! My brother and I were usually a bit later than our cousins because we'd moved to Carlisle by then – we all used to live up Glen Lednock, near Auntie Nan at Balmuick, but when that lease ended, Helen's Dad got a job at Locherlour Farm and my Dad got a job as the cattle-man on Barclay Sharp's big farm; it's just as you go up towards Muthill there from Crieff on the left hand side. Then Dad got a job as poultry manager on a farm in Carlisle, so Norman and I went to school at Carlisle and the school holidays in England were a bit later – we would still be on holiday with Auntie Nan when our other cousins went back to school. Aunt Jean used to be home on weekends because she was the school-teacher in Bridge of Earn, and boarding all week. We just loved being there. Auntie Nan would take us to the beach at Lower Largo, and we'd all go in for a dook. She'd go in too. And after we came out, if it was a cold day we'd stop for a poke of chips to eat on the way home, or if it was a hot day we'd have an ice-cream. We'd have a wee bit of pocket-money from our parents – a few pennies went a long way in those days! Auntie Nan was only 17 years older than me, and she was great fun.

Nan Doig [1912–2014]: When we were in Fife we were only about a mile and a quarter away from the water so of course we took the children down to the sea. We couldn't swim but we all had bathing suits and we'd all hold hands, and we would go out knee deep and then dip down. And we used to play 'Three times round the ship' – we'd all sing and go three times round the ship and then sink to the bottom, (singing):

> Three times round went the gallant, gallant ship
> And three times round went she.
> Three times round went the gallant, gallant ship,
> And then sank to the bottom of the sea.

The water would be up to about their knees, then you'd sink down you see, you sat with the children, and that took them up to their necks. Oh, we'd grand times with them.

MB: *And did it have any other verses?*[3]

ND: No, that was all I ever heard, but we'd sing it over and over and over and over again. 'Three times round went the gallant, gallant ship, and sank to the bottom of the sea.' [laughter] We had a lot of fun.

214

MB: Did you play any other games or songs with the children?

ND: Oh, we used to get up to a lot of tricks with the children. And Duncan, my brother, enjoyed his game of cricket so they played cricket. We had a homemade bat and we'd always a good ball, a tennis ball, and for the wickets they'd have a shoe-box or something like that. And they'd play out on this field and Duncan would run very fast between the points. They'd learn the rules, like they'd shout L.B.W. if they had their legs in front of the wicket. And we played rounders with the children – I enjoyed them, you see. And they'd be tired out and they'd go up to their bed quite happily.

Elma: Then they moved to Blairnroar – she and Uncle Dunc and Auntie Jean were farming at the Straid so we spent holidays there too.

Helen D: Then, after they retired and moved to Comrie, Auntie Jean died and we all kept going to Auntie Nan's for our holidays. Bobby will remember the holidays – he was a good bit younger than us. This photo [see photo section] was taken in Comrie in 2012, at her hundredth birthday – we have wonderful memories.

When we were young, back then, nobody thought of going abroad for a holiday – people in the cities thought a week in the countryside and fresh air was a real holiday. A lot of our visitors would book up for the next year before they went home.

I left school when I was fifteen; I enjoyed school and got on well – my friends used to call me the 'teacher's pet'! [laughter]. And when I left, I was offered a job in the bank and I was also offered one in the Headmaster's office, but, as girls did in these days, I stayed home to help my mother. There's always a lot to be done on a farm – the hens, the milking and butter-making, the planting and harvesting, not to mention feeding everyone; it's non-stop.

MB: Did Ardtrostan have electricity when you lived there?

Helen D: No. Crieff had electricity but there was no supply at Quoig, or up the glens and there was none in Ardtrostan either. In fact, there was none on that side of the loch. We had a Tilley lamp in the kitchen and paraffin lamps for the other rooms, and you'd always keep candles. In the kitchen there was a beautiful old range; it had two ovens, and the big flat surface for all the cooking pots, and it heated the water in the hot water tank – a beautiful cooker but it burned a ton of coal a week. Then one day when I was standing beside the kitchen table, preparing something, I said to my mother, "My feet are getting wet −". The boiler had burst, and there we were with a house full of guests! Fortunately, we kept a paraffin cooker for emergencies − it had a wee gas fire, so we managed to cook on that till the old range was replaced. We got an Aga then, which was a wonderful cooker. It also burned coal, but not as much as the old range, and it was plumbed into the hot water, and we had the separate boiler to give us more hot water seeing we had the visitors.

MB: *When the house was full of summer visitors where did the family sleep?*

Helen D: The upper floor was for the guests, and the family was on the ground floor. There was another bedroom and a maid's room, and I slept in the dairy sometimes, or even in the scullery, with a mattress on the table.

Bobby: The first holiday that we had, when I was young, was with Helen and her mum and dad up at Ardtrostan. We started going there in the 1950s when my dad was on holiday from work, during the Forfar fortnight. We went for a week, but we were there as family, not as guests, so we didna eat in the dining room, we ate with the family in the kitchen.

MB: *Do you remember the house?*

Bobby: Oh, aye, it was a big house, a beautiful house, and when they were busy all the bedrooms were occupied. Helen slept in the dairy, and it was a very cold room, of course. There was another bedroom downstairs, and Helen's parents slept there, and all the guests were upstairs. I too was very taken by the size of the bathroom; it had originally been a bedroom so was extraordinarily spacious. At home in Forfar we just had an outside 'lavvy' in the garden, so this was luxury!

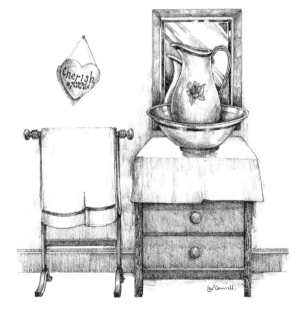

MB: *And during these years, did the house still have just one bathroom?*

Helen D: Yes, one bathroom, but we had basins and ewers in all the bedrooms and anybody that wished hot water to wash in the bedroom got it. There was no extra toilet, just the one, but sometimes there was lots of long faces when they went to the bathroom door and found the 'Occupied' sign on the door. We had an outside privy we could use when the house was busy.

MB: And what about refrigeration? You'd need to keep things cool in the summertime.

Helen D: There was an outside larder, where you stored the game and whatever meat you had. It had louvre sides and sort of mesh windows. And the dairy, being on the north side of the house, was always cool, and after we milked we'd carry the milk into the dairy, where it was strained. There was the daily routine with your milk pails and everything, as they had to be sterile – there had to be a good supply of hot water, so we washed them, dried them, and turned them upside down on a rack. There was a cream separator, so we always had cream to serve, and we made our own butter – we used to have a wooden butter churn then we got a glass one. The milk and cream would keep cool enough in the dairy, but when you're making the butter if you didn't whip the cream at the right temperature it didn't thicken. Sometimes it was too cool and we'd to put a wee spot of boiling water, because if it's too cold that's just as bad as being too hot – about room temperature or blood heat is best. In the summer when there's plenty of cream we made plenty butter, but some of the visitors didn't like the home-made butter – they weren't used to it, so some wanted bought butter, they preferred it.

Bobby: I used to help Uncle Dave at milking-time, taking the cows out, and bringing the cows back in again, that kind of thing. The cows were milked by hand in those days, and Uncle Dave did all the milking.

MB: Did he just milk enough for the household or did they sell any milk?

Bobby: They sold some, because Uncle Dave rented out caravan sites on the field about a third of the way down towards St Fillans, on that back road, and the people in the caravans used to buy milk and eggs from them. The whole family were busy, but they always employed folk for serving the tables at mealtimes, doing cleaning work, making up the beds, and all that. They needed that help because they had all the cooking to do and Helen's mum was a wonderful baker, she was tremendous, and that was why Helen was so good, she learned it off her mum.

Helen D: We also made ice-cream.

MB: Ice-cream! Even when you had no electricity or freezer?

Helen D: Yes [laughter] A few years ago, on my way to visit Auntie Nan, I was on the bus one Friday and I got talking to a woman going to Perthshire – she said she belonged to Comrie, and I said, "Oh, perhaps you'll know my aunt, Nan Doig?". "Ah, Doig," she said, "I remember that name. There's a place up Lochearnside, they used to sell ice cream on a Sunday [laughter]. That was us, I told her! How did we make ice cream? You got the big slab of ice, and we had a special ice-cream maker – it was like a wooden barrel and it had the container for the ice-cream that fitted inside it. You had to make your custard first and let that cool – two cups of cream to one of milk, half a cup of sugar, a pinch of salt and about six egg yolks. Then when it was cold you put it into the container, put the lid on it, and you filled up the barrel with ice and salt and water and fastened down the top so then you cawed the handle till it was ready. It made delicious ice cream!

Bobby: I remember the ice-cream making, and when we were there I had the job of cawing the handle. It was delicious stuff, and they were run off their feet on Sunday afternoons with folk out for a run in their car, which was a very popular activity in those days.

Billy: There used to be ice-hooses on the estates, arched buildings, sunk intae a bank – north-facing, I suppose. I remember there was one at Dunira, no far fae the big hoose; there's just a mound o earth now, where it was. And there was one at Lawers – it'll still be there yet. That one was on the left-hand side, goin up the drive tae Lawers Hoose. They had a curlin pond doon there, Lawers Pond, an in the winter when the ponds would aw be frozen, they'd saw up lumps o ice and put them in the ice-hoose. I've never actually seen the one at Dunira, so I'm no certain where they wid get the ice – it wouldnae be the Boltachan because that goes at an awfie rate; I don't think that would freeze so mebbe it was the curling pond.

Helen D: You could buy ice. And on a Sunday afternoon we did afternoon teas for one and six, and high teas for two and six[4], and these were served in the dining room. For the high teas it was just bacon and egg, and of course we had bread and my mother's baking, her scones and her cakes. She was a beautiful baker.

MB: *So you learned from your Mum, Helen. And for less than a pound, twelve people could have afternoon tea with home-baking! Can you remember what the tariff was for B&B or full board at Ardtrostan?*

Helen D: It was mostly full board that the visitors wanted. And every morning I'd go into the dining room and say, "Good morning. Porridge, corn flakes or fruit juice?". A lot of them came for the fly fishing, and if they were going out for the day we'd pack them a picnic

and a flask, and they'd be back for the evening meal, dinner. In 1961, the year we left Ardtrostan, it was eight guineas a week full board – I still have the tariff card somewhere.

MB: *Eight guineas a week, that's 8 pounds 8 shillings (£8.40) – less than a tenner for a week's holiday, with full-board!*

Bobby: I've still got a menu – we weren't paying guests but I kept it as a souvenir.

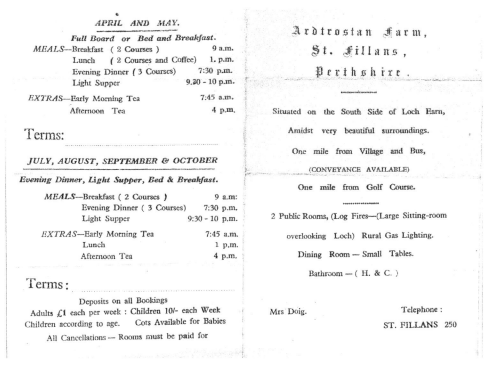

APRIL AND MAY.

Full Board or Bed and Breakfast.

MEALS—Breakfast (2 Courses)   9 a.m.
    Lunch   (2 Courses and Coffee)   1. p.m.
    Evening Dinner (3 Courses)   7:30 p.m.
    Light Supper   9.30 - 10 p.m.

EXTRAS—Early Morning Tea   7:45 a.m.
    Afternoon Tea   4 p.m.

Terms:

JULY, AUGUST, SEPTEMBER & OCTOBER

Evening Dinner, Light Supper, Bed & Breakfast.

MEALS—Breakfast (2 Courses)   9 a.m:
    Evening Dinner (3 Courses)   7:30 p.m.
    Light Supper   9:30 - 10 p.m.

EXTRAS—Early Morning Tea   7:45 a.m.
    Lunch   1 p.m.
    Afternoon Tea   4 p.m.

Terms :

Deposits on all Bookings
Adults £1 each per week : Children 10/- each Week
Children according to age.   Cots Available for Babies
All Cancellations — Rooms must be paid for

Ardtrostan Farm,
St. Fillans,
Perthshire.

Situated on the South Side of Loch Earn,
Amidst very beautiful surroundings.
One mile from Village and Bus,
(CONVEYANCE AVAILABLE)
One mile from Golf Course.

2 Public Rooms, (Log Fires—(Large Sitting-room
overlooking Loch) Rural Gas Lighting.
Dining Room — Small Tables.
Bathroom — (H. & C.)

Mrs Doig.   Telephone :
           ST. FILLANS 250

MB: What prompted the decision to leave Ardtrostan?

Helen D: In 1960 the Ancaster Estate sold the farm to the Forestry Commission, and without the hill we had only a hundred acres or something, so it wasnae worthwhile for sheep-farming.[5] My brothers had always wanted a farm in Lanarkshire because it's better land, not nearly so rocky, so that's why we moved into Dykehead. There was 763 acres, and it was all grazing, 350 sheep and later we upped it to 600. I remember it well, because the day we went to see Dykehead I said to my brothers, "Look, don't ever expect me to live here, in this wee hoose – just the two rooms upstairs and a kitchen and a bathroom!". So you can imagine after being in a beautiful house like Ardtrostan, beside Loch Earn, moving down into the bings of Lanarkshire! And when we gave up Ardtrostan it was the Edinburgh Merchant schools that took it over as an adventure centre – the last time I was up there, just going past it, the old steading was still there. The hill is all trees, and now the area near the loch is the big caravan park across from St Fillans, the one with all the static caravans so a lot more people now go there on holiday.

MB: *Muriel, you were saying you worked with Helen's mum when you were still at school.*

Muriel: Yes, I used to work at the weekends for Mrs Doig when she kept the bed-and-breakfast house at Ardtrostan. I would have been 14 or 15, and I worked there on Saturdays and Sundays. I'd leave Comrie on Saturday morning on the 7 o'clock bus to St. Fillans and I kept my bike just behind where the Post Office used to be, so I would cycle all the way up to Ardtrostan – it was a big sheep farm. And Mr Doig's brother Duncan farmed across the glen [at the Straid] and the two brothers used to walk the sheep all the way to Ardtrostan for clipping day. I can mind when they'd all be at the fank and Mrs Doig would feed all the shearers and shepherds. She used to have a big, long table outside, with a white cloth on it and everything. She was a beautiful cook, and everything done without electricity, and she fed everyone.

MB: *Helen was also a very good cook.*

Muriel: She'd have learned from her mother, Mrs Doig. There used to be a lot of American tourists would stay there, and Mrs Doig did all the cooking. Her scrambled eggs were the best I've ever tasted, but I don't know how she managed it – I've never been able to make scrambled eggs quite like she did.

Elma: I remember that after they had a season of so many visitors, Helen went to Glasgow and took a catering course at the 'Dough School'. But she was already a good cook.

MB: *So, while Helen and her mum were cooking, what were your main jobs, Muriel?*

Muriel: I used to wait at the tables, at the meals, carrying the food and dishes back and forth to the kitchen, then I'd help with the washing up. Plenty to do! And Mrs Doig was so neat, always so well turned out – in the morning she had her working apron on, then in the afternoon, when she'd done her work and the B&B guests would be coming back for the evening meal, she would change into a nice fresh blouse, and a little frilly apron. She was always beautifully dressed when the tourists came back from fishing, or whatever they were doing. It was mostly Americans who came, and Mrs Doig would be all ready for them.

MB: *Did you stay overnight at their house?*

Muriel: Yes, I had my own wee room at the very top of the house, up a wee stair; it was a tiny wee room with just enough room for the bed and little else – it was mair like a cupboard!

MB: *Did you do any other tasks around the farm?*

Muriel: Yes, I used to collect the eggs – they had a lot of hens to keep them going with the bed-and-breakfast. I enjoyed that, except one day Helen's younger brother Duncan gave me such a fright – he jumped out and he thought it was a joke, but I didn't! He liked to play pranks – that's boys for you! But we all used to have a lot of fun – the whole family was still at home when I was there; there was Helen, and Dunc (as we called him) and their brother Bob. And on a Saturday night we used to go to the dancing in Lochearnhead – we went on our bikes, the four of us, and cycled down to St Fillans, then all along the loch to Lochearnhead, then after the dance we'd cycle back home again. Never thought anything of it! We had a great time in those days. Duncan was a really good accordion player. He was in a band too, and they used to travel to all sorts of places. There was a lot of really good players in thae days – my brother John was a bit younger, and he was a really good player, and Hamish Reid – you'll know him – he had a band. He's a lovely player and he still plays at local events like the Comrie Burns lunch in the local church hall – and he played at the Monzievaird Burns Supper. And everyone loves to hear him. You'll need to talk to my brother John – he's long since retired and lives just a couple of miles from me. He won the Scottish championship, then he lived in Edinburgh for a long time. He had a dance band and they went all over the world playing, but he hasnae played for years.[6]

Alistair Work: Muriel's brother John and I were in the same class at school – he was a quiet lad, and we used to play football. I saw a lot o John because, like me, he was one of the boys at school who was keen on animals and birds. And he was really good on the accordion – John had his own band an everything, and Muriel was the best jiver you ever saw – by God, she could move! You could've watched her all night – there was nobody on the dancefloor could touch her when it came to jiving! She was fantastic!

Muriel: When we were young, everybody went to the dances – that's where you met folk and there were some really good bands. And I loved jiving! I won a competition in Auchterarder, dancing wi a waiter – I dinna ken where he was from, but oh, he was good at jiving! So were the soldiers at Cultybraggan camp, and the Glasgow boys were all braw dancers.

Annie Young: I met my husband jiving – we both went to a jazz club in Glasgow on a Monday night. After we were married, we'd occasionally visit Comrie with my mother – her people were farming folk from Comrie, Comries – and Ian and I would go dancing. Sometimes we went dancing in the Monzievaird Hall, a lovely wee corrugated tin hall – it was there in my mother's day.

Nigel Gatherer: I used to play for dances in the Monzievaird Hall with a local accordion player Eileen Anderson, from Crieff – the last one we did was a couple of years before the pandemic. I also did a few concerts there with my ukulele group, so I composed a tune, 'Monzievaird Hall'.[7] Then Ian [Young] wrote a song to the tune – it's on his last CD, 'Time and Tide'.[8]

Ian Young (based on his CD notes): *Annie and I had visited Monzievaird over 40 years ago ... So I felt the urge to add words which reflected this nostalgic, romantic mood ...*

Monzievaird Hall

Words by Ian Young,
tune by Nigel Gatherer

The day is fading and the wind sings its song,
The Ochils are lit, but that will not last long.
With a tune in the breeze, I can follow its call
And I find mysel' drawn back to Monzievaird Hall

Chorus:
      Reach for the day and hold the hour,
      See the sorrel and bluebell in flower.
      And Spring is here in each blossom and shoot,
      My heart is a-flutter an' there's dancin' afoot.

Alone in the dusk I hear a strathspey,
It draws me inside to see the band play
Wi' a snap and a swing, they gi'e it their all,
I fair missed you last night at Monzievaird Hall.

Chorus:
      Reach for the day ...

Dae ye mind o' the old days in Crieff?
We played t' gether frae mornin' till nicht,
The walks o'er tae Comrie, The Sma' Glen and a',
An' dancin wi' you at the Monzievaird Hall.

Chorus:

      Reach for the day and hold the hour,
       See the sorrel and bluebell in flower.
      And Spring is here in each blossom and shoot,
       My heart is a-flutter an' there's dancin' afoot.

      I fair missed you last night at Monzievaird Hall
      Oh, I missed you last night at Monzievaird Hall.[9]

Endnotes

1   According to the Merriam-Webster Dictionary, a *staycation* is a stay-at-home vacation. The word appeared in print appeared during the Second World War: 'Take a Stay-cation instead of a Vacation, this year' in the *Cincinnati Enquirer*, 18 July 1944. See <https://www.merriam-webster.com/words-at-play/staycation-date-meaning>.

2   Queen Victoria kept a journal of this and subsequent visit (see *Leaves from the Journal of our Life in the Highlands from 1848-1861* and *More Leaves from the Journal of a Life in the Highlands from 1862 to 1882*). She appointed the bard Mary MacKellar to translate the second journal into Gaelic. Strathearn became so popular that a 200-page tourist guidebook was published: C. Rogers, *The Beauties of Upper Strathearn: Described in Six Excursions from the Town of Crieff.* Edinburgh, 1854. Updated in 1860 by G. McCulloch, with plates and a fold-out map; a 'limited edition' facsimile was published by Alan Colquhoun in 1988.

3   Nan's 4-line verse occurs in variants of the ballad 'The Mermaid' which is also known as 'Our Gallant Ship', (Child No. 289; Roud 124: <https://mainlynorfolk.info/martin.carthy/songs/themermaid.html>) 'Gallant, Gallant Ship' was also popular as a children's singing game; see Iona and Peter Opie, *The Singing Game,* pp. 231–32.

4   One shilling and sixpence (1s.6d.) is seven and a half pence (7.5p.) in today's currency, and two shillings and sixpence (2s.6d.) is twelve and a half pence (12.5p.)

5   See also Chapter 9, Alistair Work's discussion on the Forestry Commission's compulsory purchases of land and the effects it had on estates and farms.

6   In 1970 Muriel's brother John MacGregor was the 'All Scotland Senior Traditional Accordion Solo Champion'.   <https://www.perthaccordionfestival.co.uk/senior-traditional-scottish-accordion-champions/>. His recordings include 'The John MacGregor Scottish Dance Band: Invitation to a Scottish Dance" (vinyl, 12-inch LP), Louden Records, LDN453.

7   'Monzievaird Hall' is included in *The Nigel Gatherer Collection,* with notation available online: <https://nigelgatherer.com/tunes/tunes/zComposers/MNO/MonzH.html>.

8   'Time and Tide' by Ian Young and Friends (Birnam CDs) was issued as a fund-raiser and all proceeds to St Columba's Hospice and Parkinsons (UK), Edinburgh. The words of all the songs are on the CD booklet and an online description can be accessed online: <https://www.birnamcdshop.com/product/ian-young/>.

9   In 2019 Ian and Nigel were joint winners of the song-writing competition held annually by Edinburgh Folksong Club. Sadly, Ian died of cancer in 2023.

Chapter 12

There's Something that Draws You Back

Duncan McNab: My parents left Glenartney in 1953 when Dad got a job shepherding at the foot of the Tinto Hills, so, unlike my brother and two sisters, who started life in Glenartney, I started off in Lanarkshire as the family lived at Bowdenlea Farm when I was born. Helen Doig and her brothers also moved to Lanarkshire after the Drummond Estate sold Ardtrostan – they leased a farm near Tarbrax. There's a lot of big sheep farms in the area, hill farms, and we used to visit one another, just like in Glenartney. As often as not, Duncan Doig would bring his accordion – he was a really good player. He was a member of the Tarbrax Badminton Club so when I joined I saw Duncan at least once a week.

Bowdenlea is near Roberton – on some maps it's 'Boddenlea' but it was Bowdenlea to us and I was christened in Roberton Church. After that we moved to Howgate Farm, then Dad got a job shepherding at Fallburns – they're all within a few miles. He liked it there until they got a new farm manager who knew that my father had a reputation as a shepherd that was second to none – Dad was at home in the hills, good with dogs, he knew how to build up a good breeding stock and severe winters didn't bother him. But when the new manager decided to put a herd of cattle on the sheep grazing ground, Dad said, "That's it!" So he picked up The Scottish Farmer, 'Shepherds Wanted', and the next thing we were moving to Crosswoodhill Farm in Midlothian – it's about half a mile over the county boundary with Lanarkshire and the local school was in West Calder. Anyway, in 1974, just when I was about to leave West Calder High School, Dad decided to go back to Glenartney. Fisher Fergusson was the manager of the Drummond Estate, and he was needing a shepherd who could handle a hill farm of Blackface sheep. So I was uprooted and had to leave all my friends to live in the wilds of Perthshire where there was nobody my own age. We moved to Mailermore and the farmhouse was the family home until Dad retired.[1]

Margaret Bennett: Mailermore Farmhouse? Isn't that the same farm Peter Grewar leased, the same big house Helen Gardiner lived in?

Duncan: That's right, but when we were at Mailermore the glen had electricity – there was none when Helen was growing up or all the years our family were in Glenartney. So that made a big difference, especially for Mum. And though I was reluctant to leave all my friends behind, I don't think I'd ever been drawn to Lanarkshire the way I'm drawn to Perthshire. I felt at home in Glenartney and Comrie, and I can understand how my Dad felt, and the Doigs too – when they moved to Lanarkshire they were always back and forth to visit Nan. There's just something that draws you back.

MB: Did you spend any time in school after you flitted?

Duncan: Yes, we moved in late spring, so I had a few months at Perth High School, getting up at 6 to catch the school taxi then the bus from Comrie to Perth – by the time I got home after school it was about 6 o'clock, so it was a long day. But I soon made friends, although when we wanted to meet up, it was quite a hike from Glenartney back down to the village. When I left school, I had the whole summer months to fill before leaving home in September. The option was either stay home and help my dad on the farm, or find something to get out from underneath his feet. I managed to get a job as a labourer in the Cultybraggan Camp. At that time the camp was housing the CCF, the Combined Cadet Force, with army cadets from all over Britain coming for a fortnight at a time and given training by the regular army – they were stationed there to run the whole show effectively. When I was there, it was the Fourth Royal Regiment of Wales that organized these fortnight blocks of training and everything at the camp. Then there was a change-over, when the King's Own Scottish Borderers took over and did a stint.

MB: What was the accommodation like for the CCF and all the army folk who were there?

Duncan: The whole camp was made up of brown Nissen huts with a bit of creamy colour at the end. Just the corrugated iron, no insulation, and depending on the length of the hut there was either one or two log-burning stoves in each of the huts. They all slept in these Nissen huts, and it was just military-style metal bedsteads. During the summer there was never any issues, but in the winter if you got cold the best you were going to have to keep you warm was an army blanket. The huts were numbered, like, the officers' mess was hut 26, and the catering huts had their own numbers. And there was a Nissen hut for the squad of labourers that I was working with – we'd leave our stuff there. If my memory serves me right, there were about six of us in the squad, of which I was undoubtedly the youngest by a considerable margin. When I joined them, the first job assigned to our squad was creating a rifle range for the cadets to do their weapons training on. You know when you head out of Comrie and pass the road to the camp? You carry on up the hill and as the road sweeps around before you get to Auchingarroch there's an area down below on your right-hand side, and that was where we constructed the shooting range. Basically, behind it is a blooming great hill, so that's where the target was, and if you missed, it was only gonna hit the hill – that's where the shooting range was. A large section of Glenartney on the south side of the glen was used by the army for training operations. Various parts of the hill had flag poles – I suspect they're still there – and if the red flag was flying you'd to stay clear because there was live firing going on.

MB: *I remember when I first came here about 30 years ago, there was a big, big sign just where you turn off to Comrie on the Langside road – a warning notice indicating Danger when the red flags were flying. Drivers were warned not to go through that area as there was live ammunition in use. But I never did see the flags flying so I'd just drive on through the hills.*[2]

Duncan: Yes, that's the way it was. The cadets who came were getting put through an assault course and there was sports and such like, but to be honest, I didn't really have a great deal to do with them. As things turned out, I found I was mixing with the officers, the catering and the office staff. After working on the rifle range I had about a week of emptying dustbins and doing other menial tasks, then I was approached and asked, "Do you want to earn a few extra bits of cash for yourself? There's an officers' mess dinner, and I'm looking for somebody to help out in the kitchens." Well, at that age, anything that brings in extra money – I was up for that, so I agreed to go and I spent the weekend scrubbing pots and pans and washing dishes. And at the end of it I was approached again, because another staff member had said something along the lines of, if you're looking for somebody who's quite happy to work, the young lad that was in the kitchen should be handy. They were looking for a runner for the Adjutant, who was the officer in charge of the whole place. As you come in through the main gates, the first Nissen hut on the left was the adjutant's office, and I was asked if I'd like to go and become the adjutant's runner. I had no idea what I was letting myself in for, but it seemed a promotion from labourer and dishwasher. So I said, "I'm your man," and I ended up working in the office. The job? Basically, if he had any messages to be delivered around the camp, I did that. There was a secretary and I remember her surname was Cruickshank because her father was a shepherd and knew my dad – the pair of us got on really well. And as well as being the secretary, she ran the telephone exchange for the whole camp. It was one of the old styles where you plugged in lines, and you move them around various sockets – it was somewhat antiquated. So she taught me to operate the telephone exchange, and when she went for lunch, I covered the camp telephone exchange for that period of time.

Every day in the office they published a Daily Order for everyone in the camp so that everybody knew exactly what the routine would be for the following day. The secretary typed it out on a duplicating skin and my job was to take the skin and put it onto the Gestetner – this is probably a foreign language to the younger generation, but basically, it was a 'skin' that you typed on, but instead of printing, the keys cut the shape of the letter into the skin, then you would take the whole skin off, and it got wrapped around a drum, which was inked up and then you cranked the handle, and the paper would go through the bottom. It was an early edition of a printer.

MB: *I remember them well from my own school days and also as a teacher, cranking the handle, or standing in the queue to use the Gestetner.*

Duncan: Yes, they were very common in schools and offices, and I would make 50 to 60 copies of Daily Orders. And then I would be off round the camp delivering them to all the various places. It's a big camp but I got to know it quickly and I became the camp postman as well. I used to go down to Comrie in the morning to the Post Office with one of the workers and we'd collect all the mail for Cultybraggan Camp. And then once we got back to the office, I'd sort all that out and deliver it round the various departments – just jumped on my bike and pedaled round it, and I did that right through till September. I was kept on the go, but it was a very relaxed and informal atmosphere, lots of good humour, and as I say, I got on really well with the secretary. The only drawback for me was the early start because I'm never the quickest off the mark in the morning, and from Mailermore Farm, it's about two miles downhill to the camp. I would jump on my bike and with very little effort and some considerable speed, I could make it down to my work. It wasn't so quick going home – all uphill! But I remember one morning just towards the end of my time at Cultybraggan, things didn't go so well.

All the workmen would gather in their Nissen hut first thing in the morning, and they would have cups of tea and plan out the day ahead. I'd leave my stuff there and I'd go back there to have my lunch, and in the morning I'd put my bike in this hut rather than leave it at the main gate. But one particular morning, I was running behind schedule, so I was pedaling furiously down the hill, then flew in through the main gates. My routine was to turn left, which was the quickest way to get to the hut where all my stuff was, but that took me across the middle of the parade-ground. But unfortunately, on this occasion, the Fourth Royal Regiment of Wales was out on parade and they were there with their

regimental mascot, which is a goat. The goat didn't exactly turn into a bucking bronco, but it took fright when I suddenly had to do a diversion around it. Though the Adjutant didn't see it, word got back to him, so I had, eh, words in my ear from him – probably best not repeated here!

Another thing that comes to mind happened after the officers' mess dinner: for reasons unknown to me, there was a mountain of foodstuff left over. And the chaps in the kitchen said, "Listen, this stuff's all just gonna get chucked out, so if you want it, it's yours." And so over a series of nights, I cycled up the glen with bags hanging off my bike, all full of the stuff from the officers' mess. I remember there were several tins of turtle soup, and my mother had never come across the likes. Turtle soup? There was I, bringing home so many bits and pieces you can't imagine they'd give that away, and I'm sure my mother thought I was nicking the stuff, but no!

MB: Do you remember if there were students working in the camp during the summer?

Duncan: I'm not sure about that, because I was the only young person in my squad. But there might well have been. It's a huge camp and it was a busy, busy place.

David Campbell: When I was a student in the late Fifties quite a few of us got summer jobs at Cultybraggan. I was working as a sort of kitchen assistant – I think we saw the jobs advertised in the university, and we were working for the NAAFI, in the kitchen.[3] There were hundreds of army cadets there as well as some kind of regular army people, so we worked very hard feeding all the Cadets in the camp.

Ed Miller: They had a Cadet Corps in Daniel Stewart's (in Edinburgh).[4] It was all boys when my brother and I were there; now it's co-ed and they also changed the name to Stewart's-Melville. The thing was, when you were in your third year of school, the third form, you had to join the Corps for a year, and after that you could choose whether to be in it or not.

MB: *What year was this, approximately?*

Ed: I'd be about fourteen, fifteen, so it'd be about 1959, 60. And if you stayed in the Corps and did your four years, then if you ever joined the army you were taken as an officer.[5] My brother, for example, decided to stay in – he liked it (though he didn't join the army), but I hated all this marching and uniforms and all that stuff.

MB: *Did you sing or chant rhymes when you marched?*

Ed: Ehm, just this one: [then chants:]

> Left! right! left, right!
> I had a good home but I left,
> Right! Left!
> Right! Left!

That was one –

MB: *I remember reciting a similar one in Portree, mid-fifties, when I was in the Brownies,*

> Left! right! Left! right!
> I had a good job but I left,
> Left, left, left, right, left
> I left, it serves me jolly well right,
> Right, right, right, left right   and so on.

And do you remember what the uniform was?

Ed: It was kinda Second World War stuff – thick, khaki-coloured stuff. Very uncomfortable ... with a shirt and a hat and gaiters that we'd to wear, and the boots had to be polished of course. I think we had our own socks – can't quite remember, but you couldn't see the socks anyway. And every Monday you had to wear the uniform to school – polish up, wear khakis and big tackety boots that were shined up. Terrible, but the only thing I liked about the Corp was that we went for a one-week camp to Cultybraggan.

MB: *And did they give you any history of the camp?*

Ed: No.

MB: *How did you travel from Daniel Stewart's to Cultybraggan?*

Ed: On a bus, a special charter bus. The year that I went, most of the kids had never been to a camp and never done any hiking, but I was a Scout and I really loved that. On the first day they took us on a road march, it must have been at least three miles and for me it was a wee dawdle but for most of them it was the hardest thing they'd ever done, and they were all blisters and crying and things like that.

MB: *Do you have any recollection of your first sighting of the camp?*

Ed: It was a dull-looking place, a collection of Nissen huts, and it was surrounded by barbed wire because even then I think they were nervous about the IRA or somebody getting in, cos there were guns and stuff there that they could have stolen so there were sentries at night. And our big adventure was to sneak out at night and run round the dormitory and sneak back in again without being seen by the sentries. But that was quite dangerous, cos those guys had guns and they were supposed to shoot! [laughs]

MB: *And what sort of sleeping quarters did you have?*

Ed: It was Nissen huts with double-tier bunks right along either wall. Very spartan and very bare, probably about twenty in each dorm. I don't remember it being that warm [laughs]; they provided you with a sheet and a blanket, and that was it. And in the morning, you had to fold them up neatly, military stuff, aye. And we got up to all kinds of hi-jinks at night, which boys do, all crowded together – but I won't go into any detail about that, not in ladies' company.

[Ed's wife Nora and daughter Maggie]

MB: *Now you have us wondering what you got up to at night.*

Ed: You heard of the phrase 'black-balling'? Literally – with shoe-polish.

MB: *Oh gosh! Were you a victim?*

Ed: Eh, only after I had been a perpetrator!

MB: *So it was pay-back time? I daren't ask about the washing facilities.*

Ed: Those were the days when you had a bath once a week, whether you needed it or not! [laughs] I really don't remember the washing facilities, but, for fifteen year-old boys washing was not a big issue, I'm sure my mother put me straight in the bath when i got home. [Laughter] Certainly when I came back from Scout camp she'd just say, "Put your clothes there. The bath'll be ready."

MB: *And did you sing in those days?*

Ed: Yes, we sang all those camp songs – I'd learnt a lot in the Boy Scouts so, I was probably one of the leaders of the songs. [Ed starts to hum the tune of 'Mademoiselle from Armentières' then sings a verse of their camp version[6]]:

> The German officers crossed the Rhine, parlez-vous
> The German officers crossed the Rhine, parlez-vous
> The German officers crossed the Rhine, parlez-vous
> [Tra-la-la-la] and drank the wine,
> Inky-pinky-parlez-vous

That's just the first verse – censored – and there were several more. But this is mixed company – they probably don't want to hear the one about how many testicles these guys had. [Nora and Maggie are laughing and Ed starts to hum the marching tune of 'Colonel Bogey'] That was great for marching to [laughter] and we had different ones like 'Roll me over in the clover, Roll me over, lay me down and do it again' and so on.

MB: *So singing was an incentive to march?*

Ed: Hm-mm, oh yes.

MB: During all this marching, and routine drill and stuff, was there any mention of ammunitions?

Ed: Well, there was a mention that there was ammunition at the camp, so it had to be guarded, but no, we never used anything. We did have a shooting gallery at school where you practised with old World War Two rifles, but I don't remember doing anything at camp. We had a day off and we went into Comrie, Crieff, or wherever. But I remember the scariest thing was, walking back we saw a whole group of people, away over, about half a mile from us and we waved at them. And it turned out it was a group of kids from Glasgow, from the slums. And they'd been at some camp somewhere and they thought we were being rude to them and we were toffs. So they ambushed us on the road and we were almost – they wanted a big battle, they had sticks and chains and stuff. I remember saying, "Do nothing. Keep walking, keep walking" so we did [laughs]. And for some reason all we got was one wee kick from one of them. And they were so surprised that we didn't hit back or attack them, all we did was keep walking – otherwise we'd a-got murdered cos we were nice, middle class Edinburgh boys, we'd no idea how to fight!

MB: Were you unaccompanied or was there a teacher with you?

Ed: No, that was our day off. We went to see the pictures or something, right after supper [dinner/tea] – there was a big canteen with food cooked in the kitchen, but some evenings we'd walk into Comrie to get a fish supper – that was a major treat!

David: When I was at Cultybraggan we had a great team of university students working in the kitchen and we were all living in Nissen huts – one hut for the boys and one for the girls, with very basic bunks, but that was fine in those days. And we had the use of a barn so we'd get together in the evenings – I don't think we drank, but we had fun. We didn't do anything outrageous or scandalous, maybe just an occasional prank, but I remember one time, just for a dare, I ran as a streaker round the girls' hut! We enjoyed our time there, and on the weekends we went to the dance in Comrie. It's just a couple of miles from the camp and for some reason I remember one time just as we were leaving Comrie one of the girls was singing Stuart MacGregor's song, "The West winds blow to Coshieville," and there he was, the man himself, just walking along the road with his guitar! Stuart was a medical student, and he ran Edinburgh University Folk Club, so we knew one another.[7]

He didn't work at Cultybraggan that year because he got a summer job as a labourer on one of the hydro dams. So that's where his song comes from:

> The big wheels rumble up and down,
> The lorries know the way ...

I think Stuart had relatives in Comrie so he might have stopped over on his way to the hydro scheme. But we had a great time in Comrie, although I have a very sad memory of one of those dances because I was called to the door to be told that my dad was dead.

MB: Very sad indeed. Did you ever come back to the area?

David: Yes, I did; I came back again in the Seventies when I was a member of the Edinburgh group, 'The Heretics' and we were invited to perform at Ochtertyre Theatre – Doli [Maclennan] and Adam McNaughtan were with us.[8] But that's another story.

Endnotes

1. When Pat retired in 1980 he and his wife Isobel moved to Escullion near Blairnroar. Isobel died in 1988 and Pat moved from the glen into the village. Comrie was his home until his death in 2010.

2. The flags were there until 2004 when the Ministry of Defence sold the camp and surrounding area to the Comrie Development Trust.

3. Founded by the British Ministry of Defence in 1920, the NAAFI (*Navy, Army, and Air Force Institutes*) was set up to provide catering and social facilities for British military personnel.

4. The Cadet Corps, founded in 1913, was officially known as "Daniel Stewart's Training Corps," or C Company of the 1st (Highland) Cadet Battalion, The Royal Scots Regiment. A detailed description of the Corps and the expectations of the boys is included in "The Cadet Corps" in *Stewart's College Magazine,* Vol. III, No. 2, April 1913, pp. 53–55. Thanks to the Stewart's Melville College's Archive, online: <https://archives.esms.org.uk/PDFViewer/web/viewer.html?file=%2fFilename.ashx%3ftableName%3dta_magazines%26columnName%3dfilename%26recordId%3d24>.

5. The school's WW1 Role of Honour lists the names of over 1000 former pupils who served in the 1914–18 war.

6. 'Mademoiselle from Armentières' became popular during World War 1 when it was recorded c. 1915 by music-hall singer Jack Charman (Decca Records) and other recording artists. The song, or versions of it, has been sung ever since, parodied in barracks and bars, trenches and on route marches, through World War 2. Parodies are still part of the repertoire sung at Boy Scout camps and in school playgrounds.

7. Born in Edinburgh in 1935, Stuart MacGregor was the son of Thomas MacGregor, a shopkeeper from Comrie, and Janet Redpath, from the Borders. While he was a medical student in Edinburgh, he got to know folklorist and poet Hamish Henderson and in Stuart's 5th-year (1958) they co-founded one of Scotland's earliest folk-clubs, Edinburgh University Folk Song Society. The club brought together international students, giving them an opportunity to sing and to meet and learn from invited guests such as Jeannie Robertson and Flora MacNeil. (H. Henderson, *Alias MacAlias,* pp. 13–15 and 137.) Stuart MacGregor's untimely death in 1973 was a great blow to the Scottish 'folk scene'. In a letter to fellow-poet Tom Scott (Feb. 1973) Hamish wrote 'I valued [Stuart] greatly as a friend and on top of that he was for long my most resourceful ally in the Scottish folk revival'. (H. Henderson, *The Armstrong Nose: Selected Letters,* p. 213.) See also The Scottish Poetry Library online, <https://www.scottishpoetrylibrary.org.uk/poet/stuart-macgregor/s>.

8   'The Heretics' was a performance group founded in 1970 by Stuart MacGregor and Willie Neil, giving a platform to writers and musicians who, at the time, received little recognition from mainstream media mainly because of their political views. See, Chapter 6, note 15.

A final note from a student who helped transcribe the recordings …

From: Macaulay Ross
Date: Wednesday, 9 March 2022 at 16:08
To: Margaret Bennett
Subject: Re: recording local traditions, family and community

Hello Margaret,

I was so sad to read your last email about Billy and it's a sad thought that he can't tell us any more. But the recordings you made of conversations with him will always be there – in 20 or 30 years' time, his voice will still be heard.

Reading your email got me thinking that I need to get back up North and get recording. I'd been telling my dad about Billy – I'd just finished transcribing your recordings of him and I was laughing out loud about the man stopping him in the road and claiming that Joey the Jackdaw had been into his bedroom and stole his wife's diamond ring… an put it back again half an hour later. Brilliant! Dad's a tractor mechanic an he was telling me about an old engineer from Tomintoul back home, a great character, so it would be brilliant to meet him and record him – he's up in years now.

Meanwhile I'd love to hear even just a wee snippet of other recordings you have of Billy or the gamekeeper from Glenartney! It would be great to try and transcribe some bits and pieces too!

A right bonnie night here in Glasgow, so a hope it's the same wi you in Perthshire.

Aa the best,
Macaulay

Epilogue

Goodbye.

Goodbye, my family, my life is past,
I loved you all to the very last,
Weep not for me, but courage take
Love each other for my sake.
    For those you love don't go away,
They walk beside you every day.

Diary, Nan Doig, Comrie, [1912–2014]

References and Further Reading

Adams, David G. *Bothy Nichts and Days: Farm Bothy Life in Angus and the Mearns.* Edinburgh: John Donald, 1997.

Allen, Arthur C. 'Features of Lednock Dam, Including the Use of Fly Ash' in *Proceedings of the Institution of Civil Engineers,* Vol. 13 (2): pp 179–196, Jan. 1959.

Banks, Mary MacLeod. *British Calendar Customs: Scotland,* Volume II. London: The Folk-Lore Society, 1939.

Bennett, Margaret, Simpson, Gladys, and Simpson, Charles. 'Weather Sayings from Banffshire' in *Tocher: Tales, Songs, Traditions,* No. 47, School of Scottish Studies, Edinburgh University, 1994, pp 310–313.

Bennett, Margaret. 'A Balquhidder Farm with Mrs. Jean Innes' in *Tocher: Tales, Songs, Traditions,* No. 46, School of Scottish Studies, Edinburgh University, Summer 1993, pp. 209–215.

Bennett, Margaret. 'Calendar Customs in Scotland' in *The Oxford Companion to Scottish History,* ed. Michael Lynch. Oxford: OUP, pp. 60–64

Bennett, Margaret. 'Céilidh', in *The New Grove Dictionary of Music and Musicians,* London, 2000.

Bennett, Margaret. *'In Our day...' Reminiscences and Songs from Rural Perthshire,* illustrated by Doris Rougvie, with CD of Perthshire songs, Ochtertyre: Grace Note Publications, 2010.

Bennett, Margaret. *Robert MacLeod: Cowdenbeath Miner Poet. An Anthology by Arthur Nevay.* Ochtertyre: Grace Note Publications, 2015.

Bennett, Margaret. *Scottish Customs from the Cradle to the Grave.* Edinburgh: Polygon, 1992, Birlinn, 2004, New edition. 2012.

Bennett, Margaret. *"See When You Look Back": Clydeside Reminiscences of the Home Front, 1939–45.* Glasgow: Mitchell Library, 2005.

Bonser, Wilfrid. *A Bibliography of Folklore for 1958-1967 Being a Subject Index Vols 69-78 of the Journal 'Folklore'.* London: The Folklore Society, 1969.

Bonser, Wilfrid. *A Bibliography of Folklore. As Contained in the First Eighty Years of the Publications of the Folklore Society.* London: The Folklore Society, 1961.

Brennan, Mary. *Scottish Ballet: Forty Years*. Glasgow: Saraband, 2009

British Library Oral History collaboration (Charlie Morgan, Oral History Archivist with Rob Perks, Mary Stewart, Camille Johnston et al). 'Advice on remote oral history interviewing during the Covid-19 pandemic' online, <https://e554ji8k8hn.exactdn.com/wp-content/uploads/2021/02/Advice-on-remote-interviewing-during-the-Covid-19-Pandemic-v.70DOA-FINAL.pdf>.

Bruford, Alan (Ed.). *Tocher: Tales, Songs, Traditions*, No. 47, School of Scottish Studies, Edinburgh University, 1994.

Burnett, Peter and McCaffery, Richie (Eds.). *Not Dark Yet: A Celebration of John Herdman*, Edinburgh: Leamington Books, 2021.

Cameron, David Kerr. *The Ballad and the Plough: a Portrait of the Life of the Old Scottish Farmtouns*. London: Gollancz, 1978; Edinburgh: Birlinn, 2008.

Cameron, David Kerr. *The Cornkister Days: A Portrait of a Land and Its Rituals*. London: Gollancz, 1984; Edinburgh: Birlinn, 1995.

Cameron, David Kerr. *Willie Gavin, Crofter Man: A Portrait of a Vanished Lifestyle*. London: Gollancz, 1980.

Cameron, Ian, and Shepherd, Robbie (foreword). *The Jimmy Shand Story*. Edinburgh: Scottish Cultural Press, 1998.

Campbell, David. *Minstrel Heart: A Life in Story*. Edinburgh: Luath Press, 2021.

Chambers, Robert. *Popular Rhymes of Scotland*, Edinburgh: W. & R. Chambers, 1826.

Clydebank Life Story Group and Stewart, Liam (Ed.). *Untold Stories: Remembering Clydebank in Wartime*, Clydebank College, 1999. <https://education.gov.scot/media/lvlbn5wy/soc4-untold-stories.pdf>.

Comrie Primary School Centenary, 1909–2009, booklet introduced by Headteachers Ruth Billingham & Fiona Lowson, Comrie: n.p., 2009.

Coutts, Ben. *A Stick, Hill Boots and a Good Collie Dog: A Shepherd's Life Fifty Years Ago*. Edinburgh: Mercat, 1999.

Coutts, Ben. *Auld Acquaintance: Great Scots Characters I Have Known*. Edinburgh: Mercat, 1994.

Davies, O. 'Aughentaine Castle', in *Ulster Journal of Archaeology* 2 (1939): pp 72–82.

Douglas, Sheila. 'Perthshire Scots' in Omand, Donald (Ed.), *The Perthshire Book*. Edinburgh: Birlinn, 1999, pp 219–226.

Drummond, Peter Robert. *Perthshire in Bygone Days: One Hundred Biographical Essays.* London: W.B. Whittingham & Co. 1879.

Fergusson, Jean (narrator) & MacKenzie, Leslie (compiler, editor & publisher). *Balquhidder in Transition: Life on a Balquhidder Sheep Farm in the 1960s and 1970s.* Tuarach, Balquhidder: L. MacKenzie, 2022.

Foster, J. 'Strathearn' in Omand, Donald (Ed.), *The Perthshire Book.* Edinburgh: Birlinn, 1999, pp 115–123.

Fraser, Ian A. 'Place-Names [of Perthshire]', in D Omand (ed.) *The Perthshire Book.* Edinburgh: Birlinn, 1999, pp 199-210.

Fraser, Norrie. *Sir Edward MacColl: A Maker of Modern Scotland,* Edinburgh: Stanley Press, 1956.

Gordon, J. ed. *The New Statistical Account of Scotland* by the ministers of the respective parishes, under the superintendence of a committee of the Society for the Benefit of the Sons and Daughters of the Clergy. 'Comrie, Perth', Vol. 10, Edinburgh: Blackwoods and Sons, 1845, p. 578–596. University of Edinburgh, University of Glasgow. (1999) *The Statistical Accounts of Scotland* online service: <https://stataccscot.edina.ac.uk:443/link/nsa-vol10-p578-parish-perth-comrie>.

Gordon, J. ed. *The New Statistical Account of Scotland* by the ministers of the respective parishes, under the superintendence of a committee of the Society for the Benefit of the Sons and Daughters of the Clergy. 'Monivaird and Strowan, Perth', Vol. 10, Edinburgh: Blackwoods and Sons, 1845, pp 723–747. University of Edinburgh, University of Glasgow. (1999) *The Statistical Accounts of Scotland* online service: <https://stataccscot.edina.ac.uk:443/link/nsa-vol10-p723-parish-perth-monivaird_and_strowan>.

Gordon, J. ed. *The New Statistical Account of Scotland* by the ministers of the respective parishes, under the superintendence of a committee of the Society for the Benefit of the Sons and Daughters of the Clergy. 'Crieff, Perth', Vol. 10, Edinburgh: Blackwoods and Sons, 1845, pp 487–526. University of Edinburgh, University of Glasgow. (1999) *The Statistical Accounts of Scotland* online service: <https://stataccscot.edina.ac.uk:443/link/nsa-vol10-p487-parish-perth-crieff>.

Grant, I. F. *Highland Folk Ways.* London: Routledge & Kegan Paul, 1961.

Gregor, Rev. Walter. *Notes on the Folk-Lore of the North-East,* London: The Folk-Lore Society, 1881.

Hall, M. A., and Lowe, A. 'Twenty Shilling Wood, Comrie, Perth and Kinross, Construction Workers' Camp, Temporary Cinema' in *Discovery and Excavation in Scotland* 3, 2002. P. 92. <https://archaeologydataservice.ac.uk/archiveDS/archiveDownload?t=arch-753-1/dissemination/pdf/2000/2002.pdf >.

Hawthorne, Peter. *The Animal Victoria Cross: The Dicken Medal.* Barnsley: Pen & Sword Military, 2012; 80th anniversary edition, 2023.

Henderson, Hamish. *Alias MacAlias: Writings on Songs, Folk and Literature,* ed. by Finlay, Alec, Edinburgh: Polygon, 1992.

Henderson, Hamish. *The Armstrong Nose: Selected Letters of Hamish Henderson,* ed. by Finlay, Alec, Edinburgh: Polygon, 1996.

Holmes, Heather, and Ayrshire Archaeological & Natural History Society. *Tattie Howkers: Irish Potato Workers in Ayrshire.* Ayrshire Monographs; No. 31. Ayr: Ayrshire Archaeological & Natural History Society, 2005.

Holmes, Heather. *'As Good as a Holiday': Potato Harvesting in the Lothians from 1870 to the Present.* East Linton: Tuckwell Press, 2000.

Innes, Jean, School of Scottish Studies Archive, Tobar an Dualchais/Kist o Riches, <https://www.tobarandualchais.co.uk/track/99875?l=en>.

Knight, Rev. G.A. 'Archaeological Notes from Perthshire and Argyllshire' in *Transactions of the Perthshire Society of Natural Science*, Vol. 5, pp. 142–161. Perth: Perthshire Society of Natural Science at the Perthshire Natural History Museum, 1914.

Lea, K. J. 'Hydro-Electric Power Generation in the Highlands of Scotland.' *Transactions of the Institute of British Geographers*, no. 46 (1969): 155–65. <https://doi.org/10.2307/621414>.

Lockhart, G. W. *Highland Balls and Village Halls.* Edinburgh: Luath Press, 1985.

Macara, Duncan and Kippen, D. *Crieff: Its Traditions and Characters. With Anecdotes of Strathearn.* Edinburgh, 1881.

MacDougall, Ian. *Onion Johnnies: Recollections of Seasonal French Onion Sellers in Scotland,* Edinburgh: Birlinn, 2023.

MacDougall, Ian. *Hoggie's Angels: Tattie Howkers Remember,* East Linton: Tuckwell Press, 1995.

MacGill-Eain, Sorley, et al. *Four Points of a Saltire: the poetry of Sorley MacLean, George Campbell Hay, William Neill, Stuart MacGregor.* Edinburgh: Reprographia, 1970.

MacGregor, Alexander M., and Campbell, David. *Gaelic Topography of Balquhidder Parish as given in the Ordnance Survey Maps. Edinburgh: Printed for Private Circulation*, 1886. (In Mrs Jean Innes's collection; see also NLS catalogue).

MacGregor, Stuart. *Poems and Songs*. Loanhead: MacDonald, 1974.

MacGregor, Stuart. *The Myrtle and Ivy*. Edinburgh: MacDonald, 1967.

Mackellar, Mary. *Tuilleadh Dhuilleag Bho M' Leabhar-latha Mu Chunntas Mo Bheatha Anns A' Ghaidhealtachd: Bho 1862 Gu 1882*. Duneideann: U. Blackwood, 1886.

Maclennan, Dolina, Gilchrist, Jim and Eydmann, Stuart. *Dolina: An Island Girl's Journey*. Laxay, Isle of Lewis: Islands Book Trust, 2014.

McNeill, F. Marian. *The Scots Kitchen: Its Traditions and Lore. with Old-Time Recipes*. London: Blackie & Son, 1929.

McNeill, F. Marian. *The Silver Bough: A Calendar of Scottish National Festivals, Candlemas to Harvest Home*. Vol II, Glasgow: MacLellan, l958.

MacPhail, I. M. M. *The Clydebank Blitz*. Dumbarton: West Dunbartonshire Libraries & Museums, 1974.

Mayall, Colin. *Around Crieff and Strathearn*. Stroud: Tempus, 2004.

McEwen, John. *Who Owns Scotland? A Study in Land Ownership*. Edinburgh: Edinburgh U Student Publication Board, 1970; 2nd ed. Edinburgh: Polygon, 1981.

McNaughton, David B. *Upper Strathearn: From Earliest times to Today: A Study of Its Places and People*. Edinburgh: Jamieson & Munro, 1989.

McNaughton, Peter. 'Highland Strathearn', online: <https://www.highlandstrathearn.com/>.

Miller, James. *The Dam Builders: Power from the Glens*. Edinburgh: Birlinn, 2002.

National Library of Scotland 'Scottish Water Mills Project': <https://maps.nls.uk/projects/mills/project.html>.

Omand, Donald. *The Perthshire Book*. Edinburgh: Birlinn, 1999.

Opie, Iona and Peter. *The Singing Game*. Oxford: Oxford University Press, 1988.

Palmer, Roy. *Britain's Living Folklore*. Newton Abbot: David & Charles, 1991.

Payne, Peter Leslie. *The Hydro: a study of the development of the major hydro-electric schemes undertaken by the North of Scotland Hydro-Electric Board,* Aberdeen: Aberdeen University Press, 1988.

Perth & Kinross Archive, Acc11/52; Acc21/12; Acc23/30: Interviews by Margaret Bennett, audio and transcriptions.

Perth & Kinross Archive, MS140: Mott MacDonald, civil engineers, 1951-1972.

Perth and Kinross Fabian Society, 'The Acreocracy of Perthshire: Who Owns Our Land?' Perth: Perth and Kinross Fabian Society, 1971.

Perthshire Advertiser, 'Power Station Deep Under Perthshire Hill: St Fillan's Project will be started up today', June 28, 1958.

Pinney, Thomas (Ed.). *The Letters of Rudyard Kipling*, Vol 4; 1911-19, Iowa: University of Iowa Press, 1999.

Radford, E and Radford, M. A. *Encyclopaedia of Superstitions.* Rev. and Enl. ed. By Hole, Christina, London: Hutchinson, 1961.

Royle, Trevor. 'The Watcher by the Threshold: John Herdman and the Scottish Literary Tradition' in Burnett & McCaffery (eds.) *Not Dark Yet: A Celebration of John Herdman.* Edinburgh: Leamington Books, 2021, pp. 208–226.

Sinclair, Sir John. *The Statistical Account of Scotland, Comrie, Perth*, Vol. 11, Edinburgh: William Creech, 1794, pp 178–188. University of Edinburgh, University of Glasgow. (1999) *The Statistical Accounts of Scotland* online service: <https://stataccscot.edina.ac.uk:443/link/osa-vol11-p178-parish-perth-comrie>.

Sinclair, Sir John. *The Statistical Account of Scotland, Crieff, Perth*, Vol. 9, Edinburgh: William Creech, 1793, pp 583–602. University of Edinburgh, University of Glasgow. (1999) *The Statistical Accounts of Scotland* online service: <https://stataccscot.edina.ac.uk:443/link/osa-vol9-p583-parish-perth-crieff>.

Sinclair, Sir John. *The Statistical Account of Scotland, Monivaird and Strowan, Perth*, Vol. 8, Edinburgh: William Creech, 1793, pp 567–577. University of Edinburgh, University of Glasgow. (1999) *The Statistical Accounts of Scotland* online service: <https://stataccscot.edina.ac.uk:443/link/osa-vol8-p567-parish-perth-monivaird_and_strowan>.

Slimon, Campbell. *Stells, Stools, Strupag: A Personal Reminiscence of Sheep, Shepherding, Farming and the Social Activities of a Highland Parish.* Laggan: Laggan Heritage, 2007.

Smith, Norman. *The Centenary of the Aswan Dam, 1902-2002.* London: Thomas Telford, 2002.

Smith, W. McCombie. *The Romance of Poaching in the Highlands of Scotland, as Illustrated in the Lives of John Farquharson and Alexander Davidson, the Last of the Free-foresters.* Stirling: E. Mackay, 1904, 1946.

Stephens, Henry. *The Book of the Farm: Detailing the Labours of the Farmer, Farm-Steward, Ploughman, Shepherd, Hedger, Farm-Labourer, Field-Worker, and Cattle-Man.* 4th ed. rev. by James MacDonald. Edinburgh and London: Wm Blackwood & Sons, 1891.

Stewart, Alexander. *A Highland Parish, or the History of Fortingall,* Glasgow: Alex Maclaren & Sons, 1928.

Stewart, Alexandra. *The Glen that Was,* Inverness: Club Leabhar, 1975.

Strathearn Herald: general advertiser for Crieff, Comrie, Auchterarder, Braco, Muthil, Fowlis, Aberfeldy, Killin, Dunning, Blackford. 'To Let: Earnhope, Comrie' in *Strathearn Herald,* Dec. 10, 1938, p.11.

Strathearn Herald. 'Hydro-Electric Station Opens at St Fillans' in *Strathearn Herald,* July 5, 1958, p. 2.

Swainson, Charles. *The Folk Lore and Provincial Names of British Birds.* London: The Folk-lore Society, 1886.

The Courier (Laura Devlin, reporter). 'Broughty Ferry war-hero Winkie the Pigeon honoured with new statue at town's flood defences' (with photos) in *The Courier,* Dundee, Nov. 9, 2023. <https://www.thecourier.co.uk/fp/news/dundee/4807060/broughty-ferry-war-hero-winkie-pigeon-honoured-statue-flood-defences/>.

The Oral History Society, <https://www.ohs.org.uk/>; (See also British Library Oral History, above).

University of St Andrews Libraries and Museums Photographic Collections, <https://www.st-andrews.ac.uk/library/special-collections/photographs/>

Victoria, and Clark, James (ed). *Leaves from the Journal of Our Life in the Highlands, 1848 to 1861.* London, 1865.

Victoria. *More Leaves from the Journal of a Life in the Highlands from 1862 to 1882.* New ed. London: Smith, Elder, & Co, 1885.

Weir, Tom. 'My Month: The Shepherd of Artney' in *The Scots Magazine,* June 1977.

Wightman, Andy. *Who Owns Scotland?* Edinburgh: Canongate, 1996.

Wilson, James. *Lowland Scotch as Spoken in the Lower Strathearn District of Perthshire.* London: OUP, 1915.

Wood, Emma. *The Hydro Boys: Pioneers of Renewable Energy.* Edinburgh: Luath, 2002.

Index

Printed in Great Britain
by Amazon

49854914R00159